Hidden Treasures

CULTURAL, SOCIAL, AND
POLITICAL COMMENTARY
IN MAHLER'S SONGS FROM
DES KNABEN WUNDERHORN

Hidden Treasures

CULTURAL, SOCIAL, AND POLITICAL COMMENTARY IN MAHLER'S SONGS FROM *DES KNABEN WUNDERHORN*

MOLLY M. BRECKLING

CLEMSON UNIVERSITY PRESS

© 2023 Clemson University
All rights reserved

First Edition, 2023

ISBN: 978-1-63804-040-8 (print)
eISBN: 978-1-63804-041-5 (e-book)

Published by Clemson University Press
in association with Liverpool University Press

For information about Clemson University Press,
please visit our website at www.clemson.edu/press.

Library of Congress Cataloging-in-Publication Data
Names: Breckling, Molly M, author.
Title: Hidden treasures : cultural and political commentary in Gustav
Mahler's songs from Des Knaben Wunderhorn / Molly M Breckling.
Description: First edition. | Clemson : Clemson University Press, 2023. |
Includes bibliographical references and index. | Summary: "This study
explores Mahler's songs based on poetry from an 1806 collection of
German folk poetry entitled Des Knaben Wunderhorn: Alte deutsche Lieder,
collected by Arnim and Brentano, and identifies the connections the
composer found between these products of Germany's folk past and his own
cultural, social and political environments"-- Provided by publisher.
Identifiers: LCCN 2023007168 (print) | LCCN 2023007169 (ebook) | ISBN
9781638040408 (hardback) | ISBN 9781638040415 (ebook)
Subjects: LCSH: Mahler, Gustav, 1860-1911. Songs. | Mahler, Gustav,
1860-1911--Criticism and interpretation. | Songs--Germany--19th
century--History and criticism. | Knaben Wunderhorn. | Folk poetry,
German--History and criticism.
Classification: LCC ML410.M23 B72 2023 (print) | LCC ML410.M23 (ebook) |
DDC 782.42168092--dc23/eng/20230221
LC record available at https://lccn.loc.gov/2023007168
LC ebook record available at https://lccn.loc.gov/2023007169

Typeset in Minion Pro by Carnegie Book Production.
Printed and bound by CPI Group (UK) Ltd, Croydon CR0 4YY.

Contents

List of Musical Examples		vii
List of Tables		xi
Preface		1
1	Gustav Mahler's Lieder from *Des Knaben Wunderhorn*: Questions of Conception, History, and Genre	5
2	"A final remnant of a sense of duty": Mahler's Anti-Militarist Commentary	21
3	"Vehement and consuming longing, mixed with dread and anxiety": Mahler's Thoughts on Love and Romantic Fidelity	57
4	"Wrestling with God": Mahler and Spirituality	89
5	"The risky obstacles in society which are quite dangerous for women": Commentary on Gender Roles in the *Wunderhorn* Songs	117
6	"Highly complicated activity of the mind": Songs with a Freudian Slant	137
7	"The brutal bourgeoisie": Mahler and Socioeconomic Equality	171
8	"The misery of a pioneer": Mahler's Responses to Critics and Audiences	197

v

9	Conclusion	221
	Notes	233
	Index	259

List of Musical Examples

2.1. "Revelge," mm. 3–6   33

2.2. "Revelge," mm. 29–32   34

2.3. (a, b, and c) "Revelge," mm. 13–15, 40–44, and 104–6   35

2.4. "Revelge," mm. 44–48   36

2.5. "Zu Straßburg auf der Schanz," mm. 1–3   40

2.6. "Zu Straßburg auf der Schanz," mm. 14–16   40

2.7. "Zu Straßburg auf der Schanz," mm. 12–14, refrain   41

2.8. "Zu Straßburg auf der Schanz," mm. 7–10   42

2.9. "Zu Straßburg auf der Schanz," m. 61   43

2.10. "Der Tamboursg'sell," mm. 33–36   49

2.11. "Der Tamboursg'sell," mm. 102–10   50

2.12. "Der Tamboursg'sell," mm. 110–14   50

2.13. "Der Tamboursg'sell," mm. 22–26   51

2.14. "Nicht Wiedersehen!" mm. 1–4   54

2.15. "Nicht Wiedersehen!" mm. 16–20   54

2.16. "Nicht Wiedersehen!" mm. 55–59   55

viii HIDDEN TREASURES

3.1. (a and b) Cuckoo calls from "Lob des hohen Verstandes,"
m. 126 and "Um schlimme Kinder," mm. 5–6   62

3.2. Unusual cuckoo call from "Um schlimme Kinder," mm. 33–34   63

3.3. "Um schlimme Kinder artig zu machen," mm. 1–3   63

3.4. "Ich ging mit Lust," mm. 1–6   67

3.5. "Ich ging mit Lust," mm. 6–8   67

3.6. "Trost im Unglück," vocal melody mm. 12–18   71

3.7. "Trost im Unglück," piano reduction mm. 7–9   73

3.8. "Trost im Unglück," piano reduction mm. 1–4   74

3.9. "Aus! Aus!" mm. 49–52   79

3.10. "Aus! Aus!" mm. 19–26   80

3.11. "Aus! Aus!" mm. 11–18   81

3.12. Schubert: "Der Erlkönig," mm. 1–3   84

3.13. "Scheiden und Meiden," mm. 1–4   84

4.1. "Urlicht," mm. 1–2   98

4.2. "Urlicht," mm. 3–7   98

4.3. "Das himmlische Leben," mm. 60–62, oboe melody   104

4.4. "Das himmlische Leben," mm. 67–69, bassoon melody   104

4.5. "Das himmlische Leben," mm. 25–26, violin II melody   108

4.6. "Das himmlische Leben," mm. 25–26, flute melody   108

4.7. "Des Antonius von Padua Fischpredigt," mm. 52–56   113

5.1. "Starke Einbildungskraft," mm. 4–7   120

5.2. "Starke Einbildungskraft," mm. 13–16   121

5.3. "Starke Einbildungskraft," folk melody   121

5.4. "Starke Einbildungskraft," Mahler's piano introduction   122

5.5. "Starke Einbildungskraft," mm. 9–11   122

LIST OF MUSICAL EXAMPLES   ix

5.6. "Verlor'ne Müh'!" mm. 11–13   130

5.7. "Verlor'ne Müh'!" mm. 33–40, piano arrangement   130

5.8. (a, b, and c) "Verlor'ne Müh'!" mm. 30–33, 65–68, and 102–5   131

5.9. "Verlor'ne Müh'!" mm. 82–86   132

5.10. "Verlor'ne Müh'!" mm. 26–29   132

5.11. "Verlor'ne Müh'!" mm. 90–93   132

5.12. Brahms: "Vergebliches Ständchen," mm. 2–6   133

6.1. "Selbstgefühl," mm. 1–6   143

6.2. "Selbstgefühl," mm. 6–9   143

6.3. "Selbstgefühl," mm. 16–20   144

6.4. "Lied des Verfolgten im Turm," mm. 99–101   149

6.5. "Lied des Verfolgten im Turm," mm. 11–14   150

6.6. "Lied des Verfolgten im Turm," mm. 88–95   151

6.7. "Lied des Verfolgten im Turm," mm. 25–28, violin line   152

6.8. "Wo die schönen Trompeten blasen," mm. 15–20   153

6.9. "Wo die schönen Trompeten blasen," mm. 36–43   158

6.10. "Wo die schönen Trompeten blasen," mm. 170–73   159

6.11. "Wo die schönen Trompeten blasen," mm. 5–8   160

6.12. "Der Schildwache Nachtlied," mm. 1–4   163

6.13. "Der Schildwache Nachtlied," mm. 17–21   167

6.14. "Der Schildwache Nachtlied," mm. 9–12   168

6.15. "Der Schildwache Nachtlied," mm. 66–68   169

7.1. "Das irdische Leben," mm. 1–3   181

7.2. (a and b) "Das irdische Leben," mm. 7–14 and 75–82   183

7.3. "Das irdische Leben," mm. 132–35   183

7.4. Schubert: "Erlkönig," mm.1–3   184

7.5. "Das irdische Leben," mm. 27–32	185
7.6. "Das irdische Leben," mm. 15–18, piano arrangement	185
7.7. "Rheinlegendchen," mm. 10–14	189
7.8. "Rheinlegendchen," mm. 18–24	190
7.9. "Wer hat dies Liedlein erdacht?" mm. 35–46, vocal line	195
7.10. "Wer hat dies Liedlein erdacht?" mm. 46–53, piano reduction	195
8.1. "Lob des hohen Verstandes," mm. 25–26	209
8.2. "Lob des hohen Verstandes," mm. 65–69	210
8.3. "Lob des hohen Verstandes," mm. 86–90	211
8.4. "Ablösung im Sommer," m. 1	216
8.5. "Ablösung im Sommer," mm. 10–11	216
8.6. "Ablösung im Sommer," mm. 17–21	216
8.7. "Ablösung im Sommer," mm. 39–41	217
8.8. "Ablösung im Sommer," mm. 63–67	217
8.9. "Des Antonius von Padua Fischpredigt," mm. 16–24	219
8.10. "Des Antonius von Padua Fischpredigt," mm. 148–54, clarinet melody	220

List of Tables

1.1. List of Mahler's songs from *Des Knaben Wunderhorn* with dates and poetic anthology edition   6

2.1. Text comparison for "Revelge"   31

2.2. Text comparison for "Zu Straßburg auf der Schanz"   38

2.3. Text comparison for "Der Tamboursg'sell"   45

2.4. Text comparison for "Nicht Wiedersehen!"   52

3.1. Text comparison for "Um schlimme Kinder artig zu machen"   60

3.2. Text comparison for "Ich ging mit Lust"   65

3.3. Text comparison for "Trost im Unglück"   72

3.4. Text comparison for "Aus! Aus!"   76

3.5. Text comparison for "Scheiden und Meiden"   83

4.1. Text comparison for "Urlicht"   99

4.2. Text comparison for "Es sungen drei Engel"   101

4.3. Text comparison for "Das himmlische Leben"   105

4.4. Text comparison for "Des Antonius von Padua Fischpredigt"   110

5.1. Text comparison for "Starke Einbildungskraft"   119

xii   HIDDEN TREASURES

5.2. Text comparison for "Verlor'ne Müh'!"   128

6.1. Text comparison for "Selbstgefühl"   140

6.2. Text comparison for "Lied des Verfolgten im Turm"   146

6.3. Text comparison for "Wo die schönen Trompeten blasen"   154

6.4. Text comparison for "Der Schildwache Nachtlied"   164

7.1. Text comparison for "Das irdische Leben"   179

7.2. Text comparison for "Rheinlegendchen"   187

7.3. Text comparison for "Wer hat dies Liedlein erdacht?"   192

8.1. Text comparison for "Lob des hohen Verstandes"   206

8.2. Text comparison for "Ablösung im Sommer"   214

Preface

The songs of Gustav Mahler have long been relegated to the position of the lesser of his works, overshadowed by his symphonies. As such, few scholarly works have examined the songs in and of themselves, and even fewer have explored the songs as anything more than adjuncts to their symphonic brethren. This study is an attempt to remedy part of that oversight by looking at Mahler's songs composed to texts from the 1806 anthology entitled *Des Knaben Wunderhorn: Alte deutsche Lieder*, collected and edited by Achim von Arnim and Clemens Brentano. Mahler's twenty-four songs were completed over the course of fourteen years, between 1887 and 1901.

I began this process as an investigation into Mahler's narrative techniques in his songs based on texts from *Des Knaben Wunderhorn*, which has largely shaped the trajectory of this study. The majority of these songs conform to the definition of a ballad—a song that tells a clearly defined story with a specific beginning, middle, and end, using a combination of the epic, dramatic, and lyric poetic modes, in contrast to songs that merely describe a scene or an emotional state. As such, the storytelling aspects, such as narrative voice and the temporal trajectory of the stories, soon became vital tools for investigating how Mahler used his songs to comment on his cultural, social, and political environments.

No project can be completed by a single person without help from others, and this is no exception. I owe debts of thanks to many people

1

2   HIDDEN TREASURES

without whom this project would never have seen completion. As the seeds of this work were sown during my own work as a vocalist, I must thank Sharon Mabry for introducing me to Mahler's songs and her guidance in shaping my performance of them. Scholars such as Charles W. Dill, Jon W. Finson, Annegret Fauser, Mark Evan Bonds, Mark Katz, and Felix Woerner helped me cultivate my love of singing Mahler into scholarly work during my time in graduate studies at the universities of Wisconsin and North Carolina. Without their wisdom and patience, my thoughts on these songs would never have stretched beyond mere appreciation and enjoyment.

Materials from numerous libraries contributed to the analyses for this study, and no list of acknowledgments would be complete without thanking the many librarians who worked with me to obtain these materials. Robert Parks and the staff of the Pierpont Morgan Library and Museum hosted me and allowed me to view numerous manuscripts of these songs first-hand before making them available as microfilm. Monica Fazekas with the Music Library at the University of Western Ontario delivered materials to me by hand after a flooding incident made their collection unavailable to visitors. Bob Kosovsky of the New York Public Library for the Performing Arts, Bergit Busse from the Staatsbibliothek in Berlin, and Ilse Kosz from the Gesellschaft der Musikfreunde in Vienna also supplied images, without which this work could not have been completed. Finally, Alena Parthonnaud of the Médiathèque Musicale Mahler in Paris transcribed text from an unpublished source for my use. I was once told that any decent scholar must recognize and value the work of librarians, and these individuals have my sincere thanks.

Other people's generosity contributed to this process as well. Rufus Hallmark and Timothy Freeze shared unpublished writings for my use. Mechtild Vogt, Shelly Hay, and Jennifer Bienert offered their expertise in untangling subtleties of the German language that allowed me to further my interpretations of Mahler's songs. Tereza Petranova, manager of the Hotel Gustav Mahler, provided detailed information on the history of the property and its significance in the composer's childhood. I also thank J. P. E. Harper Scott and Julian Rushton for their editorial guidance with an earlier version of this project.

An academic should never overlook the importance of casual conversation with colleagues and the influence it will have on their work. My love and thanks go out to the many friends who have taken time at conferences, on social media, and in private correspondence to offer insights, suggestions, and encouragement whenever needed. While there are too many individuals that meet these criteria to list them all, special thanks must be extended to Caroline Kita, Arved Ashby, and James Zychowicz for taking the time to answer some of the stranger questions that have arisen during this project.

Of course, this work would never have reached the page without the confidence and guidance of my editor Alison Mero. Thank you for believing in this project and for having the patience and wisdom to walk me through the process of bringing my vision for this work to life. Your assistance has been invaluable, and your friendship has proven to be a delightfully unexpected bonus.

Lastly, I must acknowledge the people closest to me who have stood by while this work has evolved from a repertoire set from a recital through its many intermediary steps before becoming the work it is today. My husband Jason has been a constant source of support, encouragement, and at times pushing as my work has evolved. Thank you for always believing that this work had merit and for insisting that I give it my best effort. My mother, Sarah Dudley, has been the cheering section that filled me with confidence and a quest to succeed since day one. Though the subject of my work holds little interest for her, knowing that she supports it simply because it is mine has always driven me to achieve my goals.

Mahler's songs based on the poetry of *Des Knaben Wunderhorn* tell stories that not only comment on the composer's cultural, social, and political environments, but offer lessons for living a better life. Though these lessons were embedded into poetry with roots stretching back to the Middle Ages and were adopted by Mahler eighty years after being collected and published by Achim von Arnim and Clemens Brentano, these pearls of wisdom possess a universal quality, and it is my sincere hope that you will find the value in them even today.

CHAPTER ONE

Gustav Mahler's Lieder from
Des Knaben Wunderhorn
Questions of Conception, History, and Genre

In the summer of 1893, Natalie Bauer-Lechner, long-time friend and confidant of Gustav Mahler, noted in her diary that the composer believed, "With song you can express so much more in the music than the words directly say. The text is actually a mere indication of the deeper significance to be extracted from it, of the hidden treasure within."[1] Many such "hidden treasures" can be unearthed in Mahler's songs based on the poetry from Achim von Arnim and Clemens Brentano's 1806–8 anthology *Des Knaben Wunderhorn*. This study identifies the poetic and musical qualities of these songs, examines the stories they tell, and proposes how these songs and their chosen poetry, which itself dates back to Germany's medieval folk history, held such treasures in their observations on Mahler's cultural, social, and political environments.

Mahler turned to the verses in Arnim and Brentano's anthology on numerous occasions, setting the poetry he described as "blocks of marble which anyone might make his own"[2] in 1887–90, 1892–96, and 1899–1901 (see Table 1.1).[3] Of his extended relationship with the poetry, he wrote to his friend Ludwig Karpath, "Up to the age of forty I took the words for my songs… exclusively from that collection." He went on to write, "I have devoted myself heart and soul to that poetry—which is essentially different from any other kind of 'literary poetry' and might almost be called something more like Nature and Life."[4] The narrative processes found in Mahler's twenty-four songs are almost as variable as the works

5

6   HIDDEN TREASURES

Table 1.1: List of Mahler's songs from *Des Knaben Wunderhorn* with dates and poetic anthology edition

	Composed
"Um schlimme Kinder artig zu machen"	1887
"Ich ging mit Lust"	1887
"Aus! Aus!"	1887
"Starke Einbildungskraft"	1887
"Zu Straßburg auf der Schanz"	Summer 1890
"Ablösung im Sommer"	Summer 1890
"Scheiden und Meiden"	Summer 1890
"Nicht Wiedersehen!"	Summer 1890
"Selbstgefühl"	Summer 1890
"Der Schildwache Nachtlied"	January 28, 1892
"Verlor'ne Müh'!"	February 1, 1892
"Trost im Unglück"	February 22, 1892
"Wer hat dies Liedlein erdacht?"	February 6, 1892
"Das irdische Leben"	April 1892–August 1893
"Des Antonius von Padua Fischpredigt"	July 8, 1893
"Rheinlegendchen"	August 9, 1893
"Lied des Verfolgten im Turm"	July 1898
"Wo die schönen Trompeten blasen"	July 1898
"Lob des hohen Verstandes"	June 21–28, 1896
"Revelge"	July 1899
"Der Tamboursg'sell"	August 1901
"Das himmlische Leben" (Finale, Sym. No. 4)	February 10, 1892
"Urlicht" (Mvt. 4, Sym. No 2)	July 1893
"Es sungen drei Engel" (Mvt. 5, Sym. No. 3)	June 24, 1895

themselves. But looking directly at the literary and musical techniques that the composer utilized to bring these stories to life lends them broader significance, carrying them beyond the realm of folk-inspired art song to become stories that offer valuable life lessons, both to Mahler's contemporaneous audience and to today's listeners as well.

QUESTIONS OF CONCEPTION, HISTORY, AND GENRE   7

Orchestrated	Published	Publisher	Anthology Edition
	1892	Schott	Boxberger
	1892	Schott	Boxberger
	1892	Schott	Boxberger
	1892	Schott	Boxberger
	1892	Schott	Boxberger
	1892	Schott	Boxberger
	1892	Schott	Boxberger
	1892	Schott	Boxberger
	1892	Schott	Boxberger
April 1892	1899	Weinberger	Boxberger
April 1892	1899	Weinberger	Boxberger
April 1892	1899	Weinberger	Boxberger
April 1892	1899	Weinberger	Boxberger
1893	1899	Weinberger	Boxberger
August 1, 1893	1899	Weinberger	Boxberger
August 10, 1893	1899	Weinberger	Boxberger
May 1899	1899	Weinberger	Boxberger
July 1898	1899	Weinberger	Boxberger
June 1896	1899	Weinberger	Boxberger
1899	1905	Kahnt	Bremer
1901	1905	Kahnt	Bremer
March 12, 1892	1901	Universal	Boxberger
July 19, 1893	1897	Hoffmeister	Boxberger
May 8, 1896	1899	Weinberger	Boxberger

The folk-song lyrics preserved by Arnim and Brentano share several functions with other remnants of the *völkisch* past being preserved near the turn of the nineteenth century. These poems, and the fairy tales collected by Arnim and Brentano's good friends Jacob and Wilhelm Grimm, were instrumental in the Pan-Germanism movement that began during the

8   HIDDEN TREASURES

Napoleonic Wars, but the stories and scenes depicted in this literature also had a more basic impact—they were used as tools for teaching life lessons to the young.

Children are drawn to these kinds of stories and songs because they allow them to be entertained and to use their imagination. The didactic nature of the literature works in an almost subliminal way. Jack Zipes, a scholar of German comparative literature and culture, describes the process:

> The narrative voice [the protagonist within a poem or story] probes and tries to uncover the disturbing, repressed sociopsychological conflicts [solving the conflict brought about by the story] so that the young reader might imagine more clearly what forces operate in reality to curtail freedom of action. Uncomfortable questions about arbitrary authoritarianism, sexual domination, and social oppressions are raised to show situations which call for change and can be changed.[5]

The fantastic imagery and adventures experienced by the figures in these works provide young people with a "safe space" in which they can wonder how they themselves would deal with the problems encountered by the fictional characters. And while this mental work is often performed subconsciously, the lessons we learn from the stories of our childhood stay with us forever.

Arnim and Brentano recognized the didactic power of their poems. In his 1803 essay "Von Volksliedern," Achim von Arnim described his work as containing "centuries of wisdom,"[6] and of folk song in particular he wrote, "The image of the highest life or the highest life itself... can only reveal itself from the mouth of the human being."[7] Whether one is actively aware of the lessons these texts provide while reading them (or setting them to music, or listening to that music), they are nonetheless imparting their wisdom.

There is no evidence to explicitly suggest that Mahler was actively aware of the instructive nature of the poems he chose for the lyrics of his *Wunderhorn* lieder. However, two facts indicate that he saw something significant in these poems that remained meaningful and relatable

QUESTIONS OF CONCEPTION, HISTORY, AND GENRE   9

decades after the anthology was first published: first, that he remained preoccupied with these texts for well over a decade, and second, that he created for these songs musical settings that far surpassed the humble, simplistic settings commonly associated with folk songs at the time. Combining these "centuries of wisdom" with modern-sounding music allowed the lessons embedded in the poems of *Des Knaben Wunderhorn* to continue instructing new generations of listeners.

The mere act of setting poetry to music assumes multiple layers of narrative potential. We can examine the story in any given song as being told by the text on its own, through the music, and also by way of the subtle interactions between them. Each layer can provide information unavailable elsewhere, and, in the most interesting examples, these voices can contradict one another, creating hermeneutic friction and offering even deeper levels of meaning. While in some of his *Wunderhorn* lieder Mahler's music serves to support and enhance the story being told by the text, other songs feature musical cues that seem to thwart the progress of the poem's story, allowing the musical narrative to take on a life of its own. Examining these works through the lens of their stories and the ways they are told through word and music allows each poetic and musical nuance to function as a narrative tool, and in this way we can ascertain novel ways of interpreting and understanding them.

As products of the German folk tradition, the poems Mahler selected for these works speak to universal themes such as love, death, war, suffering, fantasy, and art. The ubiquity and universality of these ideas inspired the composer almost one hundred years after the poems were first published, and possessed intangible qualities that resonated with his own time and place. The very purpose of folk songs and fairy tales has always been to teach lessons to the young, and the fact that Mahler composed these songs in a style that was forward-looking (rather than in an artificially "once-upon-a-time" style) indicates that he saw that the lessons embedded in the songs were still relevant to audiences of his day, as they were for those when the poetic anthology was published decades earlier and for the people who originated the songs in their folk past. In the pages that follow, this study will argue that Mahler's textual and musical choices provide intriguing interactions with and embedded commentary upon topics as diverse as military life, love and fidelity, spirituality and religion,

10   HIDDEN TREASURES

gender roles, Freudian theory, economic justice, and the critics and audiences who looked negatively upon his work.

Des Knaben Wunderhorn: Alte deutsche Lieder by Achim von Arnim and Clemens Brentano

Before a close examination of Mahler's settings of the poetry from *Des Knaben Wunderhorn* can begin, it is essential to understand the origins of the text itself. The creation of the poetic anthology known as *Des Knaben Wunderhorn: Alte deutsche Lieder* started simply enough. Clemens Brentano, the older of the two folklorists, was born in Ehrenbreitstein, now part of Koblenz, on September 9, 1778 to an Italian family. As a young man, he became involved in the Romantic literary scenes in Jena, Göttingen, and Heidelberg. Ludwig Achim von Arnim, the more active of the two *Wunderhorn* collectors, was born in Berlin on January 26, 1781 into Prussian nobility. He began his studies in law and natural science before eventually devoting himself to his love of literature. Arnim and Brentano met in Göttingen in 1801, and in Heidelberg they began their collaboration on the collection of folk poetry entitled *Des Knaben Wunderhorn*.[8] Mohr and Zimmer of Heidelberg published the first volume of the anthology in 1806, and Arnim and Brentano dedicated the volume to Goethe. The remainder of the collection, in Volumes Two and Three, and a collection of *Kinderlieder* (Children's Songs) followed in 1808. By the time Mahler began composing his *Wunderhorn* lieder, the anthology had already seen numerous reprints and editions, and it continues to be published in new editions today, most recently in 2003 in a critical edition by Heinz Rölleke (who has extensively studied the anthology and its use by Mahler) and as a basic reprinted edition in 2014 edited by Karl-Maria Guth.[9]

Des Knaben Wunderhorn was not the first published anthology of German folk poetry. Many of the poems found in the collection had their roots in the traditions of the *Bänkelsänger*, poets and singers active since the sixteenth century who traveled about, spreading news and gossip by way of public singing performances atop wooden crates or benches and the distribution of broadsides, known in German as *fliegende Blätter*.[10] In 1765, such folk poetry began to be recorded in England with the publication of Thomas Percy's *Reliques of Ancient English Poetry*.[11]

QUESTIONS OF CONCEPTION, HISTORY, AND GENRE 11

This anthology inspired Johann Gottfried Herder, who published the first volume of German folk poetry, *Stimmen der Völker*, in 1779.[12] The success of this volume had two major consequences: it inspired Arnim and Brentano's collection, and it also began a vogue in Germany for all things folk that resulted in a new poetic genre known as the *Kunstballade*, in which contemporary poets such as Goethe and Bürger began writing new literary poetry that imitated folkloric content. Whereas the texts of the *Bänkelsänger* and Herder's collection arose as folk song lyrics (though the accompanying melodies were only rarely preserved with the texts), the writers of the *Kunstballaden* simply created poems, which did not receive musical treatment until discovered by composers. This shift began to blur the distinctions between art and folk traditions and between poem and song text, and explains, in part, why Arnim and Brentano included some self-authored verse and did not provide melodies for their texts.

The poems in *Des Knaben Wunderhorn* represent folk songs and stories from throughout the German-speaking lands, stretching from Switzerland to Swabia. Works such as this and other manifestations of the German folk movement of the early nineteenth century promoted the ideals of Pan-Germanism, which aimed to unify the German-speaking nation-states into one large country, united by a common folk culture. Arnim wrote of the need for an anthology such as this:

> Only because of this linguistic separation and the disregard of the poetry's better qualities is there in large part a lack of folk poetry in Newer Germany. Only where the people lack education through books do folk songs originate and come to us, unpublished and unwritten, simply floating through the air, like a white crow.[13]

All of the anthologies of folk poetry that emerged during this time served to fan the flames of Pan-German nationalism. And following several political uprisings resulting from the Napoleonic Wars, these poems allowed "the discouraged and frustrated Germans [to turn] toward the people, who seemed to represent the only hope for reunification after the country had been betrayed by the lack of patriotism of its princes."[14] Mahler would become involved in a later incarnation of the Pan-Germanist campaign

12   HIDDEN TREASURES

through his involvement as a university student with a politically active reading group known as the Pernerstorfer Circle.[15]

The poems in *Wunderhorn* represent a hodgepodge of sources: *Kunstballaden* written by Arnim and Brentano, previously published works, and those collected directly from the *Volk*. Henry-Louis de La Grange describes Brentano traveling about, "questioning old people of all classes, peasants, servants, nurses, artisans, and schoolmasters and writing down the poems that still lived in their memory."[16] Few of the poems collected for the anthology escaped the editors' hands without some degree of orthographic modification—typically a question of spelling, removal or standardization of dialects, and modernization. Some critics saw this tampering as an abominable act of editorial artifice inimical to the collection of historical texts, while others, such as Goethe, recognized that when recording the artifacts of an oral tradition, no one particular variation of a text holds primacy over any other. Goethe wrote of the anthology's authenticity:

> These songs were then carried over time, in their own sonic element from ear to ear and mouth to mouth, they gradually returned, living and glorified, to the folk, with whom they got their start, so to speak... Who knows what a song must endure as it goes through the mouths of the people, and not only the uneducated! Why is he who records it, in that last instance, not also granted that certain right?[17]

The precise wording of these texts underwent changes, similar to what happens in the children's game of "Telephone" where alterations occur with new tellings over time. The wording of texts from the folk tradition only become concretized once they are committed to writing. Karl Bode[18] and Ferdinand Reiser[19] have extensively detailed Arnim and Brentano's sources for and adaptations to the *Wunderhorn* poetry.

Des Knaben Wunderhorn represented an idealized conception of a folk culture, modernized for easy consumption by a nineteenth-century German-speaking society, and promoting a specific Pan-Germanist agenda. At no time did Arnim and Brentano actively seek to have their work recognized as an accurate historical representation of Germanic folk

QUESTIONS OF CONCEPTION, HISTORY, AND GENRE   13

traditions, claiming the collection had been "collected from the lips of the people, from books and from manuscripts, *arranged and completed.*"[20] While this was widely debated by critics of the anthology upon its original publication, it is unlikely that even if Mahler was aware of the "inauthentic" nature of these poems it would have dampened his enthusiasm, some seventy-five years later. Mahler's interest laid in the musical potential of the poems and their resonance with his current environment rather than their historical accuracy.

Mahler and *Des Knaben Wunderhorn*: Issues of History

Before beginning a closer examination of Mahler's engagement with the *Wunderhorn*, one must determine when he first encountered the poetry. This in and of itself has long posed a problem. Scholars have been unable to agree on precisely when Mahler first came in contact with the anthology, and this challenge stems, in part, from Mahler's own conflicting accounts (and subsequent misinterpretations of his remarks) on the matter. Henry-Louis de La Grange evocatively describes one theory, based on a claim by Mahler's childhood friend Guido Adler:

> Mahler accidentally came across Achim von Arnim's and Clemens Brentano's poetic anthology *Des Knaben Wunderhorn* at the Webers' [roughly 1887]. He discovered with delight a naïve medieval universe peopled by soldiers and children, animals and brightly colored saints. A universe filled with humanity, love and sorrow, *Sehnsucht*, and eternal farewells, but filled also with a fresh humour that enchanted him.[21]

Donald Mitchell cites communication with the daughter of one of Mahler's childhood friends to assert that Mahler would have become familiar with the poetry as early as 1875.[22] Herta Blaukopf observes that Mahler pursued courses in German literature during his brief studies at the University of Vienna (intermittently from 1877 until 1880), suggesting that he made acquaintance with the anthology there.[23] Ida Dehmel records that Mahler told her that "from earliest childhood his relationship to the book had been particularly close."[24] And, finally,

14   HIDDEN TREASURES

Mahler wrote to Bauer-Lechner regarding his 1878 cantata *Das klagende Lied*, "You will... see that at a time when I did not even suspect the existence of the *Wunderhorn*, I already lived completely in its spirit."[25] Amid these conflicting accounts, the fact remains that two of Mahler's earlier major compositions, *Das klagende Lied* and the *Lieder eines fahrenden Gesellen*, are, to use the composer's words, "completely in [the *Wunderhorn*] spirit," dealing with strikingly similar themes and featuring comparable language. The truth of the matter, most likely, lies somewhere in the middle of these accounts; while Mahler may not have been familiar with Arnim and Brentano's complete published collection, he seems to have had at least a passing familiarity with many of the texts contained within, or at least others of the same style, as lyrics to traditional folk songs. Such songs would no doubt have rung through the Mahler home when, as a young boy, he and his family lived in a home connected to the tavern owned by his father, where singing was among the common pastimes. Stuart Feder states of the influence of music in the composer's childhood home:

> For some artists the human era of childhood itself becomes a leitmotif in the content of the adult oeuvre, appearing repeatedly in the most manifest representations as well as in the subtlest transformations. We find that is one of the characteristic features of the music of Gustav Mahler.[26]

And the influence of this childhood soundscape echoes through each and every one of the *Wunderhorn* lieder.

Mahler's Sources for his *Wunderhorn* Texts

One of the major questions pertaining to Mahler's *Wunderhorn* lieder concerns the precise nature of his poetic sources. Before exploring the changes Mahler made to the poetry to create his song texts, it is vital to know exactly what Mahler saw that inspired him to set these specific poems to music. Without this information, one cannot accurately gauge the extent of his manipulations and how those changes impacted the outcome. By the time Mahler composed his first *Wunderhorn* songs, the

QUESTIONS OF CONCEPTION, HISTORY, AND GENRE   15

anthology had appeared in numerous editions throughout Germany, including the first edition from 1806–8, an 1878 edition edited by Friedrich Bremer (published by Philipp Reclam, Leipzig), an 1883 edition edited by Robert Boxberger (published by Gustav Hempel, Berlin), and many others. Many scholars have worked to determine which editions Mahler used to create his songs.[27] The composer's tendency to freely adapt the poetry for his own musical and narrative aims complicates this issue. We know that, due in part to his love of the text and also to his forgetful nature, Mahler owned at least six copies of the *Wunderhorn* anthology throughout his lifetime, including at least one first edition, but when he acquired each of them is unknown; nor do we know which other editions were in his collection, and unfortunately only his first edition copy has survived, without any annotations, eliminating any conclusive final proof as to his sources for a given text or insight into his practice of modifying the texts themselves.[28] Heinz Rölleke and Renate Hilmar-Voit have determined that Mahler most likely used the Bremer, the Boxberger, and the first editions. One of several singers with whom Mahler was connected romantically throughout his career, Anna von Mildenburg, presented the latter to him in 1895.[29] He wrote to her of this gift, "You cannot imagine what joy I have found with this attractive book. It is so beautiful that its contents are almost new to me."[30] The primary differences between the editions concern changes in orthography, dialect, and punctuation rather than the poetry itself. For my analyses, I have compared these factors in Mahler's texts to a first edition, three contemporaneous editions available during Mahler's life, and Rölleke's 2003 edition.[31]

Using spelling and punctuation as criteria, none of Mahler's texts appears to have come directly from the first edition, leading me to believe that he valued his first edition more as a treasured *objet d'art* than as a tool for working out song texts. By comparing these editions to the texts Mahler set, I have concluded that the overwhelming majority of Mahler's texts originated from the Boxberger edition, and that only his final two *Wunderhorn* songs, "Revelge" and "Der Tamboursg'sell," emerged from the Bremer edition. These versions most closely resemble the texts as they appear in each of Mahler's songs, and thus seem the obvious sources for closer comparison.

16   Hidden Treasures

Mahler and *Des Knaben Wunderhorn*: Issues of Genre

Mahler referred to his *Wunderhorn* songs using a number of different genre designations, including *Gesänge, Lieder, Humoresken*, and *Balladen*. At no time, however, did he clearly indicate unique meanings and characteristics for each of these generic terms. Such information would clarify why he used this varied terminology, what each label actually meant for him, and how these conceptions impacted his compositional process. Contemporaneous music dictionaries offer us some insight as to the generally accepted meanings of these genre identifiers during Mahler's time, which in turn may inform our notions of what the composer understood these classifications to indicate and why he chose to use them to describe his works.

Oddly, while otherwise plentiful, German music dictionaries experienced a mysterious dearth of publication during the *Wunderhorn* years. Perhaps this is due to the overwhelming success and thoroughness of Hugo Riemann's 1882 *Musik-Lexikon*. Nonetheless, if we look to dictionaries published before and after the time of Mahler's compositions, we can attempt to zero in on contemporaneous notions for these generic labels, which can contribute to our understanding of what they may have meant for Mahler.

A sampling of dictionaries published between 1802 and 1923 provide various insights into how these specific genres typically conveyed their texts poetically and musically. *Balladen* were thought to narrate events of "adventurous, wonderful, frightening, tragic, comic" content,[32] using "declaimed presentation,"[33] and a "musical form... as variable as the poetic form,"[34] though it was "characteristically set either in through-composed form or strophically."[35] *Gesänge* sought to achieve "a common representation through mutual understanding" of poetry and music,[36] in a way "either natural or artistic,"[37] though it was often merely "enhanced speech" delivered "through parlando and recitative, in a simple, descriptive way,"[38] by "the rhythmic combination of human voices."[39] *Lieder* were typically thought to be less artistically elevated than *Gesänge*—it was a genre that "everyone can sing without having to learn the art of singing,"[40] presented "in simple, unaffected ways that are not overly artistic,"[41] where "the sung word takes the place of the spoken word."[42] The use of the term

Questions of Conception, History, and Genre   17

Humoresken to indicate a musical genre did not appear until the piano works of Schumann in the early nineteenth century, and thus did not appear in music dictionaries until some time later, but in the few dictionaries sampled that defined the term, they are described as having "witty description or narration,"[43] depicting the *humoristisch*, which was "ridiculous, which is explained with moody seriousness."[44] Before Mahler, the term *Humoreske* had almost exclusively been used to describe instrumental music. Mahler's views on humor in art stem from the writings of Jean Paul,[45] who wrote in his *Vorschule der Ästhetik*:

> The understanding and the object-world know only finitude. In the Romantic we find only the infinite contrast between the ideas (or reason) and all finitude itself. But suppose just this finitude were imputed as *subjective* contrast to the idea of *objective* contrast, and instead of the sublime as an implied infinity, now produced a finitude applied to the infinite, and thus simply infinity of contrast, that is a negative infinity. Then we should have humor or the romantic comic.[46]

Romantics derived humor from an individual's inability to comprehend his/her own limitations compared to the vastness of the sublime. In 1892, Mahler wrote to his sister Justine regarding his *Humoresken*, "They are stranger still than the former ones, they are all 'humor,' in the best and truest sense of the word; something for which only a few exceptional men are created."[47] Ultimately, we know, however, that he understood the term *Humoreske* to be related to the ballad because in the summer of 1899, Mahler and Natalie Bauer-Lechner were speaking about the famed ballad composer Carl Loewe when the composer said, "He would have understood my Humouresques, for in fact, he is the precursor of this form of writing."[48]

So, given these definitions, seemingly common before, during, and after Mahler's life, can we assume that Mahler shared these precise conceptions of genre? Not necessarily. If we did make that leap, would that tell us any more about how his understanding of such terminology impacted his compositional process? Perhaps not. In fact, we frequently find Mahler utilizing genre markers for works that do not possess the characteristics

18   HIDDEN TREASURES

that define the specific genres themselves, as we witnessed in the case of the *Humoreske*. What this exercise demonstrates is that by his failing to conform to the parameters implied by the commonly held meanings of these labels, Mahler appeared to understand genre as something elastic that could be manipulated and expanded as various creations required.[49] The musical and narratological needs of his songs held primacy over any preconceived notions of what a song of a certain type "ought to be." These genre markers, rather than confining his artistic impulses, merely served as references or symbols, indicating outside sources that inspired his ideas.

Further difficulties in specifying the genre of these works came into play when Mahler began composing his mature *Wunderhorn* songs in arrangements for voice and piano simultaneously with versions for voice and orchestra. This question of timing is an important distinction, as these orchestral versions were not simply arrangements made at a later date; rather, the timbral qualities of the orchestra informed Mahler's compositional process from inception. These are truly "orchestral songs" rather than merely "orchestrated songs," though neither Mahler nor his contemporaries had yet fully drawn that distinction, as evidenced by the fact that Mahler published the songs in both piano and orchestral versions.[50]

Critics, scholars, and composers of Mahler's time were engaged in a lively debate regarding genre and the tradition of the German lied with the emergence of orchestral song.[51] While the distinctions between *Gesang, Lied, Humoreske*, and *Ballade* tend to be equally based on poetic and musical concerns, this discussion looked at musical and performative qualities as the basis for genre designation. Traditionalists argued that lieder possessed an inherent intimacy that was disrupted by orchestral accompaniment, and as such orchestral songs were not part of the family of lieder, but something new and different. Progressives, among whom we should consider Mahler, felt that providing lieder with the additional tone colors of the orchestra offered an expanded palette of expressive capabilities. Continuing to refer to these songs as lieder connected the works to an already established tradition of German song, while at the same time pushing conceptual boundaries and providing something new and innovative.

Mahler's seemingly flexible view of genre had been developing among other poets and musicians for quite some time. Even nearly a century earlier, in Goethe's time, such terms were not concrete in meaning.[52] It would seem that generic labels were in large part based on the whim of the poet, and subsequently the composer who set his texts to music.

This study views the *Wunderhorn* not simply as art songs, but as stories of significance that span across time and place when told through song. Viewing the songs through this lens broadens our understanding of the narrative potential of lieder in general and also of the symphonies that these works so heavily influenced. As seen from the poems that Mahler chose to set from *Des Knaben Wunderhorn*, he clearly believed them to be capable of telling stories that he could relate to himself and to his audience. The simple fact that Mahler chose to set these poems to music, and that he returned to the anthology for inspiration for fourteen years, resulting in twenty-four songs which heavily influenced three of his symphonies, implies that his music is a vital part of the storytelling process, as he himself once stated: "One can often add a great deal, and can deepen and widen the meaning of the text through music."[53]

CHAPTER TWO

"A final remnant of a sense of duty"
Mahler's Anti-Militarist Commentary

Mahler left little to no written evidence of his views on politics, yet it would seem obvious that the notion of war and military life held some fascination for him. During his fourteen-year engagement with *Des Knaben Wunderhorn*, Mahler composed ten lieder based on militaristic themes, comprising almost 42 percent of the total songs he based on the anthology. By comparison, only about 10 percent of the poems found in Arnim and Brentano's collection present wartime scenarios. Given this incongruity, evidently some intangible quality must have attracted Mahler to this subject matter. Scholars such as Donald Mitchell, Kordula Kraus, Peter Franklin, Stefan Hanheide, and Albrecht von Massow have devoted numerous studies to Mahler's militaristic *Wunderhorn* songs.[1] Many of these scholarly works examine Mahler's depictions of army life, his representation of soldiers and the sweethearts they leave behind, or the relationships between these songs and the *Wunderhorn* symphonies. These scholars commonly attribute the sheer quantity of these works to the composer's frequently reported childhood fascination with military music. He reportedly told Natalie Bauer-Lechner that he frequently heard music emanating from the barracks near his childhood home in Iglau and that "Even as a boy, I was thrilled by it!"[2] Contemporaneous biographer Paul Stefan tells this colorful tale of the composer's childhood fascination with military music:

22   HIDDEN TREASURES

> The bugles ring out from the barracks. The regimental band marches past. And the tiny youngster sings each and every tune after them. At the age of four, someone buys him a concertina, and now he plays them himself, especially in the military marches. These latter have so much attraction for him that one morning, hastily dressed, he hurries away after the soldiers, and gives the market-women who come to fetch him a regular concert on his instrument.[3]

The pervading theory suggests that Mahler's youthful interest in militaristic music stirred a desire to create works that allowed him to experiment with those sonic elements, and he lends credence to this by attributing many of his musical experiments to his childhood love of military-band music.[4] This theory, however, is more complicated than it might seem.

Scholars have reported a great deal of conflicting information regarding the actual troops and military bands that young Mahler would have had the opportunity to hear, making a true understanding of his childhood soundscape difficult.[5] Perhaps some of the confusion stems from contradictory accounts by other Iglau residents from the time of Mahler's childhood. Neighbor Theodor Fischer recalled that "An infantry garrison was permanently stationed at the Iglau garrisons."[6] Musicologist Guido Adler, also from Iglau but five years older than Mahler, remembered that troops were not a permanent feature of the town until 1866.[7] Most recently, Henry-Louis de La Grange and Sybille Werner have identified that the Austrian Imperial 13th Battalion of Light Infantry, with their eight-piece band led by Dominik Matzek, was stationed in Iglau from 1862 to 1867, and was replaced by the 5th Infantry Regiment briefly thereafter.[8] La Grange reports that the band included a drum major, who led players of the trumpet, cornet, baritone horn, tuba, cymbals, triangle, side drum, and kettledrum. They performed ten concerts per year at local schools and occasionally paraded through the town, providing the instances which Mahler spoke of most frequently and which have since captured the imagination of scholars.

We also find a paradox in the composer's partiality for these texts because, contrary to the pleasant memories Mahler reportedly associated with military music, none of his militaristic songs paints the soldier's life in an entirely positive light. This is striking, given that roughly half of the military poems from Arnim and Brentano's anthology explore the pleasurable aspects of service, such as camaraderie among soldiers and fighting for a divine purpose.[9] This type of poetry is not entirely surprising, given the nineteenth-century tendency to romanticize notions of war as acts of nation-building and fighting for a noble cause.[10] Nonetheless, somehow Mahler's views appear to be different.

Mahler, for the most part, did not live during a time of war. Indeed, contemporaneous novelist and playwright Stefan Zweig describes the unusually peaceful environment of Austria-Hungary in the late nineteenth century:

> Catastrophes as took place outside on the world's periphery never made their way through the well-padded walls of "secure" living. The Boer War, the Russo-Japanese War, the Balkan War itself did not penetrate the existence of my parents. They passed over all reports of war in the newspapers just as they did the sporting page. And truly, what did it matter to them what took place outside of Austria, what did it change in their lives?... They did not know war, they had hardly given it a thought. It had become legendary, and distance had made it seem romantic and heroic. They still saw it in the perspective of their school readers and of paintings in museums; brilliant cavalry attacks in glittering uniforms, the fatal shot always straight through the heart, the entire campaign a resounding march of victory.[11]

The seven-week Austro-Prussian War took place when Mahler was only six years old, and it came to a climax only just over one hundred kilometers way from Iglau.[12] Herta Blaukopf notes that during the war, Mahler's hometown was briefly occupied by Prussian troops.[13] She suggests that this experience may have colored his views toward militarism, despite his often positive descriptions of it later in life, but there are no recorded instances of him discussing the occupation or any awareness he may have even had of the war, so if this experience caused the deep-seated trauma Blaukopf claims, the composer never spoke of it, even to his closest confidants.

24   HIDDEN TREASURES

But given his own description of military music as "thrilling," it remains perplexing that he chose to only examine the darker sides of military life in his songs. Where and when did he develop his seemingly negative opinions on militarism? We must answer these questions before we can interpret examples showing how Mahler expressed these attitudes musically. Part of the answer lies in Mahler's political engagement as a young man at the University of Vienna.

Mahler's involvement with the Pernerstorfer Circle will be discussed at length in Chapter 7. Pertinent to our understanding of Mahler's views on war, however, are the philosophical readings with which he engaged during this period of his life. The Pernerstorfer Circle's outward political leanings changed over time, but the writings Mahler encountered during his affiliation with the group informed his worldview for years to come.

Pan-Germanism was at first, for Mahler and other Jewish members of the Circle, a particularly compelling aspect of the group's political agenda.[14] At the point that Mahler joined it, the Circle considered national identity to be a product of a shared culture, and Mahler and other Viennese Jews consequently envisioned themselves as part of that cultural community of Germans, though not necessarily among the German *Volk*, its native people.[15] In fact, Carl E. Schorske wrote that Mahler's motives for joining the group were never political, but merely "multinationalist" in origin.[16] Nonetheless, the Circle exposed Mahler to significant philosophical ideals.

While precise dates are not evident, Jens Malte Fischer proposes that Mahler joined the group in 1879, if not the year before.[17] By 1880, after Mahler returned to the university after a brief hiatus in his studies and again took up his acquaintance with the Circle, the group had begun to split into two distinct factions with very different perspectives. The Jewish members were more inclined to uphold the philosophical ideas of the group, seeking "a metaphysical community of will."[18] Meanwhile, the more politically active (and largely Gentile) members borrowed the same ideas in order to create a sense of national belonging, which benefited them in the political arena.[19] These more politically active members eventually began to transform the Circle's ideals of Pan-Germanism into extreme cultural nativism, which eventually evolved into isolationism and then to anti-Semitism, leaving several members of the Circle to become disillusioned and leave the group.[20] These political members of the Circle began to view Judaism as biological, a problematic and irradicable marker of racial identity. By a logic which also construed Germanness in biological rather than cultural terms, Jews could therefore never be true Germans. An honorary member of this growing anti-Semitic side of the Circle was Karl Lueger, who went on to form the Christian Social Party in Vienna. The party used the Catholic Viennese population's fear of economic disaster (which had lingered since the bank crisis of 1873 and reemerged with the Panic of 1893) and stereotypes of the "money-grubbing Jew" as bait to lure anti-Semitic voters and to assure Lueger's election as mayor of Vienna in 1895. The ideals of equality and acceptance once promoted by the Circle gradually became poisoned by bigotry and hatred.[21]

The abandoned Jewish members of the Circle primarily sought refuge in the aesthetic and philosophical values of the group and lived according to the metaphysical and artistic values outlined in their readings of Schopenhauer, Nietzsche, and Wagner (including vegetarianism, which Mahler followed ardently until his departure from the Circle). These young men viewed language and a common cultural history as markers of German identity and worked toward a nationalist state with a culture personified by an idealized notion of the *Volk* that was blind to biology and bigotry.

In 1883, Mahler officially resigned from the Pernerstorfer Circle and abandoned his outward political activism. While we have no documented evidence regarding his motives for leaving the group, one can infer that he was becoming increasingly uncomfortable with the growing divisiveness among its members. His interest in the group's founding ideals, however, remained, as his attraction to the poems of *Des Knaben Wunderhorn* demonstrates. As mentioned in Chapter 1, the anthology itself was collected in an earlier phase of Pan-Germanist sentiment that arose in the aftermath of the Napoleonic Wars.[22]

Given the importance of the writings of Wagner, Nietzsche, and Schopenhauer during Mahler's time with the Pernerstorfer Circle, it stands to reason that perhaps their views on militarism may have played a part in Mahler's evident change of heart regarding military service, as evidenced by his choices of *Wunderhorn* texts. One must also consider the implications of selective reading, as written evidence of views on war from these figures is not necessarily consistent, particularly in the case of Richard Wagner.

26   HIDDEN TREASURES

Wagner's views on war tended to change over time, depending on his concurrent circumstances and political alliances. He recorded an early instance of anti-militaristic sentiment in his autobiography, reflecting on the 1848 Revolutions as they broke out in Dresden:

> During my hasty return to Friedrichstadt I recognized that this portion of the town had been almost entirely cut off from the inner city by the occupation of the Prussian troops; I saw in my mind's eye our own suburb occupied, and the consequences of a state of military siege in their most repulsive light.... While the larks were soaring to dizzy heights above my head, and singing in the furrows of the fields, the light and heavy artillery did not cease to thunder down the streets of Dresden. The noise of this shooting, which had continued uninterruptedly for several days, had hammered itself so indelibly upon my nerves, that it continued to re-echo for a long time in my brain.[23]

In 1873 Wagner wrote an essay entitled "On State and Religion," responding to inquiries from his patron, King Ludwig II of Bavaria, about his views on violence and militarism following the Franco-Prussian War (which he initially supported with great fervor, mostly due to his hatred of the French):

> This fact that one's own quiet can be ensured by nothing but violence and injustice to the world without, must naturally make one's quiet seem always problematic in itself: thereby leaving a door forever open to violence and injustice within one's own State too. The measures and acts which show us violently disposed towards the outer world, can never stay without a violent reaction on ourselves. When modern state and political optimists speak of a state of International Law, in which the [European] States stand nowadays toward one another, one need only point to the necessity of maintaining and constantly increasing our enormous standing armies, to convince them, on the contrary, of the actual lawlessness of that state. Since it does not occur to me to attempt to show how matters could be otherwise, I merely

record the fact that we are living in a perpetual state of war, with intervals of armistice, and that the inner condition of the State itself is not so utterly unlike this state of things as to pass muster for its diametric opposite.[24]

In this essay Wagner opposes war and militaristic pursuits; rather than bringing peace, violence only begets more violence. Whether war is officially declared or not, the inherent tensions and compulsion toward violence remain.

History has somewhat skewed our understanding of Wagner. Modern readers must take into consideration his work's mistreatment by the Nazis and their frequent misinterpretations of his writings. When considering how Mahler might have viewed Wagner's writings, we can surmise that the younger composer would have been drawn to those works that resonated with his own youthful idealism. Of course, the writings that would most have concerned Mahler dealt with the arts and metaphysics, but he read Wagner's political writings as well. It is likely that the anti-Semitic essays such as "Judaism in Music" were more or less disregarded by Mahler, as Wagner's prejudices did not dampen the younger composer's enthusiasm for the Master and his music.

Friedrich Nietzsche's views on militarism have also suffered from misinterpretation due to their misuse by Hitler and the Nazis. Nietzsche's assertions that mankind is predestined to be violent power-seekers can easily be interpreted as condoning warfare; however, his later admonition that man should strive to become the *Übermensch* gives mere humans the ability to develop beyond our innate violent tendencies.[25] As Nietzsche gradually developed his theory over the course of many works, we see a relatively consistent perspective on concerns of war and violence. In his 1878 book *Human, All Too Human*, the philosopher quipped, "Against war it may be said that it makes the victor stupid and the vanquished revengeful."[26] In 1882's *The Gay Science*, he claimed, "Certainly the state in which we hurt others is rarely as agreeable, in an unadulterated way, as that in which we benefit others."[27] Sometimes, however, Nietzsche actually promoted the cause of fighting, but only in defense of the intellect. Also in *The Gay Science*, he promoted "heroism into the search for knowledge...

28   HIDDEN TREASURES

that will wage wars for the sake of ideas."[28] He carried this idea into *Also sprach Zarathustra*, writing, "Your enemy you shall seek, your war you shall wage—for your thoughts!"[29] And finally, in *Beyond Good and Evil* (1886), he wrote, "How poisonous, how crafty, how bad, does every long war make one!"[30]

Among all of his writings, Nietzsche never completed a work specifically dedicated to his views on war and violence. In 2009, Rebekah S. Perry collected all of the philosopher's writings referring to militarism, and, blending that with his writings on Christianity, extrapolated this hypothesis:

> There is every reason to assume that Nietzsche would have assembled these same ideas in forging an assault against hostile, violent war. I believe he would have applied them similarly, and that he would have arrived at the same conclusions. War, like Christianity, had played a dominant role in effectively bringing about the degradation and devastation of Western culture.... As with his unmasking of the real nature of Christianity, so it would be, or have become, with Nietzsche's unmasking of war. It is a lie, a fabrication engendered to transform what is incomprehensibly vile and vicious into its opposite—something virtuous, glorious, heroic, necessary, justified—a brilliant act of alchemy.[31]

If we accept Perry's theory of Nietzsche the pacifist, his influence on Mahler may go a long way toward explaining the young composer's views on militarism as expressed in his choices of texts from *Des Knaben Wunderhorn*.

Arthur Schopenhauer, much like Mahler, wrote very little pertaining explicitly to politics. Indeed, Cesare Vasoli, an Italian Marxist charged with creating an Italian edition of *The World as Will and Representation*, described his work as "a perfect theory for extreme disengagement."[32] Nonetheless, we do find a few references to war in his writings, and in these cases, they serve as warnings of the destructive potential of religion and of greed.

In Volume Two of *The World as Will and Representation*, first published in 1844, Schopenhauer describes war as the inevitable result of strict adherence to religious belief:

Look back also at the wars, disturbances, rebellions, and revolutions in Europe from the eighth to the eighteenth century; how few will be found that have not had as their essence, or their pretext, some controversy about beliefs, thus a metaphysical problem, which became the occasion of exciting nations against each other. Yet is that whole thousand years a continual slaughter, now on the battlefield, now on the scaffold, now in the streets, in metaphysical interests![33]

Here he described war as a state of "continual slaughter"—surely not a positive reflection of militarism—brought about by Christianity and its adherents.

In his 1851 *Parerga and Paralipomena*, he goes on to describe war as an outcome of greed. He writes:

The whole unnatural condition of society, the universal struggle to escape from misery, sea navigation with so much loss of life, the complicated interests of trade, and finally the wars to which all this gives rise—all these things have their sole root in luxury which does not even make happy those who enjoy it, but rather makes them unhealthy, delicate, and bad tempered.[34]

This relates to Schopenhauer's notion of greed leading to suffering, which can best be eased by aesthetic contemplation. In essence, Schopenhauer suggests that a healthy appreciation of the arts, especially music, which he sees as the purest form of art, can ease human suffering and bring about an end to greed and war. It is little wonder that Mahler and his friends in the Pernerstorfer Circle found themselves so drawn to Schopenhauer's theories, as they essentially transformed aesthetics into its own form of religious practice.

While we know little about Mahler's specific activities during his impressionable years at the University of Vienna with regard to politics, the writings to which he was introduced during this time do express anti-militaristic sentiment. Because Mahler was never recorded speaking of any firsthand experience with military violence he may have had, and he reportedly held positive memories of the soldiers he knew in childhood

30   HIDDEN TREASURES

from the barracks in Iglau, his engagement with the new philosophical ideals of Richard Wagner, Friedrich Nietzsche, and Arthur Schopenhauer provides a logical explanation for the negative perspective of militarism reflected in the *Wunderhorn* lieder, even as he maintained a fascination with military subject matter.

We find three primary types of military stories among Mahler's chosen song texts. The first three songs discussed here deal explicitly with military life. The first song, "Revelge," depicts the horrors that await men on the battlefield. Two others, "Der Tamboursg'sell" and "Zu Straßburg auf der Schanz," reveal the punishments inflicted on young men who try to abandon their military duties. Many of Mahler's military songs explore the pains of separation from loved ones when a young man is called off to war, and we will see an example of this type with "Nicht Wiedersehen."

Rather than expressing his anti-militaristic views through wordy philosophical rhetoric, Mahler chose to paint more descriptive images of the evils of war by focusing in on specific instances, in this case, folk stories, that vividly illustrated his ideas. The soldiers depicted in many of these songs share obvious traits: their stories occur in the midst of wartime, many have left sweethearts back home, and those sweethearts often serve as their motives for the stories that unfold. None of them can be entirely certain what their future holds for them, whether they are envisioning happy reunions with their loved ones, are trapped in a seemingly endless cycle of fighting a battle as a ghost, or are awaiting execution.

"Revelge"

The soldiers in Mahler's "Revelge" possess a far stronger sense of loyalty to their military duties than most might even find logical. These young men meet death through their devotion to an obviously lost cause. "Revelge" establishes its militaristic scenario from the very start with its strong marching rhythms in the strings and drum and fanfare-like trumpet passages, but by measure 3 we can already see that something is not right with this group of soldiers. A chromatic descending passage played by the woodwinds establishes an eerie foreboding of what follows (see Example 2.1).

MAHLER'S ANTI-MILITARIST COMMENTARY 31

Table 2.1: Text comparison for "Revelge"

Rewelge (Bremer)	Revelge (Mahler)	Reveille
Des Morgens zwischen drein und vieren	Des Morgens zwischen drei'n und vieren,	In the morning between three and four o'clock,
Da müssen wir Soldaten marschieren	da müssen wir Soldaten marschieren	We soldiers need to march Up and down the alley,
Das Gäßlein auf und ab;	Das Gäßlein auf und ab,	Tralalala,
Tralali, Tralalei, Tralala,	Trallali, Trallaley, Trallalera,	My darling looks down!
Mein Schätzel, sieht herab!	mein Schätzel sieht herab!	
"Ach, Bruder, jetzt bin ich geschossen,	Ach Bruder, jetzt bin ich geschossen,	Ah brother, just now I was shot,
Die Kugel hat mich schwer getroffen,	Die Kugel hat mich schwere, schwer getroffen,	The bullet has hit me hard, Carry me to the quarters,
Trag mich in mein Quartier,	trag' mich in mein Quartier,	Tralalala,
Tralali, Tralalei, Tralala,	Trallali, Trallaley, Trallalera,	It is not far from here!
Es ist nicht weit von hier."	es ist nicht weit von hier!	
"Ach Bruder, ich kann Dich nicht tragen,	Ach Bruder, ach Bruder, ich kann dich nicht tragen,	Ah brother, ah brother, I cannot carry you,
Die Feinde haben uns geschlagen,	die Feinde haben uns geschlagen,	The enemy has us beaten, May our loving God help you,
Helf dir der liebe Gott;	helf' dir der liebe Gott,	May our loving God help you!
Tralali, Tralalei, Tralala,	helf' dir der liebe Gott!	Tralalala,
Ich muß marschieren in Tod."	Trallai, Trallaley, Trallali,	I must, I must march until death!
	Trallaley, Trallalera,	
	ich muß, ich muß marschieren bis in' Tod!	
"Ach, Brüder, ihr geht ja vorüber,	Ach Brüder, ach Brüder,	Ah brother, ah brother, You're passing over me
Als wär es mit mir schon vorüber,	ihr geht ja mir vorüber, als wär's mit mir vorbei,	Like it is all over for me, Like it is already all over for me!
Ihr Lumpenfeind seid da;	als wär's mit mir schon vorbei!	(Like it is all over for me!)
Tralali, Tralalei, Tralala,	(als wär's mit mir vorbei!)	Tralalala,
Ihr tretet mir zu nah.	Trallali, Trallaley, Trallali,	You are stepping too close to me!
	Trallaley, Trallalera,	Too close to me!
	ihr tretet mir zu nah!	
	Ihr tretet mir zu nah!	

32 HIDDEN TREASURES

Table 2.1: continued

Rewelge (Bremer)	Revelge (Mahler)	Reveille
Ich muß wohl meine Trommel rühren,	Ich muß wohl meine Trommel rühren,	I must play my drum to wake them,
Sonst werde ich mich ganz verlieren;	ich muß meine Trommel wohl rühren,	I must play my drum to wake them,
Die Brüder dick gesäet,	Trallali, Trallaley, Trallali, Trallaley,	Tralalala, Tralalala,
Tralali, Tralalei, Tralala,	sonst werd' ich mich verlieren.	Otherwise I will lose myself.
Sie liegen wie gemäht."	Trallali, Trallaley, Trallala.	Tralalala,
	Die Brüder, dick gesät,	The brothers, far and wide,
	Die Brüder, dick gesät,	The brothers, far and wide,
	Sie liegen wie gemäht.	Like they were mowed down.
Er schlägt die Trommel auf und nieder,	Er schlägt die Trommel auf und nieder,	He played his drum far and near.
Er wecket seine stillen Brüder,	er wecket seine stillen Brüder,	He woke his silent brothers,
Sie schlagen ihren Feind,	Trallali, Trallaley, Trallali, Trallaley,	Tralalala,
Tralali, Tralalei, Tralala,	sie schlagen und sie schlagen	They attacked and they attacked
Ein Schrecken schlägt den Feind.	ihren Feind, Feind, Feind,	Their enemy, enemy, enemy,
	Trallali, Trallaley, Trallalerallala,	Tralalala, Tralalala,
	ein Schrecken schlägt den Feind,	A terror strikes their enemy,
	Ein Schrecken schlägt den Feind!	A terror strikes their enemy!
Er schlägt die Trommel auf und nieder	Er schlägt die Trommel auf und nieder,	He played his drum far and near,
Sie find vorm Nachtquartier schon wieder,	da sind sie vor dem Nachtquartier schon wieder,	They are there again, In front of the night quarters,
Ins Gäßlein hell hinaus,	Trallali, Trallaley, Trallali, Trallaley, Trallalera,	Tralalala, Tralalala,
Tralali, Tralalei, Tralala,	sie ziehen vor Schätzeleins Haus, Trallali.	They end up at his sweetheart's house,
Sie ziehn vor Schätzels Haus.		Tralala.

Rewelge (Bremer)	Revelge (Mahler)	Reveille
Da stehen Morgens die Gebeine	Des Morgens stehen da die Gebeine	In the morning, there stand the bones
In Reih und Glied wie Leichensteine,	in Reih' und Glied, sie steh'n wie Leichensteine,	In rank and file, they stand like tombstones.
Die Trommel steht voran,	in Reih', in Reih' und Glied.	In rank, in rank and file.
Tralali, Tralalei, Tralala,	Die Trommel steht voran,	The drummer stands in front,
Daß sie ihn sehen kann.	die Trommel steht voran,	The drummer stands in front,
	daß sie ihn sehen kann,	So that she can see him,
	Trallali, Trallaley, Trallali,	Tralalala, Tralalala,
	Trallaley, Trallalera,	So that she can see him.
	daß sie ihn sehen kann!	

Example 2.1: "Revelge," mm. 3–6

The wounded drummer asks to be carried along with the uninjured soldiers, stating, "[My beloved's home] is not far from here." We then hear a brief anthemic interlude (see Example 2.2), demonstrating the moment when the drummer's comrade pauses to decide whether helping his friend is more important than his duty; his response shows that the mission wins out, as he replies, "I cannot carry you, the enemy has struck us!" The statement itself brings with it a softer dynamic, showing great emotion, as if choosing to move on brought the drummer's comrade great pain. Yet the allegiance of the drummer continues even beyond his own death, as after he is gone, the text speaks of his ghost: "He played the drum far and near,

Example 2.2: "Revelge," mm. 29–32

He woke his silent brothers, They attacked their enemy, A terror strikes their enemy." By this point in the song, the drum has become a constant accompaniment feature. It plays very softly behind the vocal line marked "sehr laut" (very loud), giving the impression of distance between the narrator and the ghostly battle.

Despite these soldiers' commitment to their cause, the battle is not going well, and the focus of the song gradually shifts from the living soldiers to the casualties, as the text transforms from a story of wartime into one of the supernatural. Mahler's representation of his soldiers becomes increasingly more grotesque with each successive verse, as we hear in his distortion of the men's battle cry "Tralali, Tralaley, Tralalera!," which becomes more fragmented and complex as the living soldiers are outnumbered by the dead. The refrain slowly transforms into something beyond itself, morphing and changing with each successive hearing, until it can no longer be contained to the end of the verse, but rather appears sporadically, breaking down into progressively smaller pieces and then growing into a monstrous image of its former self. Examples 2.3a, b, and c show three instances of the refrain. The first hearing of the refrain appears in measures 13–15, as shown in Example 2.3a. Here we see the refrain in its simplest state. By measures 40–44, when it is revealed that the soldiers will continue to march even in death, the refrain begins to fragment, as shown by the separation between the words and the refrain's expansion from two and one-half measures to four measures, as seen in Example 2.3b. Example 2.3c shows the refrain in its fully morphed state, where even the words have undergone a transformation. By this time, short fragments of the refrain appear in seemingly random, unexpected places, not unlike the remains of the fallen. Yet even in death, their commitment to the cause remains. The grisly image of decaying bodies marching from the battlefield into the town finds its musical equivalent in the gradual mutation of their battle cry.

Despite the simple strophic structure of Mahler's chosen poem, he adopts a much freer form for the resulting ballad. The song begins, as

Mahler's Anti-Militarist Commentary

Example 2.3a, b, and c: "Revelge," mm. 13–15, 40–44, and 104–6

do many other examples of Mahler's military-inspired songs, with two repeated verses (though the key of the second verse begins in G minor, rather than the D minor that began the ballad), but the formal structure undergoes a gradual morphing that resembles the progressive distortion of the bodies of the soldiers who refuse to stop marching long after their hearts have stopped beating.

The first dramatic shift from what initially seems like an essentially strophic structure occurs in measures 29–32. The marching rhythms of the

Example 2.4: "Revelge," mm. 44–48

strings and brass give way to a woodwind melody with anthem-like qualities. But this kinder, gentler music is soon surpassed by the line "Ich muß marschieren bis in' Tod" (I must march until death), as the lines between the living and the dead, and between battle and home front, start to break down into a macabre march of death (see Example 2.4). We also find in this section the invasion of the refrain into the middle of verses; as the legions of the dead pile up, their song expands beyond its original boundaries.

The final image of "Revelge," "In the morning, there stand the bones, In rank and file, they stand like tombstones, The drummer stands in front, So that she can see him," reveals the grisly outcome of the battle. The men's loyalty to their cause and their loved ones has not only led to their untimely deaths, but this has resulted in this gruesome and haunting scene. "Revelge" vividly demonstrates that ongoing devotion to a lost cause and resorting to violence to support it claim the innocent as victims when they surrender their lives in support of circumstances that are not meant to be.

By comparing the spelling and punctuation found in Mahler's lyric compared to the poem as shown in the first edition and numerous contemporaneous editions, a change becomes evident. "Revelge" and the final *Wunderhorn* song, "Der Tamboursg'sell," were most likely composed using the edition published by Friedrich Bremer in 1878 in Leipzig, rather than the Robert Boxberger edition (Berlin, 1883) which Mahler appears to have relied upon up until this point. What led Mahler to change from one edition to another is unclear, but given the number of copies of the anthology he owned over the years (at least six can be confirmed),[35] it may simply be that by the time he resumed composing *Wunderhorn* songs, after the hiatus following "Wo die schönen Trompeten blasen," he had misplaced his previously used copy.

The temporal qualities of this story exist in a state that is open to interpretation. At first, the story seems to be happening roughly in real time and is presented in present tense through the soldiers' dialogue, but as the numbers of fallen soldiers begin to mount, the time seems to slow, until the narrator interrupts in stanza six to describe the eerie aftermath of the battle (though still in present tense), showing through narrative reflection that the events have already taken place in the past. The events that unfold—the preparation and marching off to battle, the battle itself, and the aftermath where the drummer leads the dead troops to the home of his sweetheart—all occur within a natural succession within at least the course of a day, but the repetitive nature of the stanzas seems to extend the story over a longer period of time, giving the impression that the march to the sweetheart's home becomes a nightly ritual that is repeated time and again. The interruption of the narrator shifts the focus away from the protagonist introduced earlier in the story and broadens it to encompass all the soldiers who have lost their lives in this battle.

Donald Mitchell writes that the expansive nature of "Revelge" and its sister song "Der Tamboursg'sell," which will be discussed below, successfully reversed the relationship between song and symphony on which Mahler relied for his previous *Wunderhorn* settings. Rather than basing a symphonic movement on a preexisting song, these songs, in their expansiveness and independence from orchestral writing, took their inspiration from ideas initially intended as instrumental music.[36]

"Zu Straßburg auf der Schanz"

This song, the fifth of his earliest group of *Wunderhorn* settings, composed only in voice and piano arrangements, contains specific performance indications and sonic hints that Mahler was already thinking of these songs as works that could be expanded with orchestral accompaniment. The opening pitches of the piano accompaniment feature the marking "Wie eine Schalmei" (Like a shawm), but the dynamic markings of piano and pianissimo contrast with the notoriously loud instrument that the music is intended to emulate.[37] These conflicting directives establish from the

Table 2.2: Text comparison for "Zu Straßburg auf der Schanz"

Der Schweizer (Boxberger)	Zu Straßburg auf der Schanz (Mahler)	At Strasbourg on the Ramparts
Zu Straßburg auf der Schanz, Da ging mein Trauern an; Das Alphorn hört ich drüben wohl anstimmen, Ins Vaterland mußt ich hinüber schwimmen; Das ging nicht an.	Zu Straßburg auf der Schanz', da ging mein Trauern an! Das Alphorn hört' ich drüben wohl anstimmen, in's Vaterland mußt' ich hinüber schwimmen, das ging ja nicht an, das ging ja nicht an! in's Vaterland mußt' ich hinüber schwimmen, das ging ja nicht an, das ging ja nicht an!	At Strasbourg on the ramparts, That's where I started mourning! I could hear the tune of an alphorn over there, I had to swim over to my homeland! That was not allowed, not allowed! I had to swim over to my homeland, That was not allowed, not allowed!
Ein Stunde in der Nacht Sie haben mich gebracht; Sie führten mich gleich vor des Hauptmanns Haus. Ach Gott, sie fischten mich im Strome auf; Mit mir ist's aus.	Ein' Stund' in der Nacht sie haben mich gebracht; sie führten mich gleich vor des Hauptmann's Haus! Ach Gott! Sie fischten mich im Strome auf! Mit mir ist es aus, mit mir ist es aus!	They brought me back in the middle of the night; They led me right in front of the captain's house! Ah God! They fished me out of the river! It's all over for me, It's all over for me!
Früh Morgen um zehn Uhr Stellt man mich vor das Regiment; Ich soll da bitten um Pardon, Und ich bekomm doch meinen Lohn; Das weiß ich schon.	Früh morgens um zehn Uhr stellt man mich vor's Regiment! Ich soll da bitten um Pardon, um Pardon! Und ich bekomm' doch meinen Lohn, und ich bekomm' doch meinen Lohn! Das weiß ich schon, das weiß ich schon!	Early in the morning at ten o'clock They put me in front of the regiment! I should ask for a pardon, a pardon! And I would get my due reward, And I would get my due reward! This much I already know, I already know!

MAHLER'S ANTI-MILITARIST COMMENTARY   39

Table 2.2: continued

Der Schweizer (Boxberger)	Zu Straßburg auf der Schanz (Mahler)	At Strasbourg on the Ramparts
Ihr Brüder allzumal,	Ihr Brüder all'zumal, ihr	You brothers, especially all
Heut seht Ihr mich zum	Brüder all'zumal,	you brothers,
letztenmal.	heut' seht ihr mich zum	Today you see me for the last
Der Hirtenbub ist doch nur	letzten mal;	time;
Schuld daran,	heut' seht ihr mich zum	Today you see me for the last
Das Alphorn hat mir solches	letzten mal!	time!
angethan;	Der Hirtenbub' ist nur schuld	The shepherd boy is the only
Das klag ich an.	daran gleich!	one to blame!
	Das Alphorn hat mir's	The alphorn has done this
	angethan,	to me,
	das hat mir's angethan!	Has done this to me!
	Das klag' ich an, das klag'	I blame that! I blame that!
	ich an!	
Ihr Brüder alle Drei,		
Was ich Euch bitt: erschießt		
mich		
Verschont mein junges Leben		
nicht,		
Schießt zu, daß das Blut,		
rausspritzt!		
Das bitt ich Euch.		
O Himmelskönig, Herr!		
Nimm Du meine arme Seele		
dahin,		
Nimm sie zu Dir in den		
Himmel ein,		
Laß sie ewig bei Dir sein,		
Und vergiß nicht mein!		

outset a protagonist grappling with a situation off in the distance. His mind is elsewhere, as is the alphorn that has caused him such internal conflict. We soon learn from the text that the young soldier is homesick, and the

Example 2.5: "Zu Straßburg auf der Schanz," mm. 1–3

sounds of the distant horn have only intensified his longing, driving him to attempt to desert. However, triplets heard in measures 2 and 8 also lend a certain fanfare-like quality to the situation (see Example 2.5), showing the conflict between duty to country and longing for home with which the soldier is struggling. This, in a way, creates a sense of two competing sonic worlds, one based in the present and one lost in dreams of a far-off time and place. At measure 15, Mahler adds a low trill to the accompaniment with the instruction "In allen diesen tiefen Trillern ist mit Hilfe des Pedals der Klang gedämpfter Trommeln nachahmen" (Use the pedals in all the low trills to emulate the sound of a muted drum) (see Example 2.6). This effect instantly brings to mind the drumrolls heard at an execution, and the listener learns that the soldier has been caught trying to flee and that his plea for a pardon will not be successful; we are witnessing the final moments before his sentence will be carried out.

Clemens Brentano collected the source poem, entitled "Der Schweizer," from a broadside that Ludwig Erk located among Arnim's estate, but his version of the poem differs quite dramatically from its source. Rather than suffering from intense homesickness, the soldier in the folk song printed on the broadside leaves his post because he wishes to fight for the Prussians rather than the French. This soldier lacks the innocence and sympathetic nature of Brentano's deserter.[38]

Example 2.6: "Zu Straßburg auf der Schanz," mm. 14–16

Example 2.7: "Zu Straßburg auf der Schanz," mm. 12–14, refrain

Mahler omitted the final two cinquains of the poem, which contained a somewhat graphic representation of the soldier's end. His other poetic changes, in the form of repetitions, contractions, and removal of unnecessary words, primarily serve to destabilize the poetic rhythm, allowing his music, rather than the words, to control the flow of ideas. Mahler's version of the poem also shortens the duration of the action and leaves open the smallest glimmer of a possibility that the soldier may be released and once again see his beloved Strasbourg. This is one of many instances where Mahler omits text and, in so doing, opens avenues of interpretive ambiguity and allows the listener to speculate, though in this case, their curiosity is not satisfied.

The musical structure of Mahler's setting extends traditional bar form, using three slightly varied *Stollen* sections (the first comprised of ten measures and the second and third of eight) and a lengthy *Abgesang* section (twenty measures), each of which closes with a kind of varied refrain (see Example 2.7), creating a form that neither conforms precisely to bar form, due to the added *Stollen*, nor to strophic form, due to the length of the final section, which might in a different case be interpreted as a coda. The first of the refrains appears as in Example 2.7, and the others alternate pitch ranges, moving from B flat to E flat in the second verse, returning to B flat in the third, and back to E flat in the final section. The first verse contains a brief passage of lyrical music (see Example 2.8) that contrasts with the martial motives heard at the beginning of the song. In this lyrical passage, the soldier becomes lost in remembrance of the past

Example 2.8: "Zu Straßburg auf der Schanz," mm. 7–10

as he tells of his loneliness and how the sound of the alphorn led him to abandon his duty. The second verse is the most cohesive and rooted in the reality of the soldier's unfortunate situation, maintaining the militaristic motives. The third verse rises slightly in pitch, ratcheting up the tension felt by the doomed young man, before eventually returning, by way of the refrain, to the pitch center heard in the beginning.

The musical landscape of Mahler's setting changes most dramatically to begin the B section at measure 39, when the soldier stops simply narrating his story and shifts his address to his fellow soldiers. The key changes from G minor to C major and the drumroll and fanfare motives become more invasive, taking a more active role in the narration and telling the soldier and his friends that his end is near. As the prisoner's moments become increasingly precious, the temporal characteristics of the narrative become more urgent. Suddenly, events seem to occur much more quickly. In measures 48–51, we hear the shawm theme one last time, telling us that the time has come for the soldier to face the firing squad. This final call of the alphorn signals the coming of morning and serves to move the story forward and focus our attention away from the young man's self-pity toward the events about to take place. A series of three ascending grace notes followed by a staccato eighth note musically simulates the shots of the firing squad in the final measure (not unlike the beheading heard in the fourth movement of Berlioz's *Symphonie fantastique*) (see Example 2.9). The final instance of the alphorn heard at the execution also functions very similarly to Berlioz's *idée fixe*, when the prisoner to be executed hears the theme representing that which he

Example 2.9: "Zu Straßburg auf der Schanz," m. 61

loves most (in this case, his homeland rather than a woman) in his final moment. Finally, we hear that the soldier's remaining hopes for a pardon have gone unanswered as the piece ends on the subdominant, providing no opportunity for a last-minute stay.[39]

The protagonist narrates the story directly to the audience, telling his tale as if to serve as a warning to others. Only in the final stanza does he speak to his fellow soldiers. The direct address gives the emotional power of the soldier's story more urgency than if it had been narrated by a third person. In the verses that Mahler omitted, the soldier speaks to the firing squad and to God, and eliminating these verses provides the audience a more immediate connection to the soldier, not allowing time and emotional distance to diminish the sympathy that his plight has aroused—though one might argue that the eliminated pleas for a swift execution would also lend the soldier a certain degree of sympathy. Despite the specific temporal references (he tells us he was caught in the middle of the night, but not whether it was the night before his pending execution, the passage of time in the story is elusive; one cannot tell how long the soldier has been awaiting his pending execution, only that he will face the regiment "tomorrow morning at ten o'clock." One could easily imagine either that the soldier has had a long time to think about his actions prior to telling his tale, or that all these events have taken place within the course of one night.

Matthias Slunitschek ascribes the soldier's actions to feelings of nostalgia and homesickness. He notes that medical science had begun to recognize homesickness as a psychological malady as early as 1678, when Johannes Hofer completed his work *Dissertatio medica de nostalgia oder Heimwehe*.[40] As recently as World War I, France maintained a policy of executing soldiers who attempted to flee from their military duty.[41] In 1802, Swiss anthropologist Johann Gottfried Ebel cited that intense

44   HIDDEN TREASURES

homesickness and desertion were to be expected from those from Alpine regions, due to their longing for the mountains and being forced to fight in a flat land they perceived as a "wasteland."[42]

"Der Tamboursg'sell"

Mahler's last *Wunderhorn* setting, "Der Tamboursg'sell," displays his compositional style at its apex. Bauer-Lechner wrote of the seemingly instantaneous inspiration of the song:

> It occurred to him literally between one step and the next—that is, just as he was walking out of the dining room. He sketched it immediately in the dark ante-room, and ran with it to the spring—his favorite place, which often gives him aural inspiration. Here he had the music completed very quickly. But now he saw that it was no symphonic theme—such as he had been after—but a song! And he thought of "Der Tamboursg'sell." He tried to recall the words; they seemed made for the melody. When he in fact compared the tune and the text up in the summer-house, not a word was missing, not a note was needed; they fitted perfectly![43]

This anecdote contradicts Mahler's earlier statement, made to Bauer-Lechner in 1896, that "the melody always grows out of the words,"[44] indicating a different compositional technique from his earlier ballads. This change in approach to the act of composing *Wunderhorn* songs may account for Donald Mitchell's observation that "'Revelge' and 'Der Tamboursg'sell' in a sense reverse the established relationship in Mahler's works between song and symphony."[45] That is to say, in these two examples, the songs grew out of musical ideas initially intended for symphonic use rather than musical inspiration emerging purely from the text.

The source poem for "Der Tamboursg'sell" remained almost untouched by Arnim and Brentano's editing process. Only a few small wording changes alter their version of the poem from that on the broadside on which they found it and which remained in Arnim's collection at the time of his death.[46] Mahler then made only a few changes, only deleting some repetition, and adding some of his own. These changes

Table 2.3: Text comparison for "Der Tamboursg'sell"

Tamburusgesell (Bremer)	Der Tamboursg'sell (Mahler)	The Drummer Boy
Ich armer Tambursgesell,	Ich armer Tamboursg'sell!	I am a poor drummer boy!
Man führt mich aus dem Gewölb,	Man führt mich aus dem G'wölb,	They lead me out of the cell,
Ja aus dem Gewölb,	man führt aus dem G'wölb!	They lead me out of the cell!
Wär ich ein Tambur blieben,	Wär ich ein Tambour blieben,	Had I stayed a drummer,
Dürft ich nicht gefangen liegen,	dürft ich nicht gefangen liegen!	I would not be a prisoner!
Nicht gefangen liegen.		
O Galgen, du hohes Haus,	O Galgen, du hohes Haus!	Oh, gallows, you high house!
Du siehst so furchtbar aus,	du siehst so furchtbar aus!	You look so awful!
So furchtbar aus,	Ich schau dich nicht mehr an	I cannot look at you anymore
Ich schau dich nicht mehr an,	ich schau dich nicht mehr an!	I cannot look at you anymore!
Weil i weiß, i gehör daran,	Weil i weiß, das i g'hör d'ran	Because I know what I'm hearing.
Daß i gehör daran.	weil i weiß, das i g'hör d'ran!	I know what I'm hearing!
Wenn Soldaten vorbeimarschieren,	Wenn Soldaten vorbeimarschier'n,	When soldiers march past me,
Bei mir nit einquartieren,	bei mir nit einquartier'n.	They don't stay by me.
Nit einquartieren,	Wenn sie fragen, wer i g'wesen bin:	If they ask who I was:
Wann sie fragen, wer i g'wesen bin:	Tampour von der Leibkompanie,	Drummer for the King's Bodyguard!
Tampur von der Leib=Kompanie,	Tampour von der Leibkompanie!	The King's Bodyguard!
Von der Leib=Kompanie.		
Gute Nacht, ihr Marmelstein,	Gute Nacht, ihr Marmelstein!	Good night, you marble stones!
Ihr Berg und Hügelein,	Ihr Berg' und Hügelein!	You mountains and hills!
Und Hügelein,	Gute Nacht, ihr Offizier,	Good night, you officers,
Gute Nacht, ihr Offizier,	Korporal und Musketier!	Corporals and musketeers!
Korporal und Musketier,		
Und Musketier!		

46   HIDDEN TREASURES

Table 2.3: continued

Tambursgesell (Bremer)	Der Tamboursg'sell (Mahler)	The Drummer Boy
Gute Nacht, ihr Offizier,	Gute Nacht!	Good night!
Korporal und Grenadier,	Gute Nacht ihr Offizier!	Good night you officers!
Und Grenadier.	Korporal und Grenadier!	Corporals and grenadiers!
Ich schrei mit heller Stimm,	Ich schrei mit heller Stimm:	I cry with a clear voice:
Von euch ich Urlaub nimm,	von Euch ich Urlaub nimm!	I take my leave from you!
Ja Urlaub nimm!	Von Euch ich Urlaub nimm!	I take my leave from you!
	Gute Nacht,	Good night,
	Gute Nacht!	Good night!

appear on the piano sketch discussed by Bauer-Lechner on which Mahler worked out the drum cadence, the harmonic flow, and to some degree the melody of the song, providing us with an unusual view of the compositional process mid-stream. The final stanzas of the poem are scrawled on the bottom of the second page of the sketch, and the words are also penciled in above the text. The penciled words differ in terms of added and omitted repetitions from the text which are written at the bottom of the same page. This sketch reveals a great deal regarding Mahler's practice of text alteration as it corresponded to the act of song composition. The placement of words and erasures on the sketch seem to indicate that any alterations the composer chose to make to his song texts were completed as part of the compositional act rather than as a discrete activity. "Der Tamboursg'sell" was the last *Wunderhorn* poem set by Mahler; after this, he turned to the poems of Friedrich Rückert. Carl Schorske has proposed that the death of the drummer boy marked the end of Mahler's association with the innocence of an idealized folk tradition and paved the way for the pessimism and tragedy found in his settings of *Kindertotenlieder*.[47]

In order to set the scene for the drummer boy's impending execution, Mahler regularized portions of the poetic rhythm, that moves along at the beat of a drum cadence, through the use of contractions (e.g. "das i gehör daran" becomes "das i g'hör d'ran") and some added repetitions of text. Mahler replaces several short repeated phrases that appeared in each of the poem's five stanzas with repetition of different phrases, shifting the emphasis from the drummer boy's current situation to the things that he believes he will miss the most once he is gone.

The doomed drummer boy narrates his entire story directly, but his address changes several times throughout his tale. In his opening stanza, the boy seems to be speaking to no one in particular, as he simply bemoans his fate, then he begins to call out to various places and people that he will not see again, engaging in the literary device of apostrophe and taking the opportunity to say his goodbyes, even though those to whom he wishes to speak are not actually present—some are even inanimate objects, such as stones, mountains, and hills, as if prolonging the process of saying his goodbyes to anything and everything might somehow stall his impending doom.[48] The nature of the story makes it difficult to determine precisely how much time is passing during it. We are hearing the drummer boy's thoughts during his final night before his execution, but he does not reveal how long he has been held captive, and this blurs the temporal center of the story, making it almost lyrical in nature. He recalls being led to the gallows and his thoughts on seeing it, but only his final words are spoken in real time.

This song also holds the distinction of being the only one of the *Wunderhorn* ballads to be explicitly labeled by Mahler as a ballad.[49] He referred to many of the earlier *Wunderhorn* songs as *Humoresken*, and the drollness of those songs is absent in "Revelge" and "Der Tamboursg'sell." Indeed, there is nothing even vaguely humorous about this situation. In the folklore tradition, stories of young men being executed during military service are somewhat common. As noted above, Mahler set a poem that tells a similar story, "Zu Straßburg auf der Schanz," roughly a decade before composing "Der Tamboursg'sell." What makes the story of this drummer boy particularly poignant is that he is only a child. Given that the cause of his punishment has not been explicitly specified, one is forced to wonder what crime would be so heinous as to justify the execution of a child.

Children have been enlisted for military duties throughout history, dating back to antiquity, as noted in David's service to King Saul in the Bible. And drums had been a standard part of military campaigns almost as long, but the romanticized notion of the military drummer boy is largely

48   HIDDEN TREASURES

a product of the eighteenth century. Drummer boys of note served in the French and American Revolutionary Wars and the American Civil War. Among the earliest extant evidence of a drummer boy is a petition for service written to the Privy Council by Gawen Smithe in 1582, wherein he provides a list of "all suche marches I can sownde on the drum."[50] And these children were not spared from the penalties for desertion, as noted in the following advertisement from the May 31, 1777 edition of *The Providence Gazette*:

> Deserted from Capt. John Garzia's Company of Artillery, in Col. Elliott's Regiment Eldridge Spink, jun., a Drummer, born in West Greenwich, twelve Years of Age, 4 Feet 8 Inches one Quarter high, light blue Eyes, and light brown Hair. Had on when he went away, a blue Coat, the Seams trimmed with blue and white Saddle Trimmings. Whoever will apprehend him and return him to his Company, at Providence, or secure him in any Gaol of the United States, shall have Five Dollars Reward; and all reasonable Charges, paid by John Garzia, Capt.[51]

Petitioning the public to capture and return these children to the military for execution must have caused enormous emotional turmoil for those unfortunate enough to encounter such a deserter.

Musically speaking, "Der Tamboursg'sell" possesses a level of drama that the other *Wunderhorn* songs lack. The lone muted drumrolls come as if out of a dream or a forgotten past, then the horns and low-pitched woodwinds, playing minor chords, fill out the scenario as that of an execution. The unusual instrumentation helps to create the dark, solemn atmosphere. Mahler's string section includes only cellos and contrabass; violins and violas are omitted. The lack of higher pitches results in a sense of emptiness in the scene, a kind of musical representation of the compassion missing in the story. The mood is not unlike that heard in the fourth movement of Berlioz's *Symphonie fantastique* (especially so in measures 33–49, when a countermelody in the bassoons and horns emulates the act of marching to the scaffold, as seen in Example 2.10). Mahler adds weight to this grave situation with touches such as the addition of contrabassoon and bass clarinet, creating a dark sense of foreboding.

Example 2.10: "Der Tamboursg'sell," mm. 33–36

Marked "Mit naivem Vortrag, ohne Sentimentalität" (With naïve presentation, without sentimentality), the vocal melody remains simple and lyrical throughout. This delivery emphasizes the innocence of the drummer boy and underscores the brutality of war in which the execution of a child is considered as acceptable punishment for his crime.

Mahler utilizes a variation on typical bar form in "Der Tamboursg'sell," similar to that used in "Zu Straßburg auf der Schanz," using three varied *Stollen* sections (of twenty-two, twenty-three, and nineteen measures) followed by a lengthy *Abgesang* section (of fifty-five measures). The mood changes drastically at measure 91, the beginning of the B section, as the drummer boy begins to say his farewells, as if the truth of what awaits him has finally sunken in.[52] The key changes from D minor to C minor, and the lowering of the pitch adds weight to the scene. The tempo slows, and the low woodwinds, brass, and strings sustain long pitches over which the English horn begins its mournful song associated with the drummer boy's goodbyes. This melancholy mood remains throughout the rest of the song. It is only in this section that the boy truly realizes how little time he has left, what fate has in store for him, and what he is about to lose.

Mahler lends strong symbolic reference to the oboe and English horn and their associations with the drummer boy's former life. When the boy speaks of his life before his capture, claiming his former identity as "Tampour von der Leibkompanie!" (drummer for the king's bodyguard), the oboe proudly supports his melody in G major, and when he says goodbye to the soldiers he is leaving behind, he is preceded by a pitiable melody in the English horn marked "sehr klagend" (very sorrowful)

Example 2.11: "Der Tamboursg'sell," mm. 102–10

(see Example 2.11). Much of this section features conflicting expression marks between the vocal and instrumental melodies: a marking of "mit Gefühl" (with feeling) appears above the voice at measure 110, while at the same point the clarinet and bassoon countermelodies are marked "ohne Ausdruck" (without expression) and the strings "ausdruckslos" (expressionless) (see Example 2.12). This allows the boy's profoundly emotional response to the situation to remain separate and distinct from that of the world around him, serving as a commentary on how callous and unfeeling the outside world can be during wartime, when the impending execution of a child does not stir even the slightest pity.

Mahler uses chromatic harmony to great effect throughout the song as a marker of the drummer boy's fear and regret (see Example 2.13). The first example of chromatic pitches occurs when the boy states "Wär ich ein Tambour blieben, dürft ich nicht gefangen liegen" (Had I stayed a drummer, I would not be a prisoner), expressing his wish that things could be different. Further chromaticism appears when the boy looks out upon the gallows and during his final goodbyes, moments when his fear

Example 2.12: "Der Tamboursg'sell," mm. 110–14

Example 2.13: "Der Tamboursg'sell," mm. 22–26

would naturally be at its highest. The rest of the song remains relatively diatonic, as though the chromatic pitches represent his emotions getting the better of him and diatonic pitches symbolize emotional control.

"Der Tamboursg'sell" tells a story that lacks a temporal grounding. Neither the text nor Mahler's music provide much indication of how much time has passed from beginning to end. We can assume, given the drastic change in musical sound at the beginning of the B section, that the morning of the boy's hanging has arrived, but how long he has been forced to await his execution remains unstated. Ironically, the only example of the *Wunderhorn* lieder that Mahler explicitly identified as a ballad lacks the hallmark characteristic of the genre, that of a story passing through time with a clear beginning, middle, and end.

"Nicht Wiedersehen!"

"Nicht Wiedersehen!" speaks to the horrors of war from a different angle. It tells a tragic tale of a couple separated by patriotic duty, with devastating consequences. It begins with their parting but then immediately skips to the young man's anxious return, wherein he searches for his beloved, only to learn that she has died of a broken heart mere days earlier. Mahler dramatically alters the form of the original poem to create his lyric, changing five short stanzas into three larger verses with a refrain adapted from the opening line of the poem. Upon the soldier's return and learning of the maiden's death, he goes to her resting place, and their reunion is marked with a substantial, albeit heartrending, change in musical setting.

Table 2.4: Text comparison for "Nicht Wiedersehen!"

Nicht wiedersehen (Boxberger)	Nicht Wiedersehen! (Mahler)	Never Seen Again
"Nun ade, mein allerherzliebster Schatz! Jetzt muß ich wohl scheiden von Dir Bis auf den andern Sommer; Dann komm ich wieder zu Dir." –	Und nun ade, mein herzallerliebster Schatz! Jetzt muß ich wohl scheiden von dir, von dir, bis auf den andern Sommer; dann komm' ich wieder zu dir! Ade, Ade, mein herzallerliebster Schatz, mein herzallerliebster Schatz!	And now, farewell, my heart's most beloved! I must now go far away from you, Until next summer; Then I will come back to you! Farewell, my heart's most beloved!
Und als der junge Knab heimkam, Von seiner Liebsten fing er an: "Wo ist meine Herzallerliebste, Die ich verlassen hab?" –	Und als der junge Knab' heimkam, von seiner Liebsten fing er an: "Wo ist meine Herzallerliebste, die ich verlassen hab'?"	And when the young man came home, He thought of his beloved: "Where is my heart's most beloved that I left behind?"
"Auf dem Kirchhof liegt sie begraben, Heut ist's der dritte Tag; Das Trauern und das Weinen Hat sie zum Tod gebracht." –	"Auf dem Kirchhof liegt sie begraben, heut' ist's der dritte Tag! Das Trauern und das Weinen hat sie zum Tod gebracht!" Ade, ade, mein herzallerliebster Schatz, mein herzallerliebster Schatz!	"She lies buried in the churchyard, Today is the third day! Her grieving and crying Brought her to death!" Farewell, my heart's most beloved!
"Jetzt will ich auf den Kirchhof gehen, Will suchen meiner Liebsten Grab, Will ihr alleweil rufen, Bis daß sie mir Antwort giebt.	Jetzt will ich auf den Kirchhof geh'n, will suchen meiner Liebsten Grab, will ihr all'weile rufen, ja rufen, bis daß sie mir Antwort gab!	Now I will go to the churchyard, I will find my beloved's grave, And I will call out to her Until she gives me an answer!

MAHLER'S ANTI-MILITARIST COMMENTARY 53

Table 2.4: continued

Nicht wiedersehen (Boxberger)	Nicht Wiedersehen! (Mahler)	Never Seen Again
Ei, Du mein allerherzliebster Schatz,	Ei du, mein allerherzliebster Schatz,	Oh, you, my heart's most beloved,
Mach auf Dein tiefes Grab!	mach' auf dein tiefes Grab!	Open your deep grave!
Du hörst kein Glöcklein läuten,	Du hörst kein Glöcklein läuten,	You hear no clocks chiming, You hear no birds singing,
Du hörst kein Vöglein pfeifen,	du hörst kein Vöglein pfeifen,	You see neither the sun nor the moon!
Du siehst weder Sonn noch Mond!"	du siehst weder Sonne noch Mond!	Farewell, my heart's most beloved!
	Ade, ade, mein herzallerliebster Schatz,	
	Mein harzallerliebster Schatz!	
	Ade!	

"Nicht Wiedersehen!" makes the anguish experienced by this young soldier obvious from the first notes of the introduction, a lonely melody that foreshadows the tragedy to come. From the very outset, the slow, quiet theme informs the listener that all is not well, and in measure 3, when the soldier addresses his love for the first time, a low-pitched descending fourth appears in the piano (see Example 2.14). This motive recurs five times more in the song and soon becomes associated with the young woman's death, gradually taking on the symbol of church bells ringing to signal her burial, as noted by the marking "Wie fernes Glockenläuten" (like the distant ringing of bells). A brief respite from the sorrow takes the form of an epic narrated section in measures 16–20 (see Example 2.15), in which we learn that the soldier has returned from service and immediately looks for his love, only to discover that she has died. This section has a lighter accompaniment and lacks the dragging tempo found in the earlier parts of the song, providing a detached, more neutral point of observation. This brief passage also contracts the time that the soldier has been away into an instant, allowing the accompaniment to assume the role of narrator by taking control of the temporal progress of the story.

Example 2.14: "Nicht Wiedersehen!" mm. 1–4

Only an eighth-note rest separates the soldier's final words before parting and the narrator's announcement that he has returned. If it were not for the lightening of the texture and the return of the church bell motive, it would be easy to overlook the fact that his tour of duty has passed by in the story so quickly.

The bar form in "Nicht Wiedersehen!" is conventional, comprised of two *Stollen* and an *Abgesang*, each containing the refrain, created through repetition of the opening poetic lines, "Ade, mein herzallerliebster Schatz" (Farewell, my heart's most beloved). Mahler's *Stollen* are nearly identical, except that the pitches in the bass are doubled at the lower octave the second time they are heard. The added pitches signal to the young man and the audience that the young woman has only recently died, representing the echoes of the tolling bells from her burial

Example 2.15: "Nicht Wiedersehen!" mm. 16–20

Example 2.16: "Nicht Wiedersehen!" mm. 55–59

still hanging in the air. The echoes remain throughout the entire second verse, while the young man absorbs the knowledge of his love's death and subsequently vows to wait by her graveside until she "gives him an answer," presumably to his proposal of marriage, though that is never made clear.

A significant change in the mood of the music occurs at measure 52, the beginning of the *Abgesang*, when the key changes from minor to major (see Example 2.16). The soldier has at last gone to the graveyard to address his beloved directly. The shift from C minor to its parallel major brings an uncanny sense of comfort, as though even under the dreadful circumstances, the soldier is relieved to at last be reunited with his love. He asks her to "open her deep grave" so that she can hear bells and singing birds. During this passage, the church bell motive heard earlier in the song continues relentlessly, as if the accompaniment is speaking directly to the young man, trying to convey to him the fruitlessness of his pleas. Finally, he realizes that what is done cannot be undone, and he says his

56   HIDDEN TREASURES

final goodbyes to his beloved, the tragedy of reality reveals itself, and the final refrain returns to C minor.

The text for the song indicates that the young man would not be away for an extraordinarily long time (he states before leaving, "Until next summer, then I will come back to you!"), yet their separation was difficult enough and caused the maiden so much pain that she died from "her grieving and crying." This may strike the listener as an overexaggeration, but, as will be revealed in Chapter 3, Mahler's descriptions of his own feelings of love could often seem overly dramatic. In any case, the death of the maiden in "Nicht Wiedersehen!" brings to light one of the more easily overlooked tragedies of wartime violence, the price paid by the loved ones that the soldiers leave behind.

Through his composition of these songs Mahler paints very distinct and vivid pictures of his views on wartime violence. A clear connection can be drawn between his youthful political activities and his resulting interest in the writings of Wagner, Nietzsche, and Schopenhauer, who at various times expressed anti-militaristic views similar to those demonstrated by Mahler's songs. Given his general ambivalence toward politics, Mahler left little direct evidence pertaining to his specific views, but the sheer quantity of military themes he explored during the *Wunderhorn* years suggests that on some level, he maintained the idealistic views that he had developed during his years at the university.

CHAPTER THREE

"Vehement and consuming longing, mixed with dread and anxiety"

Mahler's Thoughts on Love and Romantic Fidelity

Mahler spent the so-called *Wunderhorn* years in and out of several romantic relationships. Several of these seem to have been brief but passionate affairs that quickly burned out; others had more lasting effects on the composer. The letters he wrote to the most important women in his life reveal a great deal about Mahler's views on love and romance, particularly those on fidelity and commitment.[1] The desperate, intense emotions he poured into his words reveal a man who took romantic faithfulness to heart. But it would seem that this was not always the case, and two of his *Wunderhorn* lieder, "Um schlimme Kinder artig zu machen" and "Ich ging mit Lust," deal with the idea of romantic infidelity, though in both cases that hermeneutic layer lies hidden below the surface. Three other examples, "Trost im Unglück," "Aus! Aus!" and "Scheiden und Meiden," tell the stories of lovers who have clearly tired of one another, further calling their faithfulness into question. From the perspective of history, we can acknowledge the irony of a bachelor in his late twenties writing multiple songs about casual infidelity, only to find his own world shattered when he would later learn of his own wife having an affair, but as Mahler would not even meet his future wife for over a decade after most of these songs were composed, we must simply chalk up these songs and the subject of them to youthful naïvety.

By the time Mahler began composing songs to the texts of *Des Knaben Wunderhorn*, he had had several clandestine affairs with sopranos singing

58   HIDDEN TREASURES

under his baton: first with Johanna Richter, who sang for him in Kassel in 1883 and inspired his first song cycle, *Lieder eines fahrenden Gesellen*, and then with Betty Frank in Prague in 1885. This tells us that from the very start of his career, his love life would serve as a vital inspiration for his song composition.

Marion von Weber

Mahler's first serious love affair that coincides with the *Wunderhorn* era was also his most indelicate. In 1886, he was hired as an assistant conductor at the Leipzig Opera House, under Arthur Nikisch. In February 1887, Nikisch became gravely ill, and from February until May, Mahler had sole control over the company's baton. During this time, he made the acquaintance of Captain Karl von Weber, grandson of composer Carl Maria von Weber. Mahler's dramatic sensitivity made such an impression on the captain that soon the composer was asked to complete Carl Maria's unfinished opera, *Die drei Pintos*. This project had been attempted without success several times before: first by Weber's friend, the composer Giacomo Meyerbeer, at the request of Weber's widow Caroline, then by Vincenz Lachner at the behest of Weber's son Max. Given the history of the piece, Mahler was initially reticent to take on the challenge, but during the summer of 1887, he had a breakthrough, telling Natalie Bauer-Lechner, "As restrained as I was in the beginning in amending the sketches, I got more and more daring during the course of the work, allowing myself to be carried away by the matter and by myself instead of worrying whether Weber would have done it that way."[2] On October 4 of that same year, he wrote to the Weber family, informing them that the score was complete.

During Mahler's time with the Weber family, he engaged in a romantic affair with Frau Marion von Weber. Four years his elder and evidently lonely due to her husband's frequent military duties that took him from the family home, she, by all accounts, seems to have been perfectly willing to give in to her longing for the composer. Mahler described her in a letter to his friend Friedrich Löhr as "A beautiful person… the sort that tempts one to do foolish things."[3] No documents survive to indicate the lengths the lovers took to keep their liaison a secret, and nor is it clear when Captain Weber learned of the relationship, but at the end of

MAHLER'S THOUGHTS ON LOVE AND ROMANTIC FIDELITY 59

the 1888 season, Mahler left Leipzig for good. English composer Ethel Smyth wrote quite melodramatically of the events leading to the couple's separation:

> In spite of his ugliness he had demoniacal charm. [Mahler], a tyrannical lover, never hesitated to compromise his mistress. Things were getting critical, when one day, traveling to Dresden in the company of strangers, [Capt.] Weber suddenly burst out laughing, drew a revolver and began taking William Tell-like shots at the headrests between the seats. He was overpowered, the train brought to a standstill, they took him to the police station raving mad—thence to an asylum. Always considered rather queer in the Army, the Mahler business had broken his brain. I afterwards heard that his wife in an agony of remorse refused to see her lover again.[4]

La Grange clarifies, saying Smyth's account is highly exaggerated, and Captain Weber did not live out his days in an asylum; in fact, he took advantage of his sway with theater management and nominated Mahler to conduct his own First Symphony at the Gewandhaus concerts a few months after the Dresden incident. However, the truth remains that a liaison did take place between Mahler and his patron's wife; the composer was evidently not overly concerned with protecting his lover's reputation and indeed hinted at the indiscretion in the song "Um schlimme Kinder artig zu machen."

"Um schlimme Kinder artig zu machen"

Mahler began to compose his earliest *Wunderhorn* songs shortly after reportedly encountering the anthology in the home of Captain Weber in 1887.[5] During the time that Mahler worked with the sketches for *Die drei Pintos*, he spent a great deal of time in the Weber home, becoming close with the Webers' three children—Katharina, age nine, Adolf, eight, and Marion, six—as he was beginning his secret intimacy with their mother. "Um schlimme Kinder" is among several songs dedicated to the Webers' children, but the result is far more than merely a children's song.

60   Hidden Treasures

Table 3.1: Text comparison for "Um schlimme Kinder artig zu machen"

Um schlimme Kinder (Boxberger)	Um schlimme Kinder artig zu machen (Mahler)	To Make Naughty Children Behave
Es kam ein Herr zum Schlößli	Es kam ein Herr zum Schlösseli	There came a man up to the castle,
Auf einem schönen Rößli;	auf einem schönen Röss'li, Kukukuk, kukukuk!	riding on a handsome horse, (Cuckoo, cuckoo!)
Da lugt die Frau zum Fenster aus	Da lugt die Frau zum Fenster aus	The woman peeks out of the window
Und sagt: "Der Mann ist nicht zu Haus,	und sagt: "der Mann ist nicht zu Haus, und niemand, und niemand,	and says, "My husband is not at home, and no one is here but my children,
Und Niemand heim als Kinder	und niemand heim als meine Kind';	and the maid who is washing!"
Und's Mädchen auf der Winden."	und's Mädchen, und's Mädchen ist auf der Wäschewind!"	
Der Herr auf seinem Rößli Sagt zu der Frau im Schlößli.		
	Der Herr auf seinem Rösseli sagt zu der Frau im Schlösseli: Kukukuk, kukukuk!	The man on his horse says to the woman in the castle: (Cuckoo, cuckoo!)
"Sind's gute Kind, sind's böse Kind?	"Sind's gute Kind', sind's böse Kind'?	"Are they good children, or naughty children?
Ach, liebe Frau, ach sagt geschwind!"	Ach, liebe Frau, ach sagt geschwind,"	Ah, dear woman, tell me quickly!"
Die Frau, die sagt: "Sehr böse Kind;	Kukukuk, kukukuk!	(Cuckoo, cuckoo!)
Sie folgen Muttern nicht geschwind."	"In meiner Tasch' für folgsam Kind'	"In my pocket, for obedient children,
	da hab ich manche Angebind," kukukuk, kukukuk!	I have presents." (Cuckoo, cuckoo!)

MAHLER'S THOUGHTS ON LOVE AND ROMANTIC FIDELITY 61

Table 3.1: continued

Um schlimme Kinder (Boxberger)	Um schlimme Kinder artig zu machen (Mahler)	To Make Naughty Children Behave
	Die Frau, die sagt: "sehr böse Kind'! Sie folgen Muttern nicht geschwind, sind böse, sind böse!" Die Frau, die sagt: "sind böse Kind! Sie folgen der Mutter nicht geschwind!"	The woman says: "Very naughty children! They don't obey their mother quickly; they're naughty, they're naughty!"
Da sagt der Herr: "So reit ich heim; Dergleichen Kinder brauch ich kein." Und reit auf seinem Rößli Weit, weit entweg vom Schlößli.	Da sagt der Herr: "so reit' ich heim, dergleichen Kinder brauch ich kein'!" Kukukuk, kukukuk! Und reit' auf seinem Rösseli weit, weit entweg vom Schösseli! Kukukuk, Kukukuk!	Then the man says: "Then I will ride home, for I have nothing to give children such as these!" (Cuckoo, cuckoo!) And he rides his horse far, far away from the castle! (Cuckoo, cuckoo!)

"Um schlimme Kinder" seems to tell a simple story on the surface: a rider approaches a castle and speaks to the woman of the house, who states that her husband is away, and her children and housekeeper are busy elsewhere. The rider asks if the children are well behaved, saying he bears gifts if they are, and she replies that they are "very naughty children. They do not listen to their mother." The rider replies, "Then I will ride home. I have nothing to give children such as these." Superficially, "Um schlimme Kinder" appears to be an admonishment for children to obey their parents, which makes sense, given for whom it was composed; however, the song carries a message hidden below the surface.

Mahler cleverly disguised a secret meaning within the text. Scattered throughout the poem he inserted an onomatopoetic cuckoo call. Musically, this reinforces the folk-like and child-friendly veneer of the song, but it also carries a private message. In German medieval literature, the cuckoo was a common emblem, "symbolic of adultery, especially by a married woman who deceives her husband. The word 'cuckold' comes from cuckoo and refers only to the husband."[6] Mahler would have known about this representation from his studies of medieval literature while at the University of Vienna.[7] He later described animal sounds as "pregnant with meaning," implying that the use of the cuckoo call was not coincidental.[8] Whether any of the Webers recognized the significance of the cuckoo is unknown, but the symbolism certainly explains its presence, which, when taken out of this context, strikes the listener as contrived and unnecessary.

Mahler uses the interval of the descending perfect fourth to symbolize this important (though physically absent) figure in the story of the rider and the *Hausfrau*. This interval appears in the opening measure of the introduction and recurs no fewer than forty-three times throughout the course of the song's forty-one measures. Several things are unusual about the prevalence of this interval. Cuckoo calls are traditionally notated using two pitches at the interval of a descending minor third, as Mahler does in his other songs that utilize the call of the cuckoo (such as "Lob des hohen Verstandes," discussed in Chapter 8), but here it is transformed into a three-note motive of a descending perfect fourth and minor third (see Examples 3.1a and b). Cuckoo calls occur in the lyrics to "Um schlimme Kinder" (though not in the source poem) three times in each verse, but in one of these instances it is not set with the unusual, but by this time established sonic signifier of the cuckoo call, but instead a descending major second and minor third, giving the new motive a more ominous tone (see

Example 3.1a and b: Cuckoo calls from "Lob des hohen Verstandes," m. 126 and "Um schlimme Kinder," mm. 5–6

Example 3.2: Unusual cuckoo call from "Um schlimme Kinder," mm. 33–34

Example 3.2). The three-note motive associated with all but this unusual cuckoo call accompanies portions of dialogue spoken by the housewife as well; in the first verse, the motive appears with the words "'*und niemand, und niemand, und niemand* heim als meine Kind'; *und's Mädchen, und's Mädchen ist auf* der Wäschenwind'" and in the third verse to the text "'*sind böse, sind böse!' Die Frau*, die sagt: 'sind böse Kind! *Sie folgen, sie folgen der Mutter* nicht geschwind!'"

One finds another unusual quality in "Um schlimme Kinder" when looking at its rhythmic and metrical qualities. The song, written in common time, begins with an eighth-note pick-up measure, played as two sixteenth notes (see Example 3.3). A piano introduction with accents on the fourth and last eighth-note beats follows, shifting the accent of the entire song ahead of where it would be expected by an eighth note. Rather than emphasizing eighth beats one and five, the accompaniment jumps the gun, accenting four and eight, giving the impression of overeagerness, as if the rider and the *Hausfrau* cannot wait to get through their flirtation and give into their attraction. This feeling remains throughout the entire song.

Both verses end in a somewhat peculiar way as well. The vocal line traces a descending arpeggiated tonic chord, but it never reaches the tonic pitch. The thought remains to be completed by the accompaniment, which promptly picks up the figure and brings it to conclusion. This could be an

Example 3.3: "Um schlimme Kinder artig zu machen," mm. 1–3

64   HIDDEN TREASURES

indication that the rider and the woman have not even bothered to wait for their story to end properly before beginning their passion.

Given the hidden meaning of the cuckoo call in "Um schlimme Kinder," the seemingly innocent encounter it describes becomes fraught with sexual innuendo. The "gifts" the rider offers to leave suddenly morph into sexual favors, and the question of "good children" and "naughty children" begins to resemble seductive pillow talk. While the traveler may not have left trinkets for the children of the house, their mother appears to have emerged well satisfied by the encounter.

So for whom was the moral of "Um schlimme Kinder" intended: the Weber children or their mother? It would appear that it held a message for both. This song, like many of Mahler's *Wunderhorn* settings, offers multiple layers of meaning. The listener is free to understand these songs in whatever ways make the most sense to them and take away the messages that most apply to their circumstances.

"Ich ging mit Lust"

In "Ich ging mit Lust," a young man spends the day walking merrily through the woods, while his lover waits at home. When he finally arrives, the maiden wonders where he has been all day. In the final line, the narrator poses the question, "Where is *your* beloved staying?" In the original poem, the maiden's suspicion is not without just cause, as the lad claims, "With beer, wine, and a dark-haired maiden, I was quickly forgetting you." Mahler, however, omits this line and completely re-writes the ending, leaving the situation ambiguous. Where has the young man been, and what has he been doing all day?

Mahler's changes to the poetry impact the meaning in this song a great deal. In the stanzas Mahler chose to omit, the maiden has the opportunity to confront her lover with her knowledge that he is lying about his whereabouts during his "walk," and he then responds by confessing to his dalliance, resulting in a comical apothegm. Mahler's revisions cast the young man's actions as more deceitful, allowing the song to serve as a warning to young girls (possibly the Webers' daughters, or, as will be discussed in Chapter 5, Mahler's younger sisters) about the wandering eyes of suitors.

MAHLER'S THOUGHTS ON LOVE AND ROMANTIC FIDELITY 65

Table 3.2: Text comparison for "Ich ging mit Lust"

Waldvöglein (Boxberger)	Ich ging mit Lust (Mahler)	I Walked with Joy
Ich ging mit Lust durch einen grünen Wald;	Ich ging mit Lust durch einen grünen Wald,	I walked with joy through a green wood;
Ich hört die Vöglein singen.	ich hört die Vöglein singen.	I heard the birds singing.
Sie sangen so jung, sie sangen so alt,	Sie sangen so jung, sie sangen so alt,	they sang so young, they sang so old,
Die kleinen Waldvöglein in dem Wald.	die kleinen Waldvöglein im grünen Wald, im grünen Wald!	those small birds in the green wood! The green wood!
Wie gern hört ich sie singen!	Wie gern hört' ich sie singen, ja singen!	How gladly I listened to their singing! Yes! Singing!
Nun sing, nun sing, Frau Nachtigall!	Nun sing', nun sing', nun sing', Frau Nachtigall!	Now sing, now sing, Lady Nightingale!
Sing Du's bei meinen Feinsliebchen:	Sing' du's bei meinem Feinsliebchen:	sing by my sweetheart's house:
"Komm schier, komm schier, wenn's finster ist,	Komm' schier, komm' schier wenn's finster ist,	just come when it's dark, when no one is on the
Wenn Niemand auf der Gassen ist!	wenn niemand auf der Gasse ist,	street –
Herein will ich Dich lassen."	dann komm' zu mir, dann komm' zu mir!	then come to me! I will let you in.
	Herein will ich dich lassen, ja lassen!	Yes, I will let you in!
Der Tag verging, die Nacht brach an;	Der Tag verging, die Nacht brach an,	The day ended, night fell; he went to his sweetheart.
Er kam zu Feinslieb gegangen.	er kam zu Feinsliebchen, Feinsliebchen gegangen!	He knocked so softly on the ring:
Er klopft so leis wohl an den Ring:	Er klopft so leis' wohl an den Ring,	"Eh, are you sleeping or are you awake, my dear?
"Ei, schläfst Du, oder wachst Du, Kind?	ei, schläfst du oder wachst, mein Kind?	I have been standing here so long!
Ich hab so lang gestanden." –	Ich hab' so lang' gestanden, Ich hab' so lang' gestanden!	I have been standing here so long!"

Table 3.2: continued

Waldvöglein (Boxberger)	Ich ging mit Lust (Mahler)	I Walked with Joy
"Daß Du so lang gestanden hast, Ich hab noch nicht geschlafen. Ich dacht als frei in meinem Sinn:	Es schaut der Mond durch's Fensterlein zum holden süßen Lieben, die Nachtigall sang die ganze Nacht.	The moon shone through the little window, On his tender, sweet love; the nightingale sang the whole night.
Wo ist mein Herzallerliebster hin, Wo mag er so lang bleiben?" –	Du schlafselig' Mägdelein, nimm dich in Acht, nimm dich in Acht! Wo ist dein Herzliebster geblieben?	You sleepy maiden, stay alert! Stay alert! Where is your beloved staying?
"Wo ich so lang geblieben bin, Das darf ich Dir wohl sagen: Beim Bier und auch beim rothen Wein, Bei einem schwarzbraunen Mädelein, Hätt Deiner bald vergessen!"		

Musically, the opening two verses reveal a great deal on the matter of the young man's behavior. The text ("I walked with joy through a green wood. I heard the birds singing") would seem to indicate a song that would progress at a lively tempo, to represent the protagonist's cheerful stroll, perhaps with a vocal line that in some way imitates the birdsong to which the text refers. The music, however, progresses not at a walking speed, but at a slow, measured tempo, marked "Träumerisch, durchaus zart" (dreamily, softly throughout), such as one might utilize in the recitation of a well-rehearsed lie. The vocal line features large, sweeping, arpeggiated chords covering intervals as large as a major fourteenth that remain sustained at a low dynamic, with very little by way of elaboration in the accompaniment (see Example 3.4). The birdsongs are kept strictly in short piano interludes of two to four measures (see Example 3.5). These

Example 3.4: "Ich ging mit Lust," mm. 1–6

Example 3.5: "Ich ging mit Lust," mm. 6–8

alternating ideas strike the listener as completely unrelated, despite the connection made through the text, hinting that the young man heard no birds at all.

The young man also hints at his dishonesty through his overexaggeration of details in the text. The first stanza lyrically recalls his environment and his enjoyment of the idyllic forest scene, but then the second stanza suddenly shifts from past tense to present, as the young man melodramatically summons the birds to sing for his beloved maiden; however, the music remains the same, betraying the scene's artificiality. The gesture smacks of a diversion tactic designed to draw the maiden's attention away from the young man's previous whereabouts and activities and to focus her on the present moment and his eventual arrival. And it would seem to have worked, if not for the narrator's final question, "Where is your beloved staying?," which re-instills the seeds of doubt between the two lovers.

After the first two verses of the AABA' form, a dramatic change occurs. The key shifts from D major to G major, an Alberti bass pattern appears

68   HIDDEN TREASURES

in the accompaniment, and the tempo slows even more. The narrative has shifted; it is no longer the young man who speaks, but rather a narrator, stating that the day has ended, and finally, after his supposed sojourn in the forest, the young man has arrived at the home of his beloved. The young man is only heard to speak directly once more, at which time the Alberti bass pattern immediately ends, as he calls out to his sweetheart, asking to be let inside. Then the narrator returns, and the A section, previously associated with the young man's journey, also returns, shifting our attention back to earlier events. While the initial vocal melody has returned, the Alberti bass associated with the detached narrative stance remains, and the birdsong, previously only heard in between phrases uttered by the young man, is allowed to continue along with the narrator's words rather than only between sung phrases, making the accompaniment much more active than that heard in the first two verses. This forms a link between the human narrator and the birdsong, giving the animal added importance as a significant narrative voice, providing the realization that the young man's attempts to deceive the maiden are so transparent that even the birds can see through his lies.

"Um schlimme Kinder" and "Ich ging mit Lust" approach the subject of romantic infidelity from opposite ends: in the first example we hear the story of the buildup to an unfaithful act, and in the second we hear the aftermath. That both songs approach the topic in such a lively, almost comical way can only be due to Mahler's youthful brashness. Roughly twenty years after the composition of these songs, Mahler found himself playing the role of the cuckold, and his response to his wife's adultery with Walter Gropius was anything but lively and cheerful. It appears that Mahler himself missed the lesson of these songs: that faith in a lover is important, but, when given too much leeway, that faith can easily be abused.

Natalie Bauer-Lechner

Another relationship with a woman that informs the period when Mahler was writing his *Wunderhorn* lieder was with his close friend and confidant Natalie Bauer-Lechner. Just like his affair with Frau Weber, Mahler's intimacy with Bauer-Lechner is complicated. Most of what we know of this relationship comes from the pen of Bauer-Lechner herself. Her detailed

MAHLER'S THOUGHTS ON LOVE AND ROMANTIC FIDELITY   69

diaries, kept from 1890 to 1901, reveal a close friendship and provide nearly verbatim conversations and a host of subjects, most significantly for scholars on Mahler's compositional process and inspirations. Of these sorts of recollections, Bauer-Lechner wrote of her need to document, "I made it my business… not only to leave aside all subjectivity in communication and representation, but also to write down only what was of objective and general interest that took place within my and another's purpose in life, that in it which was typical, universally valid, and universally edifying."[9] It was this dedication to objectivity and her impulse to document nearly all aspects of her life that have made her diaries such a highly regarded resource for Mahler scholars.

The diaries Bauer-Lechner published in 1907 did not discuss her relationship with Mahler, a mark of her discretion despite the fact that she had been barred from his social circle since shortly before his marriage to Alma. Indeed, the bulk of Bauer-Lechner's reminiscences regarding the composer did not appear in print until after her own death, and even then only a small portion of heavily edited text made the cut.

In 1917, while Bauer-Lechner was preparing her recollections to be published after her own death, she entrusted the writings to sociologist Hans Riehl. With her collected writings she enclosed a letter in which she detailed her interpretations of Mahler's love life, which she had purposefully omitted from her recollections for reasons of propriety and because she herself was helplessly in love with Mahler and undoubtedly found chronicling his affairs with other women painful. The lengthy letter from Bauer-Lechner to Riehl was discovered, translated, annotated, and published by Morten Solvik and Stephen E. Hefling in the 2014 volume of *Musical Quarterly.*

In this missive, she reveals two instances when she and Mahler made love. In 1892, they met in Berchtesgaden in late July while Mahler was delaying his return to Hamburg during the cholera epidemic. There, "love entered our hearts… We found ourselves… locked in tight quarters and separated from the rest of the world, unfolding our entire lives for each other until the early dawn in the most intimate, moving, Scheherazadian manner of telling."[10] She blames the failure of their relationship to blossom following this brief time on the meddling and jealousy of Mahler's sister Justine, "who… did everything in her power to nip in the bud any warmer

70   Hidden Treasures

relationship... that appeared to threaten her relationship with Gustav."[11] The following February, Mahler wrote to Justine that his feelings for Bauer-Lechner were indeed not as she had hoped:

> You seem right about Natalie: that after so many of the most serious tests she has not yet become "reasonable" is connected with the wholly one-sided development of her being... Already during the summer I made it perfectly clear to her solely in what sense a friendly and comradely relationship between us could be imagined. Unfortunately, she did not take the right lesson from it.[12]

If we accept Bauer-Lechner's account of their love-making, the idea of that act occurring within the same three-week span that Mahler informed her of the parameters of their "friendly and comradely relationship" would certainly have appeared inconsistent and perhaps provided Bauer-Lechner with a glimmer of hope that romance was still a possibility. Indeed, according to Bauer-Lechner's letter to Riehl, passions between her and Mahler were rekindled for one night in 1901 at his summer retreat at Wörthersee "on a sublime, magical moonlit night," where their "loving union kept [them] long awake."[13] Yet within a month, Mahler wrote to his sister, "It's starting again with Natalie. It hurts me terribly, but now I must tell her the unvarnished truth and, of course, shatter her."[14] According to harshly dramatized accounts from Justine and later Alma, Bauer-Lechner had tried to convince Mahler that they should marry after this last night together,[15] which for the composer was unthinkable, leaving her humiliated. Within months their relationship was interminably severed.

While it would be a stretch to argue that Mahler's songs about love affairs without a future were written specifically with Bauer-Lechner in mind, the fact that "Trost im Unglück" was composed during the same summer as the couple's first intimate encounter invites the possibility. As "Verlor'ne Müh'!," discussed in Chapter 5, was also composed during that summer, one might imagine the songs as a set, intended to show Bauer-Lechner that her incessant pursual of Mahler was making her seem foolish and demonstrating the most likely outcome if they were indeed to become romantically involved.

"Trost im Unglück"

"Trost im Unglück" tells a story of a pair of lovers who are about to be separated by war. As the time for the man's departure draws near, both partners downplay their feelings, claiming "I only loved you out of foolishness, Without you I will be fine." The earliest published version of this text, "Geh du nur hin, ich hab mein Teil," appeared on a broadside that Arnim collected in 1804. In the original, less pessimistic, folk song, the maiden agrees to wait one year for her lover to return, but clearly states that three years is too long.[16] Arnim chose to omit that passage from his edited version of the text, and as a result it does not appear in Mahler's adaptation either. What seems clear, however, is that while the characters in this story claim to each other that their romance will continue, both possess the awareness that their union was a temporary one.

We hear three distinctive characters presented through unique musical soundscapes: the soldier, his sweetheart, and the personified voice of patriotic duty. Patriotism sets the stage from the start with distant but accented downbeats in the strings, clarinets, and bassoons, emulating approaching horses, and a snare drum and trumpet fanfare that calls the men to arms. When the voice enters in measure 12, the soldier's rhythm is erratic, with syncopated phrases that demonstrate his lack of discipline, particularly in comparison to the steady march rhythms that we must imagine he will soon have to keep in marching (see Example 3.6).

The character personified by the orchestra takes it upon itself to comment on the lovers' exchange by way of several sequences of loudly accented ascending intervals appearing in measures 7–9, 41–42, 49–51,

Example 3.6: "Trost im Unglück," vocal melody mm. 12–18

Table 3.3: Text comparison for "Trost im Unglück"

Geh du nur hin, ich hab mein Theil (Boxberger)	Trost im Unglück (Mahler)	Consolation in Unhappiness
Husar		
Wohlan, die Zeit ist kommen, Mein Pferd, das muß gesattelt sein; Ich hab mir's vorgenommen, Geritten muß es sein. Geh Du nur hin, ich hab mein Theil! Ich lieb Dich nur aus Narrethei. Ohne Dich kann ich wohl leben, Ohne Dich kann ich schon sein.	Wohlan! Die Zeit ist kommen! Mein Pferd, das muß gesattelt sein! Ich hab' mir's vorgenommen, geritten muß es sein! Geh' du nur hin! Ich hab' mein Teil! Ich lieb' dich nur aus Narretei! Ohn' dich kann ich wohl leben, ja leben! Ohn' dich kann ich wohl sein!	Come on! The time has come! My horse, it must be saddled! I've made up my mind, It must be ridden! Go away! I have what I need from you! I loved you only out of foolishness! I can live well without you, I can be well without you!
So setz ich mich aufs Pferdchen Und trink ein Gläschen kühlen Wein Und schwör bei meinem Bärtchen, Du ewig treu zu sein. Geh Du nur hin u. s. w.	So setz' ich mich auf's Pferdchen, und trink' ein Gläschen kühlen Wein, und schwör's bei meinem Bärtchen: dir ewig treu zu sein!	So I sit on my little horse, And drink a little glass of cool wine, And I swear by my beard To be faithful to you forever!
Mädchen		
Du glaubst, Du bist der Schönste Wohl auf der ganzen weiten Welt, Und auch der Angenehmste, – Ist aber weit gefehlt! Geh Du nur hin u. s. w.	Du glaubst, du bist der Schönste wohl auf der ganzen weiten Welt, und auch der Angenehmste! Ist aber weit, weit gefehlt!	You think you are the most handsome In the whole wide world, And the most pleasant! You are far, far from that!
In meines Vaters Garten Wächst eine schöne Blume drin;	In meines Vaters Garten wächst eine Blume drin:	In my father's garden A flower grows within:

Table 3.3: continued

Geh du nur hin, ich hab mein Theil (Boxberger)	Trost im Unglück (Mahler)	Consolation in Unhappiness
So lang will ich noch warten, Bis die noch größer ist. Geh Du nur hin u. s. w.	so lang' will ich noch warten, bis die noch größer ist. Und geh' du nur hin! Ich hab' mein Teil! Ich lieb' dich nur aus Narretei! Ohn' dich kann ich wohl leben, ohn' dich kann ich wohl sein!	I will wait for you Until it is even bigger. Go away! I have what I need from you! I loved you only out of foolishness! I can live well without you, I can be well without you!
Beide Du denkst, ich werd Dich nehmen; Ich hab's noch nicht im Sinn. Ich muß mich Deiner schämen, Wenn ich in Gesellschaft bin. Geh Du nur hin, ich hab mein Theil! u.s.w.	Du denkst (glaubst), ich werd' dich nehmen! Das hab' ich lang' noch nicht im Sinn! Ich muß mich deiner schämen, ich muß mich deiner schämen, wenn ich in Gesellschaft bin!	You think (believe), I will take you! I haven't believed that for a long time! I have to be ashamed of you, I have to be ashamed of you, When I am in public!

82–83, 91–93, and 97–99 (see Example 3.7). These sequences surround moments when the soldier and the maiden are contemplating the future of their relationship, and they strike the listener as a knowing chuckle coming from the voice of experience, which has seen many couples forced into the same circumstances.

Example 3.7: "Trost im Unglück," piano reduction mm. 7–9

Example 3.8: "Trost im Unglück," piano reduction mm. 1–4

The piece opens with a fanfare motive, typically comprised of similarly arpeggiated chords associated with a call to arms (see Example 3.8, shown in piano reduction). While Dika Newlin suggests that Mahler's use of these instances of militaristic brass writing are merely the result of Bruckner's influence on Mahler's compositional style,[17] the more widely understood implication of a fanfare as a "display of power and authority, icon of the military and hunting worlds, [which] ushers in the Biblical apocalypse"[18] fits more closely with the military context of the text, as does the commonly referenced appreciation Mahler held for militaristic music, developed while growing up in Iglau, which was home to a military base.[19] Mahler's military-inspired music was discussed in greater detail in Chapter 2. Standard military usage of the trumpet fanfare calls for the sequence to be repeated three times, and this practice appears frequently in the use of the fanfare in artistic settings, such as Monteverdi's *Orfeo* and Shakespeare's *King Lear*.[20] Mahler plays with this expectation at the end of the soldier's opening stanza. At this point, we have already heard three fanfare-like passages from the trumpets, and then Mahler inserts a fourth. This leads the informed listener to believe that another stanza from the soldier will follow, but instead, the young lady begins to speak, and, with her entry in measure 53, the music changes drastically. The melodies become smoother and more conjunct, and the texture lightens dramatically as the martial qualities of the previous section give way to a calmer, more feminine sensibility. When she finally informs the soldier that his faithfulness will not be required during his deployment, the drum cadence associated with patriotic duty signals the return of the A section. It seems that both characters knew from the start that romance was not in the cards during wartime.

MAHLER'S THOUGHTS ON LOVE AND ROMANTIC FIDELITY   75

As with many of these ballads depicting a couple's final moments together before he is called off to war, the events in "Trost im Unglück" unfold rapidly while at the same time referring to the past of their time together and looking to the future as the couple attempts to determine what fate has in store for them and their relationship. As the song itself lasts just over two minutes in most performances, it would seem that the couple not only foresees no future for their love, but they see no need to devote a great deal of time to discussing the matter.

"Aus! Aus!"

Mahler's manipulations to this poem transform a somewhat sad story of lovers being separated by a war into an almost comical scene where a couple is making a melodramatic show of their faithfulness (all the while knowing that neither has any intention of keeping their word). Bettina von Arnim (sister of Clemens Brentano and wife of Achim von Arnim) collected and modified the poem entitled "Abschied für Immer" for its eventual inclusion in the anthology. Her version paints a much rosier picture than the traditional folk song in which the lovers say their final goodbyes, holding no hope (or desire, really) for a reunion.[21]

Mahler's revisions left a song text that bears only a passing similarity to the *Wunderhorn* poem. Through rearranging the lines and adding numerous instances of repeated text (particularly exclamations of excitement or despair), Mahler transforms the opening two five-line stanzas of the poem into a three-line stanza and a six-line stanza that includes a kind of refrain constructed from the opening lines. In all, Mahler adds eleven lines of newly created text and omits sixteen lines from the poem (see Table 3.4).

Both the poem and the song text present a story of lovers being parted by war. While the soldier can barely contain his excitement, the maiden has given up hope that they will be reunited and vows to go into a convent. The story is relayed entirely in the dramatic mode through dialogue between the young man and woman, with interjections of the refrain calling the soldiers and his compatriots to battle. While maintaining a constant eye on events of the future, the story passes in real time as the lovers discuss

76   HIDDEN TREASURES

Table 3.4: Text comparison for "Aus! Aus!"

Abschied für Immer (Boxberger)	Aus! Aus! (Mahler)	Over! Over!
Heute marschieren wir, Morgen marschieren wir Zu dem hohen Thor hinaus; Ei, Du wacker schwarzbraun Mägdlein, Unsre Lieb ist noch nicht aus.	"Heute marschieren wir! Juchhe, juchhe, im grünen Mai! Morgen marschieren wir zu dem hohen Thor hinaus, zum hohen Thor hinaus! Aus!"	"Today we march! Hooray! Hooray! In green May! Tomorrow we march To the high tower out there To the high tower over there! Over there!"
Reist Du schon fort? Reist Du denn schon fort? Kommst Du niemals wieder heim? Und wenn Du kommst in ein fremdes Ländchen, Liebster Schatz, vergiß nicht mein!	"Reis'st du denn schon fort? je-je! Mein Liebster! Kommst niemals wieder heim? Je! Je! Mein Liebster!" Heute marschieren wir, juchhe, juchhe, im grünen Mai! Ei, du schwarzbraun's Mägdelein, uns're Lieb' ist noch nicht aus, die Lieb' ist noch nicht aus, aus!	"Are you leaving already? Forever? My love! Will you Never come back home? Ever? Ever? My love!" "Today we march! Hooray! Hooray! In green May! You dark-haired maiden, Our love is not yet over, Our love is not yet over, Over!
Trink Du ein Gläschen Wein Zur Gesundheit mein und Dein! Kauf mir einen Strauß an hut, Nimm mein Tüchlein in die Tasche, Deine Thränlein mit abwasch!	Trink' du ein Gläschen Wein zur Gesundheit dein und mein! Siehst du diesen Strauß am Hut? Jetzo heißt's marschieren gut! Nimm das Tüchlein aus der Tasch', deine Thränlein mit abwasch'! Heute marschieren wir, juchhe,	Drink a little glass of wine To health: yours and mine! Do you see the feather on your hat? Now it's time to march! Take the handkerchief from your pocket And wipe away your tears! Today we march! Hooray! Hooray! In green
Es kommt die Lerche, Es kommt der Storch, Es kommt die Sonne ans Firmament.	juchhe, im grünen Mai! morgen marschieren wir, juchhe, im grünen Mai!"	May! Tomorrow we march, Hooray! In green May!

Table 3.4: continued

Abschied für Immer (Boxberger)	Aus! Aus! (Mahler)	Over! Over!
In das Kloster will ich gehn, Weil ich mein Schätzchen nicht mehr thu sehen, Weil nicht wiederkommt mein Schatz. "Dorten sind zwei Turteltäubchen, Sitzen auf dem dürren Aft; Wo sich zwei Verliebte scheiden, Da verwelket Laub und Gras. Was batt mich ein schöner Garten, Wenn ich nichts darinnen hab Was bat mich ein schöner Rose, Wenn ich sie nicht brechen soll? Was bat mich ein jung frisch Leben, Wenn ich's nicht der Lieb ergeb?"	"Ich will in's Kloster geh'n, weil mein Schatz davon geht! Wo geht's denn hin, mein Schatz? Gehst du fort, heut' schon fort? Und kommst nimmer wieder? Ach! Wie wird's traurig sein hier in dem Städtchen! Wie bald vergißt du mein! Ich armes Mädchen!" "Morgen marschieren wir, juchhe, juchhe, im grünen Mai! Tröst' dich, mein lieber Schatz, im Mai blüh'n gar viel Blümelein! Die Lieb' ist noch nicht aus! Aus! Aus! Aus! Aus!"	"I want to go into a convent. Hurry away, my darling! Where are you going, darling? Are you leaving today? Will you never return? Ah, how sad it will be in this little town! How soon you will forget me! I am a poor girl!" "Today we march! Hooray! Hooray in green May! Take comfort, darling, Many blossoms bloom in May! Our love is not yet over! Over! Over! Over! Over!

how the pending war will affect their relationship. Mahler's addition of the young man's exclamation "juchhe," a term translating to "hooray" or "yippee" often heard in Alpine yodeling, provides a geographical context for the action.

The story presented by Mahler's text maintains the hope that the parting lovers may yet one day be reunited, replacing the line "Weil nicht wiederkommt mein Schatz" (Because my love will not return) with "Tröst dich, mein lieber Schatz, im Mai blüh'n gar viel Blümelein! Die Lieb' ist noch nicht aus!" (Take comfort, darling, Many blossoms bloom in May!

78   HIDDEN TREASURES

Our love is not yet over!). However, the young man's excessive repetitions lend the song text a sense of irony, indicating that we should not take the lovers at their word or attribute their emotional farewell to youthful optimism—rather that the repetition strikes the listener as one lover trying to convince the other of their faithfulness while simultaneously implying that those same promises are not truthful. The entire story occurs within the dramatic mode with a glance toward the future, beginning with the initial call to arms and ending with the dialogue between the departing soldier and his distraught lover, and Mahler's deletion of the lines "Es kommt die Lerche, Es kommt der Storch, Es kommt die Sonne ans Firmament" (The lark arrives, The stork arrives, The sun arises in the firmament), markers of the arrival of spring, serves to speed along the action by eliminating an indication that the months have passed and compressing the dialogue into a much closer representation of real time.

While written in 2/4, the martial, militaristic quality of the call to arms is alternated with passages that do not quite fit into a march cadence, due to their overly emotional qualities. The enthusiasm of the soldier and the melodramatic mourning of the lover that he leaves behind are overexaggerated to the point of ridiculousness, seen most readily in the soldier's frequent outbursts of "juchhe!" We see that Mahler does not take the situation seriously through his marking above the first utterance from the devastated maiden at measure 11, "kläglich (mit Parodie)" (sorrowfully (with parody)). This excessive expression spills over into the middle sections of the ABACADA rondo form, where the mood alters dramatically as the lovers share their parting words. The melody drips with cloying chromatic inflections that overemphasize the emotions expressed (see Example 3.9). Despite what the couple tells each other, the listener knows they are hearing an act: the maiden will not join a convent, and the soldier knows that their love has reached its end.

This element of parody becomes most clear at the very end of the song. The singer repeats the word "aus!" five times that are each marked with accented offbeats, an accelerando and increasing dynamics. The overly acted farewells have dissolved into absurdity.

Based on the text alone, one cannot definitively determine how many speakers appear in the song, which significantly blurs the narrative point of view: we know that the soldier and his sweetheart are saying their

Mahler's Thoughts on Love and Romantic Fidelity 79

Example 3.9: "Aus! Aus!" mm. 49–52

farewells, but amid the chaos of such a parting, who repeats the phrase "Heute marschieren wir! Juchhe, juchhe, im grünen Mai!" (Today we march! Hooray! In green May!) could be interpreted in multiple ways. One might assume that the young soldier delivers this information himself or that the statement comes from a third party who calls the soldier and his comrades to arms and leads them off to battle. Mahler allows musical cues to take the narrative reins and clarify the situation in several places. The second occurrence of this text continues in the same musical vein to say "Ei, du schwarzbraun's Mägdelein, unsre Lieb' ist noch nicht aus" (You dark-haired maiden, Our love is not yet over). The continuation of the musical language of the A section into this passage clearly intended for the soldier to address his beloved tells us that he speaks the preceding text. Similarly, the end of the soldier's statement heard in the C section gradually builds in intensity and changes key to smoothly transition into the third occurrence of the refrain-like section. Conversely, the passages spoken by the maiden vary considerably from those which come before and after, by way of chromaticism, grace notes, more lyrical melodies, and trill figures, as seen in Examples 3.10 and 3.11. This sets up one distinctive musical style for the maiden and essentially two separate sonic spaces for the soldier, which change depending on who he is addressing at the time: in one, the highly militaristic, declamatory sections, he can celebrate the excitement of going into battle, and in the other, section C, we hear a calmer, more lyrical passage as he speaks to his love (though this passage eventually breaks down and gives way again to his enthusiasm, which he can barely contain, and the return of his militaristic sonic space). The

Example 3.10: "Aus! Aus!" mm. 19–26

narrative clarity provided by the music informs the listener that the young man is not being entirely honest with the young woman, almost as if the war has provided him with an opportunity to end a relationship that has passed its prime.

Mahler uses key to indicate changes in narrative address and intention between each successive section of the rondo. The song begins in E-flat major and returns to that key for each instance of the A section. The B section, where the maiden learns that her beloved will be leaving, shifts dramatically to C minor. The C section, beginning in measure 29, when the soldier addresses the maiden directly, assuring her that their love will continue even after his departure, moves awkwardly from E-flat major to B major, perhaps a musical marker of the discomfort one feels when trying to assure someone of facts one does not believe to be true. The abrupt change in key instantly pulls the listener into a different sonic space, but the speaker and his addressee remain the same, as the soldier encourages his sweetheart to view his departure more optimistically, stating "Trink' du

Mahler's Thoughts on Love and Romantic Fidelity

Example 3.11: "Aus! Aus!" mm. 11–18

ein Gläschen Wein zur Gesundheit dein und mein!" (Drink a little glass of wine to health: yours and mine!). Just as suddenly as the key changes to B major, after only eight measures the key shifts back to E-flat major, though strangely, Mahler does not alter the key signature and instead uses accidentals for another thirty measures.

Mahler musically traces the frenetic nature of the scene, where young men from throughout the village are rapidly gathering their belongings and rushing to say farewell to their loved ones before charging into battle. The song pushes relentlessly forward from beginning to end with no instrumental interludes or relaxed passages. While the overly emotional portions of the song delivered from the viewpoint of the maiden can be performed at a slower tempo to emphasize their pathetic nature, they are not marked as such, and the rhythm's underlying motion remains constant. The final three measures of the song are marked *accelerando*, as a musical representation of the final opportunity for the lovers to rush to say goodbye as he rides away.

82   HIDDEN TREASURES

"Scheiden und Meiden"

"Scheiden und Meiden" is a peculiar example among the *Wunderhorn* lieder, in that Mahler's textual changes and musical cues morph the original meaning of the poem into something quite different and far less straightforward. The original poem features a refrain with the text "Scheiden und Lassen thut weh" (Parting and leaving are painful). Mahler changed the word "Lassen" to "Meiden"—"leaving" becomes "avoiding" or "shunning"—causing a dramatic shift in the motivations of the characters. Rather than the war that has led to the young man's departure causing a sad farewell, it seems that these lovers are more content to use the circumstances as an excuse to end their affair.

A sizeable textual omission also blurs the distinction between geographical and mortal separation in "Scheiden und Meiden." The text Mahler discarded from the poem clearly states that three riders who leave a village are a metaphor for the departure of life; in other words, their leaving brings death. In Mahler's version of the text, it is not clear who these three riders really are or what their departure means to the people of the town. Rather than the harbingers of death, these riders seem to be sounding a call to arms and leading the town's men off to battle, in which case they may return. The original poem and the text that Mahler created from it make no direct mention of military imagery. Mahler's musical treatment, on the other hand, leaves no question that the song should be heard as a call to arms.

The story begins in the hands of a narrator who informs us of the arrival of three riders who have come and are leaving the village. The opening four measures of the piano introduction simulate the approach of the men on horseback, who are blowing trumpets in order to call out the young men to prepare for battle, with a high-pitched trill in the right hand of the accompaniment, emulating a bell used to get the attention of the village. Mahler's mimetic technique of creating the sounds of galloping horses compares oddly to that created by Schubert in "Erlkönig" (see Examples 3.12 and 3.13); both use notes in octaves, but while Schubert's accompaniment clearly shows that his rider does not pause or wait for anything while attempting to rush his dying child to a doctor, Mahler's horses are more erratic, anxiously preparing to slow down so that their

MAHLER'S THOUGHTS ON LOVE AND ROMANTIC FIDELITY   83

Table 3.5: Text comparison for "Scheiden und Meiden"

Drei Reiter am Thor (Boxberger)	Scheiden und Meiden (Mahler)	Parting and Avoiding
Es ritten drei Reiter zum Tor hinaus;	Es ritten drei Reiter zum Thore hinaus!	Three riders have ridden up to the gate!
Ade!	Ade! Ade!	Farewell! Farewell!
Feins Liebchen schaute zum Fenster hinaus,	Fein's Liebchen, das schaute zum Fenster hinaus!	Fine sweetheart, she looks out the window!
Ade!	Ade! Ade! Ade!	Farewell! Farewell! Farewell!
Und wenn es denn soll geschieden sein,	Und wenn es denn soll geschieden sein,	And, if we should be parted,
So reich mir Dein goldenes Ringelein!	so reich mir dein goldenes Ringelein!	Hand me your little golden ring!
Ade! Ade! Ade!	Ade! Ade!	Farewell! Farewell!
Ja, Scheiden und Lassen thut weh.	Ja Scheiden und Meiden tut weh, tut weh!	Yes, parting and avoiding is painful, yes painful!
	Ja Scheiden und Meiden tut weh, tut weh! Ade! Ade! Ade!	Yes, parting and avoiding is painful! Farewell! Farewell!
Und der uns scheidet, das ist der Tod;		
Ade!		
Er scheidet so manches Jungfräulein roth,		
Ade!		
Und wär doch geworden der liebe Leib		
Der Liebe ein süßer Zeitvertreib!		
Ade! Ade! Ade!		
Ja, Scheiden und Lassen thut weh.		
Es scheidet das Kind wohl in der Wiegn;	Es scheidet das Kind schon in der Wieg'!	The child dies in the cradle!
Ade!	Ade! Ade!	Farewell! Farewell!
Wenn werd ich mein Schätzel doch kriegn?	Wann werd' ich mein Schätzel wohl kriegen?!	When will I get my treasure?
Ade!	Ade! Ade!	Farewell! Farewell!

Table 3.5: continued

Drei Reiter am Thor (Boxberger)	Scheiden und Meiden (Mahler)	Parting and Avoiding
Und ist es nicht morgen, ach, wär es doch heut!	Und ist es nicht morgen, ach, wär' es doch heut'!	Oh, it is not tomorrow, If only it were today!
Es macht uns Allbeiden gar große Freud.	Es machte uns Beiden wohl große Freud'!	That would make us both very happy!
Ade! Ade! Ade!	Ade! Ade! Ade! Ade! Ade!	Farewell! Farewell! Farewell!
Ja, Scheiden und Lassen thut weh.	Ade!	Farewell! Farewell! Farewell!
	Ja, Scheiden und Meiden tut weh, tut weh!	Yes, parting and avoiding is painful, yes painful!
	Ja Scheiden und Meiden tut weh, tut weh! Ade!	Yes, parting and avoiding is painful! Farewell!

riders can inform the young men of the village of the impending battle in which they must participate.

Then the poem turns to the words of the young man, who informs his sweetheart that he must leave. Mahler marks the accompaniment in

Example 3.12: Schubert: "Der Erlkönig," mm. 1–3

Example 3.13: "Scheiden und Meiden," mm. 1–4

Mahler's Thoughts on Love and Romantic Fidelity   85

measures 5–18 "wie Trompetenmusik" (like trumpet music), evidence that he had begun to think of his earliest *Wunderhorn* songs, which were conceived as traditional lieder with piano accompaniment, as works requiring the expanded timbral palette offered by the orchestra.[22] Mahler overexaggerates the farewells between the soldier and his sweetheart. The word "Ade!" is repeated twenty-one times within the short song, and while some of these seem to be genuine, the dramatic ritardando and exaggerated crescendo at measures 26–28 seem somewhat artificial. The change in meter appearing at measure 19 sets up a musical dichotomy between triple- and duple-metered sound worlds. The triplet figures tend to more closely align with the idea of fighting and riding off into war, while the duplet figures are associated with the people who are left behind. Mahler exposes this conflict more broadly in measure 35, when the vocal line remains in 2/4 while the accompaniment returns to 6/8 (in the manuscript this is even more complex, as the vocal line and the right hand of the piano remain in 2/4 while the left hand moves back to 6/8). We can hear the struggle of the young soldiers playing out in this musical tension. While the proper military man knows that he must perform his duty, his thoughts remain with those he leaves behind. This section also represents the passing of several months in the space of nine short measures, showing that life is going on for those at the battlefront and for those at home.

We hear from the maiden in the final stanza (though this is not directly indicated in the text itself, but only through Mahler's music), who is now looking to the future and the uncertainty of her situation. In Mahler's version of the text, it seems that some time has passed between the first and second verses, as the maiden's words are much more contemplative and pragmatic than those of the soldier in the first stanza. Rather than calling excitedly in the chaotic moments before departing, she has seen enough to speak thoughtfully on the matter ("When will I get my treasure? Oh, it is not tomorrow. If only it were today, that would make us both very happy"). She also tells of a child in its cradle, to whom, presumably, she has since given birth. One can only assume that the soldier is the father. The stanza that Mahler deleted contextualizes this statement and tells us that death (in the form of the three riders) even take children from the cradle. Mahler's deletion leaves the mention of the child somewhat obscured as to its meaning.

86   HIDDEN TREASURES

The martial themes from the beginning of the song return in measure 58, indicating that no matter what takes place elsewhere, a soldier's first duty lies with nation and cause. Despite this serious message, the whole mood of the song remains somewhat tongue in cheek. The marking "Lustig" (merrily) contradicts with the issues being faced by the characters in the song, and the listener walks away feeling as though the music and the words don't quite match up, almost as if Mahler himself were standing nearby with a wink and a smile.

Mahler on Love

While these examples demonstrate somewhat brash and pessimistic views on romance, the letters Mahler wrote to the women he loved and his descriptions of them written to others paint him as a man who loved passionately, if not a bit obsessively. Some examples of his writing will serve to show that his views on love were not as casual as these songs may make him seem.

At the tender age of nineteen, Mahler entered into his first passionate romance with Josephine Poisl, the daughter of the telegraph master in Iglau. They met when Herr Poisl hired Mahler to teach Josephine and her sister Anna piano over the summer of 1879. Mahler wrote of this love to his friend Anton Krisper, "A new name is now inscribed in my heart... true, only whisperingly and blushingly, but no less powerfully."[23] Few documented details about the relationship have survived, but by Easter of 1880, it would appear that the romance had ended, as he wrote to her:

> My eternally beloved, Despair dictated these lines to me. Is it really possible? Have you already forgotten the vows that we swore to each other?... You must still love me—otherwise I must despair of the light of Heaven—yes, of everything that is beautiful and lovely![24]

The final nail in the coffin of Mahler and Josephine's love was a letter from her father dated June 14, 1880, which clearly stated that Mahler would no longer have any contact with Josephine or any other member of the Poisl family.[25] The short but seemingly intense affair remains the earliest

MAHLER'S THOUGHTS ON LOVE AND ROMANTIC FIDELITY   87

example of Mahler's romantic life from which documented evidence survives.

Unfortunately for this discussion, no love letters to sopranos Johanna Richter and Betty Frank have survived, if such letters were even written. Given the clandestine nature of these affairs, which surely would have caused Mahler problems with the executives at the Kassel and Prague opera companies, such letters would have proved damning evidence had they been discovered. The next serious relationship that sheds light on Mahler's effusively romantic tendencies is that with Anna von Mildenburg. This affair began in Hamburg in 1895 and lasted until he accepted the directorship in Vienna in 1897. While this romance postdates most of the songs discussed in this chapter, the intensity with which Mahler expresses his feelings for Mildenburg provides a backdrop for understanding his views on love and romance as a whole.

In the early days of their love affair, he wrote to her, "Quickly tell me today in a private moment whether you love me. My love, you will have to assure me many times of it before I am secure in that knowledge... I unconditionally surrender!"[26] In 1896, as he worked on his Third Symphony, Mahler wrote to the soprano of the sixth movement, which he initially called "What Love Tells Me," "You would like to know 'what love tells me'? Love tells me very beautiful things! And when love speaks to me now it always talks about you!"[27] His effusive and flowery language must have had a powerful impact on the singer, twelve years his junior. That said, their relationship was often tumultuous, and Mahler essentially used his new position in Vienna as an excuse to end the relationship, making things all the more complicated when she was hired by the Vienna Opera herself the following year. Mahler's romantic life, like so many other aspects of his world, was rarely uncomplicated.

CHAPTER FOUR

"Wrestling with God"
Mahler and Spirituality

Conventional terminology and classification could never fully characterize Mahler's spiritual and religious beliefs. We can easily acknowledge that Mahler was raised in a Jewish family and that he converted to Catholicism through his baptism in Hamburg on February 23, 1897, but the adult Mahler never graced the rosters of membership at any house of worship. One might easily assume that this fact would indicate that the composer held no stock in public religious practice or was possibly even an atheist, but, as we will see, this is not entirely accurate either. Like so many other aspects of his life, Mahler's spiritual life was complex and frequently filled with the same kinds of contradiction that we often hear in his music.

As is regularly the case with historical figures, writers of Mahler's story often label his religious identity to align to their given agendas. His wife Alma, a noted anti-Semite, described her husband as "a believer in Christianity, a Christian Jew."[1] She emphasized this by recalling, "One of our early discussions was about Jesus Christ. Although I was brought up as a Catholic, the influence of Schopenhauer and Nietzsche had made a free-thinker of me. Mahler contested my point of view with fervor. It was paradoxical that a Jew should hotly defend Christ against a Christian."[2]

These comments echoed one of the debates raging in Vienna at this time: the precise nature of Judaism. Was being Jewish merely a question of following a specific set of sacred rituals and subscribing to certain beliefs,

89

90   Hidden Treasures

and thus a religion that could be given up, or was it something hereditary and ineradicable, a race? For most anti-Semites Jewishness was purely genetic; once a Jew, always a Jew, regardless of the religion professed and practiced. Strangely, it was not only anti-Semites who held this belief. According to Sigmund Freud, himself a Jew, Jewishness entailed a biological component, a genetic compulsion to transmit an "archaic memory" from one generation to the next. Conversion to Christianity could not destroy this physiological imperative, but only allow it to simmer below the surface.[3] According to this view, Mahler would always be a Jew, despite his baptism. On the other hand, Mahler and others like him believed national and racial identity stemmed from shared culture and language, making Judaism purely a matter of faith, and as such it could be changed, at least on the outside, though he still recognized that his Jewish background created obstacles for his career goals.

Figures such as Theodor Adorno emphasize Mahler's Jewish identity as a contributor to his sense of being an outsider and to what Adorno calls the "alienation effects" of his music.[4] Many scholars also point to Mahler's reading of German philosophy, particularly that of Schopenhauer, Wagner, and Nietzsche, and the notion that experiencing great art, most of all music, had the power to regenerate one's spiritual essence.[5] To this effect, Wagner wrote:

> One might say that where Religion becomes artificial, it is reserved for Art to save the spirit of religion by recognizing the figurative value of the mythic symbols which the former would have us believe in the literal sense, and revealing their deep and hidden truth through an ideal presentation.[6]

In these views, the spiritual elevation caused by great art supersedes the need for traditional religious practice. Mahler himself seemed unable, or at least unwilling, to label his own spirituality, writing to Richard Specht in 1895 on the idea of one's actions' impact on the soul:

> We shall all return, our whole lives acquire meaning only through this certainty, and it doesn't matter in the least whether, at a later stage of our return, we remember an earlier one. What is at stake

here is not the individual and his memories and sense of wellbeing, but the great journey towards perfection, towards the purification that increases with each new incarnation. That is why I must live an ethical existence... Goethe talked endlessly about this subject, but of course I can express myself fully only as a musician... I am only a musician, nothing more: this is the gift that was bestowed on me, and it is this alone I have to account for.[7]

This view is, perhaps apocryphally, simplified by A. David Hogarth, who wrote, "When asked what his religion was, Mahler replied, 'I am a musician.'"[8] As with so many other aspects of Mahler's worldview, we must assume that the truth lies somewhere in between all these conflicting accounts, even Mahler's own, and that his true "religion" was a synthesis of ideas drawn from his Jewish upbringing, his interest in Catholic mysticism, and most importantly, genuine faith in the metaphysical power of music to elevate the soul.

This chapter will further examine Mahler's long-held misgivings regarding his conversion to Christianity, as seen through the lens of his songs "Urlicht," "Es sungen drei Engel," and "Das himmlische Leben," both within and beyond Symphonies nos. 2, 3, and 4. Granting these songs their place as movements within symphonies demonstrates the centrality of his ambivalence toward foregoing his religious upbringing for career success, and the composer's preoccupation with topics commonly associated with Christianity rather than Judaism shows his grappling with the premises of Christian practice to determine whether or not he could genuinely accept the possibility of conversion. The song "Des Antonius von Padua Fischpredigt," while conveying the story of a Catholic saint and maintaining a close relationship to Symphony no. 2, serves a different purpose, which will be further explained below.

Mahler's Religious Upbringing

The archives of the Iglau synagogue where the Mahler family worshipped were destroyed in a fire in 1939, leaving many specific details of Mahler's religious upbringing, such as the date of his bar mitzvah, lost to time. Rabbi Jakob Joachim Unger led the synagogue from 1860 until 1911 and

92   HIDDEN TREASURES

was instrumental in maintaining positive and productive relationships between the Jewish and Catholic populations in the town. Indeed, as a child, Mahler was reportedly called upon to serve as accompanist for choir rehearsals at Sankt Jakobkirche as well as those at the synagogue.[9] It is perhaps this early exposure to Catholic practice that inspired his fascination with Catholic mysticism. It is unclear how orthodox Mahler's family's practice and observance truly was, though Martin Vann suggests that the composer's father Bernhard's participation with the synagogue and local Jewish community groups served his business interests more than those of his spirit, while mother Marie was more devout in her faith.[10] Stories of young Mahler interrupting the singing of the congregants by shouting "Be quiet! Be quiet! That's not pleasant!" and his high grades in religion class at the Gymnasium attest to at least some degree of religious activity among the Mahler family.[11] In any case, there is no record of the adult Mahler participating in any kind of consistent religious practice—Jewish, Catholic, or otherwise.

Anti-Semitism in Vienna

Mahler's conversion was a direct result of anti-Semitic sentiment in Vienna at the time he was seeking a position at the Hofoper. Several factors played into the rise of these notions, common in German-speaking areas during the final decades of the nineteenth century. Fearing financial disaster after the bank crisis of 1873 and the Panic of 1893, Viennese citizens began to worry about their lack of economic security.[12] Common stereotypes associating Jews with greed and suspicious financial practices had abounded since the 1311 edict of Pope Clement V, which severely limited career opportunities for those of the Jewish faith and forbade currency exchange as an occupation for Christians, leaving banking and money-lending as one of the few available vocations for medieval Jews.[13] As these occupational associations had long since evolved into familiar stereotypes, the Jewish population of Vienna, the largest European Jewish community at the time, made a logical scapegoat for the Gentiles' financial frustrations.[14] Over time, the results of this bigoted attitude in Austria and Germany would find a stronghold in the political arena, beginning with the election of Karl Lueger as mayor of Vienna. Lueger represented the Christian

Social Party, and his election ran on a platform of anti-Semitic policy. Still, for Mahler in the 1890s, his Judaism proved primarily to be merely a barrier to social acceptance and vocational success, rather than a motive for the dangers European Jews would face in the 1930s and '40s.

Mahler was keenly aware of the impact his Jewish heritage had on his career. In late 1894, he wrote to Friedrich Löhr, "Being Jewish prevents me, as it is in the world today, from receiving employment at any court theater."[15] Since he had long striven to achieve a post at the Vienna Court Opera House, on February 23, 1897, Mahler was baptized Catholic in Hamburg. Of this choice he wrote, "I do not hide the truth… when I say that this action, which I took from an instinct of self-preservation and which I was fully disposed to take, cost me a great deal."[16] Furthermore, he had reason to doubt that the gesture would have any real effect. Regarding Leo Blech's career-motivated baptism, he wrote, "It won't work, unfortunately, even if he has been baptized. For the anti-Semites, I still count as a Jew despite my baptism, and more than one Jew is more than the Vienna Court Opera can bear."[17]

The Viennese anti-Semitic press campaign against Mahler began almost as soon as it was announced that he had been named conductor for the Hofoper in 1897. Numerous newspapers and journals in Vienna at the time had blatantly anti-Semitic leanings, including the *Deutsche Zeitung, Deutsches Volksblatt, Östdeutsche Rundschau,* and *Kikeriki.*[18] The overwhelming majority of their critics chose to remain anonymous, but others, such as Theodor Helm (who, in time, became a friend and ally of Mahler's), Camillo Horn, Maximillian Muntz, and Hans Puchstein, made their prejudices well known.[19] Often, rather than expose their own biases by attacking Mahler's Judaism outright, anti-Semitic critics criticized the music itself, indicating through use of stereotype-laden terms and with varying degrees of clarity that their views had more to do with Jewishness than any musical characteristics. The premiere of several of Mahler's *Wunderhorn* lieder, given by the Philharmonic (then directed by Mahler), garnered several violently anti-Semitic responses. "Disregarding one of your own rules, you have given lieder of a popular nature at the Philharmonic concerts. Forgive us, *O hallowed masters of the German lied*, that we even call them lieder!"[20] Helm wrote that the *Wunderhorn* lieder were "subtly orchestrated in the manner of the Secession, yet their melodic

94   HIDDEN TREASURES

invention was *anything but original*,"[21] echoing Wagner's contention in "Judaism in Music" that Jews were incapable of creating any original artistic expression but could only copy from others.[22] Muntz was the most blatant in his prejudice, completely dismissing any positive response to the concert and chalking up the success of the performance not to the quality of the work, but to the "almost wholly Jewish audience" and the "shameless enthusiasm on the part of young Israel."[23]

Yet some anti-Semitic critics could be eventually won over. In December 1901, William Ritter wrote of Mahler and his Fourth Symphony:

> Perhaps his Jewish heritage is in fact responsible for his nervous predisposition toward an often epileptical musical form of expression, and for his stubborn tenacity to fixed beliefs, whether ridiculous or sublime; for his indomitable urge to impose, at any price, his most exorbitant demands, as well as his need for beauty; his wish to prove the opposition wrong by any means, to force hate, to disgorge admiration, and for the power with which he exploits luxury, opulence and the odd and unexpected to the full; then there is his harmonious control and infallible balance in composition, which conjures up the perfect balance of a credit and debit account, and evokes expert banking operations; and finally there is that very special note of concupiscence whose affiliations with the *Song of Songs* and, at a later date, the banks of the blue Danube are evident.[24]

This critique calls upon nearly all the pervading stereotypes that *fin-de-siècle* German-speaking society had conjured up in reference to the Jewish population: nervousness; jerking, spasmodic movement; stubbornness; hyper-sexuality; and financial greed and underhandedness. Despite his views, eventually Ritter observed his strange attraction to the symphony:

> You rebel against [Mahler's] music. You reject it with all your wisdom, all your experience and all your convictions... but you're fighting against your own pleasure... you're trying to be virtuous... at bottom... there's nothing you like better. You're defeated. Whether you will or no, you admire it! It was bound to

happen that you, an anti-Semite, should be bowled over by admiration for something Jewish![25]

Ritter represents a somewhat unusual example among Mahler's anti-Semitic critics in that he was eventually able to look past his religious biases. He did what Mahler's protégé Guido Adler hoped that all men would be able to do one day: "Considering these [musical] questions, those [anti-Semitic] passions that have been so pathologically aroused in our time [should] play no role."[26] Most anti-Semitic critics, sadly, were not so open-minded.

Mahler's Baptism

Mahler wrote to numerous friends about the obstacles his family background posed for his career goals. In January 1894, he wrote his sister Justine, "It does seem that all doors are closed to me for the moment because of my Jewishness."[27] And, similarly, he wrote to Max Marschalk in January 1897, "They need a director in Vienna and have come to the conclusion that I am the right man for the job.—But the great stumbling block—my being a Jew—lies in the road and may well barricade it."[28] However, Mahler attempted to cloud the issue of the opportunistic motives of his baptism by writing to journalist Ludwig Karpath in December 1896, "It is of course untrue that I had myself baptized only when the Vienna position beckoned—I had been baptized years before that—but the fact is that the desire to escape from Pollini's Hamburg inferno awakened in me the thought of leaving the Jewish community."[29] Nonetheless, he admitted his regret, writing, "I do not deny that it cost me a great deal of effort to take an action that one may justifiably call self-preservation."[30] Yet he also referred to Judaism as "Our principal fault, our race [which] we cannot change."[31] So, regardless of his lack of active participation in the Jewish faith, acceptance into mainstream society was clearly Mahler's goal.[32] Still, it would appear that he would have preferred to not be forced to surrender an aspect of his cultural identity in order to achieve his aspirations.

Despite his views, Mahler was not above his own brand of anti-Semitism. Leon Botstein writes of a hierarchy among Viennese Jewish populations and notes that German-speaking Jews tended to avoid

96   HIDDEN TREASURES

Leopoldstadt and other Jewish districts.[33] Sander L. Gilman refers to this type of inter-cultural prejudice as "Jewish self-hatred," an attitude prevalent among German-speaking "assimilated Jews." These Jews, predominantly native-born or from Bohemia, Moravia, or Hungary, took full advantage of the emancipation written into the new constitution of the Austro-Hungarian Empire in 1867.[34] These freedoms allowed Jews to live outside the ghettos, to freely practice their religion, and to participate fully in commerce, offering them the opportunity to assimilate and gain social standing among the Gentiles. The unforeseen consequence of the emancipation was the influx of orthodox Galician Jews from Eastern Europe, known as the *Ostjuden*. This new Jewish community refused to abandon their native languages, elaborate religious practices, and customs that would have allowed them to fit more easily into the Viennese society into which the Germanic Jews had worked for decades to assimilate. "The *Ostjuden* were widely seen to be loud, coarse and dirty, immoral, and culturally backward."[35] Anti-Semitic Christians saw these very separate Jewish communities as one and the same, and this lack of distinction brought further difficulties to the German-speaking Jews striving for further acceptance. Many of the assimilated Jews responded to this threat to their acceptance into broader society by attacking their co-religionists with a level of vitriol rivaling the most adamant anti-Semite. Mahler's attitude toward the *Ostjuden* appears in this 1892 letter to his sister Justine:

> I forbid everyone to associate with Frl. Lourié in any way, and ask you to reject her brusquely, if there's no other way. Under no circumstances visit her, and if she comes, be cool and dismissive toward her. *She is a quite common Russian Jew*, who, by the way, behaved towards me in such a pushy and indecent manner, that I was obliged to snub her directly.[36]

Later, in 1903, Mahler wrote to his wife Alma while serving as a guest conductor in Lvov (modern-day Lviv, Ukraine), "Life here has a very odd look, all its own. But the oddest of all are the Polish Jews, who run around as dogs do elsewhere. It's the greatest lark just to look at them! My God, are these my relations!?"[37] So while seeing Christian society's views of his religious heritage as an obstacle to his success, Mahler's own attitudes couched their own prejudices.

Mahler, along with his sisters Justine and Emma, began the process of converting to Catholicism in 1896. This began with a series of lessons with a vicar, or more accurately two vicars—the first continued to press Justine on the reason for her conversion, and, when she simply could not bring herself to confess that her motives were not religious in nature, studies with him were abandoned and resumed with one she found more agreeable, Vicar Zygmunt Swider.[38] Their studies culminated with a baptism, with a local cobbler, Theodor Meynberg, serving as godfather. Meynberg volunteered with the Committee for the Protection of German Emigrants, an organization for Jews needing to convert for immigration purposes.[39] As such, he proved to be less a figure who would see to the Mahlers' continued spiritual growth and more a mere formality.

Before interpreting Mahler's religious *Wunderhorn* songs as explorations into aspects of Christianity, it is vital to establish the factors that led to their creation. Revisiting the statement made by Mahler that he was baptized in order to escape from "Pollini's Hamburg inferno" will shed light on these circumstances. Mahler's letter was intended to imply that he was baptized years prior to his candidacy for a position at the Vienna Hofoper, a fact that is simply not true. The claim is clearly an indication that his desire to leave Hamburg may have led him to consider his options. So, to begin with, what happened in Hamburg between the impresario Bernhard Pollini and his chief conductor?

Like most major opera companies, the Hamburg Stadttheater closed for summer breaks. It was during these breaks that Mahler focused most intently on his composition. In August 1892, before the opera season had begun, a cholera epidemic swept through Hamburg. This epidemic would ultimately kill thousands of people. However, in an effort to keep the public calm (and, no doubt, to also keep his box office receipts coming in), in September Pollini announced that the theater would reopen and sent word to all of his employees that they were to return to Hamburg immediately (the messages also heavily implied that failure to do so could result in loss of employment). Out of concern, Mahler traveled slowly, hoping to arrive after the worst had passed. This infuriated Pollini, who threatened to fine him a year's salary as punishment, despite the fact that the impresario himself had remained safely in the countryside during the entire debacle. Mahler's friend, music critic Ferdinand Pfohl, wrote of the confrontation, "From this day forward, Mahler hated and loathed his director; and Pollini in turn became obsessed with spiteful enmity towards his conductor."[40] The following July, Mahler wrote "Urlicht."

"Urlicht"

At its heart, "Urlicht" is a prayer and a testament of Christian faith. The text, drawn from a *Wunderhorn* poem of the same title, is largely untouched by Mahler, barring some changes in punctuation and repetition. The opening line, "O Röschen rot!" (Oh, red rose!), speaks to long-standing Christian connections between Jesus Christ and the rose.[41] The fact that the song, while written as an independent work,[42] was later used as movement four of Symphony no. 2 ("Resurrection") further emphasizes its Christian viewpoint. Of the song, Mahler told Natalie Bauer-Lechner, "The 'Urlicht' represents the soul's striving and questioning attitude towards its own immortality."[43] The opening line is set to a simple, slow ascending melody reminiscent of a Christian raising their eyes to the heavens to pray (see Example 4.1). An eleven-measure interlude for horns and trumpets, playing a homophonic passage that strikes the listener as an instrumental arrangement a chorale (see the piano reduction in Example 4.2). The text

Example 4.1: "Urlicht," mm. 1–2

Example 4.2: "Urlicht," mm. 3–7

MAHLER AND SPIRITUALITY · 99

Table 4.1: Text comparison for "Urlicht"

Urlicht (Boxberger)	Urlicht (Mahler)	Primeval Light
O Röschen roth,	O Röschen rot!	Oh, red rose!
Der Mensche liegt in grösster Noth,	Der Mensch liegt in grösster Not!	Humanity lies in greatest need!
Der Mensch liegt in grösster Pein.	Der Mensch liegt in grösster Pein!	Humanity lies in greatest pain!
Je lieber möcht ich in Himmel sein!	Je lieber möcht' ich in Himmel sein!	I would rather be in Heaven!
Da kam ich auf einen breiten Weg;	Da kam ich auf einen breiten Weg;	Then I came to a wide path; Then there came an angel
Da kam ein Engelein und wollt mich abweisen.	Da kam ein Engelein und wollt' mich abweisen.	who wanted to turn me away.
Ach nein, ich liess mich nicht abweisen:	Ach nein, ich liess mich nicht abweisen,	Ah no, I will not be turned away,
Ich bin von Gott, ich will wieder zu Gott.	Ach nein, ich liess mich nicht abweisen!	Ah no, I will not be turned away!
Der liebe Gott wird mir ein Lichtchen geben,	Ich bin von Gott, und will wieder zu Gott!	I am from God, and I want to return to God!
Wird leuchten mir bis in das ewig selig Leben.	Der lieber Gott, der lieber Gott wird mir ein Lichtchen geben,	Dear God, dear God will give me a little light,
	Wird leuchten mir bis an das ewig selig Leben!	It will shine me up to that eternally blessed life!

goes on to state that the ills of earthly life have made the protagonist want to seek out Heaven instead. Suddenly, the text changes from a prayer to a narrative relaying of events. The pilgrimage begins, and suddenly an angel attempts to turn the protagonist away. At this moment, the key changes from D-flat major to A major. The jarring modulation brings a feeling of foreboding, as if the protagonist's journey will end in failure. However, he refuses to be denied, saying "I am from God, and I want to return to God!" The declaration of faith brings with it a return to D-flat major and an expression marking of "drängend, sehr leidenschaftlich, aber zart" (urgently, very passionate, but tender). The text closes with the protagonist praying to be blessed with light, which will lead him to "that eternally

100   HIDDEN TREASURES

blessed life." What it does not do, however, is explicitly indicate whether or not that wish is granted.[44] Mahler uses his instrumentation to suggest that Heaven awaits, as the closing measures of the song feature only sustained strings and harps in the accompaniment. However, as with all things Mahler, an idea that seems clear may not always be the case. In 1901, the composer created a set of program notes for a performance in Dresden. Of this movement he wrote, "The moving voice of *naïve faith* sounds in our ears."[45] His description of the protagonist's conviction as "naïve" forces us to wonder whether his term implied a sense of overly eager credulity or one of sincere and faithful innocence.

While many critics of the day took issue with Mahler's exploration of seemingly Christian themes, Arthur Seidl appears to have made one of the few attempts to decipher the message of the Second Symphony. He wrote, "Mahler is a real 'God Seeker.' His most secret inner being contemplates the immensity of nature with a really religious fervor; he is inexorably drawn to the enigma if existence… I wish to God that others had the same serious, almost sacred approach to their work!"[46]

"Es sungen drei Engel"

Mahler's most unusual setting of a poem from *Des Knaben Wunderhorn* is "Es sungen drei Engel." Composed as movement five for Symphony no. 3, it includes a children's choir and a women's choir along with the alto solo and orchestra. As the full significance of the piece cannot be fully understood beyond the context of the symphony as a whole, attempting to analyze it as an independent work would be a fruitless effort. That said, the text, which Bode identifies as a "much-sung song about the Passion" that appeared in "manifold variations,"[47] features a far more explicit discussion of Christianity than "Urlicht." The poem tells of Peter's confession to Jesus at the Last Supper. Jesus tells him, "Hast du den übertreten die zehen Gebot, So fall auf die Kniee und bete zu Gott! Liebe nur Gott in alle Zeit! So wirst du Erlangen die himmlische Freud'" (If you have broken the Ten Commandments, then fall on your knees and pray to God! Love only God forever. Then you will attain Heavenly joy!). This moment in the New Testament identifies a major point of departure between Jesus'

MAHLER AND SPIRITUALITY   101

Table 4.2: Text comparison for "Es sungen drei Engel"

Armer Kinder Betterlied (Boxberger)	Es sungen drei Engel (Mahler)	Three Angels Were Singing
	CC: children's chorus *WC: women's choir* *AS: alto solo*	
	CC: Bimm bamm, bimm bamm.	Ding dong, ding dong!
Es sungen drei Engel einen süßen Gesang,	WC: Es sungen drei Engel einen süssen Gesang;	Three angels were singing a sweet song;
Mit Freuden es im Himmel klang;	Mit Freuden es selig in dem Himmel klang,	Blessed with joy, it rang through Heaven,
Sie jauchzten fröhlich auch dabei,	Sie jauchzten fröhlich auch dabei,	They cheerfully announced
Daß Petrus sei von Sünden frei,	Dass Petrus sei von Sünden frei,	That Peter was free from sin, He was free from sin.
Von Sünden frei.	Er sei von Sünden frei, Er sei von Sünden frei, Von Sünden frei.	He was free from sin, Free from sin.
Denn als der Herr Jesus zu Tische saß,	Und als der Herr Jesus zu Tische sass,	And as Jesus sat at the table,
Mit seinen zwölf Jüngern das Abendmahl aß,	Mit seinen zwölf Jüngern das Abendmahl ass:	With his twelve disciples to eat the supper:
So sprach der Herr Jesus:	Da sprach der Herr Jesus, Herr Jesus,	Lord Jesus said, Lord Jesus,
"Was stehest du hier,	Was stehst du den hier? Was stehst du den hier?	For what reason are you standing here? Why are you standing here?
Wenn ich dich ansehe, so weinest du mir,	Wenn ich dich anseh', so weinest du mir,	When I look upon you, you weep for me,
So weinest du mir."	So weinest du mir!	You weep for me!
	CC: Bimm bamm, bimm bamm.	Ding dong, ding dong!

102 HIDDEN TREASURES

Table 4.2: continued

Armer Kinder Betterlied (Boxberger)	Es sungen drei Engel (Mahler)	Three Angels Were Singing
"Ach! Sollt ich nicht weinen du gütiger Gott! Ich hab übertreten die zehen Gebot; Ich gehe und weine ja bitterlich, Ach komm, erbarme dich über mich, Ach über mich!"	*AS*: Und sollt' ich nicht weinen, Du gütiger Gott. *WC*: Bimm bamm, bimm bamm Du sollst ja nicht weinen! Sollst ja nicht weinen! *AS*: Ich hab' übertreten die zehn Gebot. *CC & WC*: Bimm bamm, bimm bamm. *AS*: Ich gehe und weine ja bitterlich.	And should I not weep, You great God? Ding dong, ding dong! You should not weep! Should not weep! I have broken the Ten Commandments. Ding dong, ding dong! I go and weep bitterly.
	CC & WC: Bimm bamm, bimm bamm.	Ding dong, ding dong!
	WC: Du sollst ja nicht weinen! Sollst ja nicht weinen!	You should not weep! Should not weep!
	AS: Ach komm und erbarme dich! Ach komm und erbarme dich über mich!	Ah, come and have mercy on you! Ah, come and have mercy on me!
	CC & WC: Bimm bamm, bimm bamm.	Ding dong, ding dong!
"Hast du dann übertreten die zehen Gebot, So fall auf die Knie und bete zu Gott, Und bete zu Gott nur allezeit, So wirst du erlangen die himmlische Freud, Die himmlische Freud."	*WC*: Hast du den übertreten die zehen Gebot, So fall auf die Kniee und bete zu Gott! Liebe nur Gott in alle Zeit! So wirst du erlangen die himmlische Freud',	If you have broken the Ten Commandments, Then fall on your knees and pray to God! Love only God forever! Then you will attain Heavenly joy,

Table 4.2: continued

Armer Kinder Betterlied (Boxberger)	Es sungen drei Engel (Mahler)	Three Angels Were Singing
	CC & WC: So wirst du erlangen die himmlische Freud'.	Then you will attain Heavenly joy.
		Heavenly joy is a blessed city,
Die himmlische Freud ist eine selige Stadt,	Die himmlische Freud' ist eine selige Stadt,	Heavenly joy has no end! Heavenly joy was given to
Die himmlische Freud, die kein End mehr hat;	Die himmlische Freud, die kein Ende mehr hat!	Peter, was given to Peter, Through Jesus, and to all
Die himmlische Freud war Petro bereit	Die himmlische Freud' war Petro bereit't, war Petro	mankind through his blessing,
Durch Jesum und allen zur Seligkeit,	bereit't, Durch Jesum und Allem sur	Through Jesus, and to all mankind through his
Zur Seligkeit.	Seligkeit,	blessing,
	Durch Jesum und Allem sur Seligkeit.	Ding dong, ding dong!
	Bimm bamm, bimm bamm.	

teachings and the practices of the Jewish people of His day, where sins had to be atoned for through sacrifice. For a man raised in a Jewish household, contemplating conversion, these biblical instances that draw clear delineation between Judaism and Christianity seem like precisely the kinds of texts he would want to understand on a deeper level. Mahler completed his choral draft of this movement in the summer of 1895.[48] As two years had passed since he had composed "Urlicht" (though his baptism would not occur for another eighteen months), "Es sungen drei Engel" stands out as a sizeable step forward in his studies, as it deals more explicitly with the concepts of Christian grace and redemption.

"Das himmlische Leben"

The third and final instance of a complete setting of a text from *Des Knaben Wunderhorn* appearing as a symphonic movement is "Das himmlische Leben." Intriguingly, however, this song was composed before either "Urlicht" or "Es sungen drei Engel," and Mahler considered adding it to the Third Symphony before finally settling on including it as the finale of his Fourth.

The text depicts a child-like view of Heaven, with descriptions of the peaceful existence, joyful singing and dancing, sumptuous food and drink, and fine entertainment available to those who dwell among the angels. Mahler's adaptations of the source poem include minor punctuation and spelling changes, numerous repetitions, and the removal of some details regarding the fish offerings at the Heavenly dinner table. Indeed, three of the five stanzas in the poem deal with food, leading some to speculate that this view of the afterlife is being provided by the very child who dies of starvation in this example's sister song, "Das irdische Leben."[49]

When Mahler first wrote and orchestrated this song in 1892, he referred to it as one of his *Humoresken*, the genre designation he used for many of his orchestrated *Wunderhorn* lieder, and he initially conceived of his Fourth Symphony as his "Symphonie Humoreske."[50] As discussed in Chapter 1, Mahler's notion of the humoresque is drawn from the ideas of writer Jean Paul and largely conforms to that of irony. Irony abounds in the text of "Das himmlische Leben." The child's innocent and joyful description of Heaven is immediately followed by the depiction of the slaughter of lambs and oxen (complete with musical representations of their bleating played by flute and bassoon—see Examples 4.3 and 4.4). All of the pleasures enjoyed by the residents of this paradise are brought about by the labor of saints. Peter manages the overall joy and catches all the fish needed for feasts. John surrenders his lamb, and Luke butchers the ox. Martha oversees the cooking, while the angels bake the bread. Cecilia leads the musicians and dancers. The underlying message becomes that leading

Example 4.3: "Das himmlische Leben," mm. 60–62, oboe melody

Example 4.4: "Das himmlische Leben," mm. 67–69, bassoon melody

MAHLER AND SPIRITUALITY 105

Table 4.3: Text comparison for "Das himmlische Leben"

Der Himmel hängt voll Geigen (Boxberger)	Das himmlische Leben (Mahler)	The Heavenly Life
	(Words in parentheses denote differences between the orchestral song and the symphonic movement)	
Wir geniessen die himmlischen Freuden,	Wir geniessen die himmlischen Freuden,	We enjoy a heavenly life,
Drum thun wir das Irdliche meiden.	Drum tun wir das Irdische meiden.	That is why we avoid all that is earthly.
Kein weltlich Getümmel	Kein weltlich Getümmel	No earthly turmoil
Hört man nicht im Himmel,	Hört man nicht im Himmel!	Can one hear in Heaven!
Lebt Alles in sanftester Ruh.	Lebt Alles in sanftester Ruh,	We live in the sweetest peace,
Wir führen ein englisches Leben,	In sanftester Ruh.	In the sweetest peace.
Sind dennoch ganz luftig daneben;	Wir führen ein englisches Leben,	We lead an angelic life,
Wir tanzen und springen,	Sind dennoch ganz lustig, ganz lustig daneben,	In it we are entirely happy,
Wir hüpfen und singen;	Wir führen ein englisches Leben,	We lead an angelic life,
Sanct Peter im Himmel sieht zu.	Wir tanzen und springen,	We dance and leap,
	Wir hüpfen und singen!	We skip and sing!
	Wir singen!	We sing!
	Sanct Peter im Himmel sieht zu!	Saint Peter sees to it!
Johannes das Lämmlein auslasset,	Johannes das Lämmlein auslasset!	St. John leaves out his little lamb!
Der Metzger Herodes drauf passet.	Der Metzger Herodes drauf passet!	Herod the butcher lurks nearby!
Wir führen ein geduldigs,	Wir führen ein gedultig's,	We lead a patient,
Unschuldigs, geduldigs,	Undschuldig's, gedultig's,	Innocent, patient,
Ein liebliches Lämmlein zu Tod.	Ein liebliches Lämmlein zu Tod!	A lovely little lamb to its death!
Sanct Lucas den Ochsen that schlachten	Sanct Lucas den Ochsen tut Schlachten	Saint Luke butchers the ox

106   HIDDEN TREASURES

Table 4.3: continued

Der Himmel hängt voll Geigen (Boxberger)	Das himmlische Leben (Mahler)	The Heavenly Life
Ohn einigs Bedenken und Achten.	Ohn' einig's Bedenken und Achten (Trachten),	Without concern or respect (artifice),
Der Wein kost kein Heller Im himmlischen Keller;	Der Wein kost' kein Heller Im himmlische Keller!	Wine costs no money in the heavenly cellar!
Die Engel, die backen das Brod.	Die Englein, die backen das Brod!	The angels, they bake the bread!
Gut Kräuter von allerhand Arten,	Gut' Kräuter von allerhand Arten,	Good herbs of every kind,
Die wachsen im himmlischen Garten:	Die wachsen im himmlischen Garten.	Grow in the heavenly garden.
Gut Spargel, Fisolen	Gut' Spargel, Fisolen	Good asparagus, beans
Und was wir nur wollen;	Und was wir nur wollen!	And anything we want!
Ganze Schüssel voll sind uns bereit,	Ganze Schüssel voll sind uns bereit!	Whole platefuls are ready for us!
Gut Aepfel, gut Birn und gut Trauben,	Gut' Äpfel, gut' Birn', und gut' Trauben!	Good apples, good pears, and good grapes!
Die Gärtner Dir Alles erlauben.	Die Gärtner, de alles erlauben!	The gardeners allow us to pick everything!
Willst Rehbock, willst Hasen?	Willst Rehbock, willst Hasen,	Want venison? Want rabbit?
Gut offener Strassen	Auf offener Strassen	On the open streets
Zur Küche sie laufen herbei.	Sie laufen herbei!	They come running up!
Sollt etwa ein Fasttag ankommen,	Sollt ein Fasttag etwa kommen Alle Fische gleich	When there is a holiday
Die Fische mit Freuden anschwommen.	mit Freuden angeschwommen!	All the fish joyfully swim up! Saint Peter is running
Da laufet Sanct Peter	Dort läuft schon Sanct Peter	already
Mit Netz und mit Köder	Mit Netz und mit Köder	With nets and with bait
Zum himmlischen Weiher hinein;	Zum himmlischen Weiher hinein!	Up to the heavenly pond! Saint Martha must be the
Willst Karpfen, willst Hecht, willst Forellen,	Sanct Martha die Köchin muss sein!	cook!
Gut Stöckfisch und frische Sardellen?	Sanct Martha die Köchin muss sein!	Saint Martha must be the cook!

Table 4.3: continued

Der Himmel hängt voll Geigen (Boxberger)	Das himmlische Leben (Mahler)	The Heavenly Life
Sanct Lorenz hat müssen Sein leben einbüssen; Sanct Martha die Köchin muss sein.		
Kein Musik ist ja nicht auf Erden, Die unsrer verglichen kann werden. Elftausend Jungfrauen Zu tanzen sich trauen; Sanct Ursula selbst dazu lacht. Cäcilia mit ihren Verwandten Sind treffliche Hofmusikanten; Die englische Stimmen Ermuntern die Sinnen, Dass Alles für Freuden erwacht!	Kein Musik ist ja nicht auf Erden, Die unsrer verglichen kann werden. Elftausend Jungfrauen Zu tanzen sich trauen! Sanct Ursula selbst dazu lacht! Kein Musik ist ja nicht auf Erden, Die unsrer verglichen kann werden. Cäcilia mit ihren Verwandten Sind treffliche Hofmusikanten! Die englischen Stimmen Ermuntern die Sinnen, Ermuntern die Sinnen, Dass Alles mit Freuden, Mit Freuden erwacht.	There is no music on earth, That can compare to ours. Eleven thousand virgins Dare to dance! Saint Ursula herself laughs at it! There is no music on earth, That can compare to ours. Saint Cecilia with her companions Are the excellent chief musicians! The angelic voices Delight the senses, Delight the senses So that all are awakened with joy!

a saintly life on earth may only earn you the "privilege" of continuing to work hard for others in the afterlife. The lengthy list of saintly tasks is enough to make the listener wonder if striving to live a saintly life is even worth the effort.

Ironic contrast also appears in the orchestration. The song is organized in an ABCABCA form, with the A sections sounding the most relaxed and calm with winds, strings, and harp. Here the text simply describes the

Example 4.5: "Das himmlische Leben," mm. 25–26, violin II melody

Example 4.6: "Das himmlische Leben," mm. 25–26, flute melody

carefree nature of the Heavenly realm. The activity level begins to rise in the B section (beginning at measure 25), as the protagonist describes the dancing and singing of the denizens. Here the second violins and violas begin a series of repeated eighth notes, played either pizzicato or muted, setting the tempo for the dance, and the flutes and piccolos begin rapid, swirling passages, embodying the dancers' motions (see Examples 4.5 and 4.6). The calm nostalgia established at the beginning and the playful atmosphere of the second section are truly disrupted by the entrance of the C theme (beginning at measure 40), when repeated eighth notes are pounded on the sleigh bells (or tambourine in the original orchestration) and further emphasized by the same beats with added grace notes from the bassoons, horns, and trumpets (oboes, clarinets, and horns in the original). A nearly seventeen-measure interlude demonstrates the struggling of the animals who are being brought forward for slaughter.

And then the cycle begins to repeat itself. The calming surroundings of the beginning re-envelop the listener at measure 80, when the text begins to explore the beautiful and bountiful gardens, but in measure 89, a notation of "allmählich—jedoch unmerklich—bewegter" (moving faster—gradually, almost imperceptibly) points to a busier and more bustling paradise than previously described. When the B section returns at measure 94, Mahler includes the indication "das Tempo ist bereits ein sehr lebhaftes geworden" (the tempo has already become very brisk). The passage attempts to guide the listener to the inevitable return of the franticness of the C theme with notes such as "Vorwärts!" (forward!)

MAHLER AND SPIRITUALITY 109

at measure 99 and odd chromatic dissonance in measures 103–5. Then Mahler surprises the listener by suddenly slamming on the brakes and inserting a refrain from the opening section in measures 106–13, wherein we learn that St. Martha is the head chef in the Heavenly kitchen. A short instrumental interlude reintroduces the C theme, and from measure 121 to the end, the soundscape returns entirely to the peaceful, idyllic setting of the beginning, as our tour ends with a description of the music of Heaven, performed by St. Cecilia and her friends and danced to by St. Ursula's eleven thousand virgins.

Mahler himself described this song as a child's depiction of Heaven. He told Bauer-Lechner, "The child—who, though in a chrysalis-state, nevertheless already belongs to this higher world—explains what it all means."[51] As the song, initially composed on February 10, 1892 and orchestrated a month later, went on to have a strong influence on the sounds of "no fewer than five movements of the Third and Fourth Symphonies," he described it to Bauer-Lechner as "a seed containing a multitude of lives,"[52] making it arguably one of the most significant examples of Mahler's *Wunderhorn* lieder.

"Des Antonius von Padua Fischpredigt"

Unlike the songs discussed previously, "Des Antonius von Padua Fischpredigt" utilizes a Christian subject, in this case the story of a saint and one of his miracles, ironically. The song tells the story of St. Anthony of Padua (1195–1231), a monk renowned for performing several miracles, including the one discussed in this story, and for advocating against "the three most obstinate vices of luxury, avarice, and tyranny."[53] On this particular day, Anthony, finding no one in his church, decides to preach his sermon to the fish at the river. At first, the fish are fascinated by his appearance, and they gather in droves at the water's surface, seeming to take in the priest's every word ("No sermon ever pleased the fish so much"), but when the preaching ends, they return to their sinful ways ("They heard the sermon, but they stayed as they were").

The poem itself is based on a story from a biography of Judas Iscariot written by Abraham a Sancta Clara, a seventeenth-century Augustinian imperial court preacher from Austria.[54] Known for his "mad wit and

110 HIDDEN TREASURES

Table 4.4: Text comparison for "Des Antonius von Padua Fischpredigt"

Des Antonius von Padua Fischpredigt (Boxberger)	Des Antonius von Padua Fischpredigt (Mahler)	Anthony's Sermon to the Fishes

Antonius zur Predig
Die Kirche findt ledig;
Er geht zu den Flüssen
Und predigt den Fischen.
  Sie schlagn mit den
    Schwänzen,
  Im Sonnenschein glänzen.
	Antonius zur Predigt
	die Kirche find't ledig!
	Er geht zu den Flüssen
	und predigt den Fischen!
	  Sie schlag'n mit den
	    Schwänzen!
	  Im Sonnenschein glänzen,
	  Im Sonnenschein,
	    Sonnenschein glänzen,
	  sie glänzen, sie glänzen,
	    glänzen.
		Anthony went to preach,
		But he found the church
		    empty!
		He went to the river
		And preached to the fish!
		  They flick their tails
		  In the bright sunshine!
		  In sunshine,
		  Bright sunshine,
		  Bright sunshine.

Die Karpfen mit Rogen
Sind all hierher zogen,
Habn d'Mäuler aufrissen,
Sich Zuhörens beflissen.
  Kein Predig niemalen
  Den Karpfen so gfallen.
	Die Karpfen mit Rogen
	sind all' hierher zogen;
	hab'n d'Mäuler aufrissen,
	sich Zuhör'n's beflissen.
	  Kein Predigt niemalen
	  den Fischen so g'fallen!
		The carp with their roe
		All came along;
		Their mouths gaped open
		And they listened attentively.
		  No sermon ever
		  Pleased the carp so much!

Spitzgoschete Hechte,
Die immerzu fechten,
Sind eilend herschwommen,
Zu hören den Frommen.
  Kein Predig niemalen
  Den Hechten so gfallen.
	Spitzgoschete Hechte,
	die immerzu fechten
	sind eilends herschwommen,
	zu hören den Frommen!
	
		Pike with sharp snouts
		Who constantly fight
		Swam there quickly,
		To hear the good word!

Auch jene Phantasten,
So immer beim Fasten,
Die Stockfisch ich meine,
Zur Predig erscheinen.
  Kein Predig niemalen
  Dem Stockfisch so gfallen.
	Auch jene Phantasten,
	die immerzu fasten,
	Die Stockfisch ich meine,
	zur Predigt erscheinen!
	  Kein Predigt niemalen
	  den Stockfisch so g'fallen!
		Even the dreamers
		That are always fasting,
		I refer to the cod,
		Appeared at the sermon!
		  No sermon ever
		  Pleased the cod so much!

Table 4.4: continued

Des Antonius von Padua Fischpredigt (Boxberger)	Des Antonius von Padua Fischpredigt (Mahler)	Anthony's Sermon to the Fishes
Gut Aalen und Hausen,	Gut' Aale und Hausen	Good eels and sturgeon
Die Vornehme schmausen,	die Vornehme schmausen,	Feasted on by the wealthy,
Die selber sich bequemen,	die selbst sich bequemen,	They condescended
Die Predig vernehmen.	die Predigt vernehmen.	To listen to the sermon.
Kein Predig niemalen		
Den Aalen so gfallen.		
Auch Krebsen, Schildkroten,	Auch Krebse, Schildkroten,	Also crabs, turtles
Sonst langsame Boten,	sonst langsame Boten,	Arrived very slowly,
Steigen eilend vom Grund,	steigen eilig vom Grund,	Rose up from the riverbed,
Zu hören diesen Mund.	zu hören diesen Mund!	To hear this voice!
Kein Predig niemalen	Kein Predigt niemalen	No sermon ever
Den Krebsen so gfallen	den Krebsen so g'fallen!	Pleased the crabs so much!
Fisch große, Fisch kleine,	Fisch' große, Fisch' kleine!	Large fish, small fish!
Vornehm und gemeine,	Vornehm' und Gemeine!	Distinguished and common!
Erheben die Köpfe	Erheben die Köpfe	Raised their heads
Wie verständge Geschöpfe:	wie verständ'ge Geschöpfe!	Like understanding creatures!
Auf Gottes Begehren	Auf Gottes Begehren	At God's command
Antonium anhören.	Die Predigt anhören!	To hear the sermon!
Die Predig geendet,	Die Predigt geendet,	The sermon ended,
Ein jedes sich wendet:	ein Jeder sich wendet!	And no one had changed!
Die Hechte bleiben Diebe,	Die Hechte bleiben Diebe,	The pike remained thieves,
Dir Aale viel lieben.	die Aale viel lieben,	The eels loved too much,
Die Predig hat gfallen,	die Predigt hat g'fallen,	They heard the sermon,
Sie bleiben wie alle.	sie bleiben wie Allen!	But they stayed as they were!

112   HIDDEN TREASURES

Table 4.4: continued

Des Antonius von Padua Fischpredigt (Boxberger)	Des Antonius von Padua Fischpredigt (Mahler)	Anthony's Sermon to the Fishes
Die Krebs gehn zurücke, Die Stockfisch bleiben dicke, Die Karpfen viel fressen, Die Predig vergessen. Die Predig hat gfallen, Sie bleiben wie alle.	Die Krebs' geh'n zurücke, die Stockfisch' bleib'n dicke, die Karpfen viel fressen die Predigt vergessen, vergessen! Die Predigt hat g'fallen, sie bleiben wie Allen! Die Predigt hat g'fallen, hat g'fallen!	The crabs walked sideways, The cod stayed fat, The carp ate too much, The sermons forgotten, forgotten! They heard the sermon, But they stayed as they were! They heard the sermon, they heard!

cleverness,"[55] Abraham published several books throughout his career, many of which contained violently anti-Semitic rhetoric, calling the Jews "Christendom's worst enemy."[56] In Abraham's telling, Anthony's miraculous summoning of the fish becomes a mockery—not only of the humans who failed to attend Mass that day, but also of Anthony himself, who proved unable to sway the fish from their sinful ways despite their rapt attention during the sermon. Commenting on this latter point, Mahler told Bauer-Lechner, "Not one of them is one iota the wiser for it, even though the Saint has performed for them! But only a few people will understand my satire on mankind."[57] Rather than using this story to further his understanding of Catholic thought, Mahler eschews veneration for symbolism.

Mahler's setting also holds another subtle hint of religious commentary. A theme similar to those heard in Jewish peasant music is heard twice, at measures 52–62 and 87–98 (see Example 4.7). The melody shows a strong influence from the *klezmer* tradition through its use of the clarinet, essentially minor tonality, and melodic intervals of the augmented second.[58] *Klezmer* is a festive style of Jewish dance music, typically heard at weddings and religious celebrations. The juxtaposition of this characteristically Jewish-sounding passage with text discussing the actions of a Catholic saint points to issues of religious difference. It remains unclear whether his insertion was intended as an observation on the impact of

Example 4.7: "Des Antonius von Padua Fischpredigt," mm. 52–56

anti-Semitism on Mahler's life and career or simply a coincidence wherein the slippery chromatic melody was used to represent the flowing of the Brenta River (which runs near the city of Padua and was the site of Anthony's miraculous sermon), but the proximity of these ideas remains nonetheless intriguing.

Like "Urlicht," "Es sungen drei Engeln," and "Das himmlische Leben," "Des Antonius von Padua Fischpredigt" holds a strong connection to Mahler's symphonic composition. The Scherzo of Symphony no. 2 is based entirely upon the melody and arrangement for the song. In a set of program notes, written for a performance in Berlin in December 1901, Mahler described the movement:

> *3rd movement—Scherzo*: the spirit of unbelief, of presumption, has taken possession of him [the deceased person whose spirit is to be resurrected through the movements of the symphony], he beholds the tumult of appearances and together with the child's pure understanding he loses the firm footing that love alone affords; he despairs of himself and of God. The world and love become for him a disorderly apparition; disgust for all being and becoming lay hold of him with an iron grip and drives him to cry out in desperation.[59]

This movement is immediately followed in the symphony by "Urlicht," so the program notes seem to imply that one can only open oneself to the

114   HIDDEN TREASURES

"naïve faith" expressed in the fourth movement after having experienced the "unbelief," "disgust," and "despair" heard in the third.

The program Mahler describes here for his Scherzo compares strangely with the failure of St. Anthony's sermon to alter the behavior of his aquatic congregation. While the fish are presented with the Gospel and refuse to accept it, the symphonic protagonist is confronted with doubt and confusion and still, somehow, finds his way to the path of salvation. Magnar Breivik published an essay in 2002 that compared the messages of the song and symphonic setting of this music.[60] In this work, he describes "Antonius" as "a story of the heavenly inspired capacity of eloquent speech. But... also a depiction of the stubborn strength of worldly disbelief."[61] In its symphonic transformation, he notes, "The song is *not* a song any longer.... The music sounds while the story has become mute. The message has been transfigured in such a way that, like the fishes of St. Anthony, we do not hear a word."[62] This interpretation fails to account for the narrative trajectory of the symphony as a whole. While the protagonist of the symphony does indeed experience "the spirit of disbelief and renunciation,"[63] similar to that of Anthony's fish, these feelings are what eventually allow him to accept the journey to faith and to the salvation promised in the final movement.

"Des Antonius von Padua Fischpredigt" will be discussed in further detail in Chapter 8 as a commentary on music critics and audiences. In that context, far more intricate and subtle commentary contained within the song will be revealed. For now, "Antonius" provides an intriguing contrast from the spiritual exploration observed in "Urlicht," "Es sungen drei Engeln," and "Das himmlische Leben."

Mahler's three *Wunderhorn* songs that were featured as movements in his symphonies all share the unusual quality of being inherently Christian in nature, as does the fourth song which inspired yet another movement. Given that all these songs were also composed prior to his baptism and conversion to Catholicism, it stands to reason to consider these songs as a kind of "dipping his toes into the water" of Christian doctrine. David Schiff has proposed that the naïve views of faith expressed in these poems show Mahler "returning to a world that was never his" as a way to claim that innocence and faith are accessible to anyone, not just Christians.[64]

It may seem tempting to simply view these songs as necessary texts to complete the narratives created by his first four symphonies, but the composer told Natalie Bauer-Lechner of the first two, "My two symphonies contain the most inner aspect of my whole life; I have written into them everything that I have experienced and endured... To understand these works properly would be to see my life transparently revealed in them."[65] He later told her that the first four symphonies create a "perfectly self-contained tetralogy."[66] If we take these ideas together, we can infer that he saw something of himself in the naïve searcher for God embodied by the protagonists in "Urlicht," "Es sungen drei Engel," and "Das himmlische Leben," as well as the confusion and struggle experienced in the movement inspired by "Des Antonius von Padua Fischpredigt." Given the monumental step that his baptism represented, in terms of public perception of his religious identity, these songs provided an opportunity for Mahler to come to know Christianity on his own terms and in the language he understood best—his music.

CHAPTER FIVE

"The risky obstacles in society which are quite dangerous for women"

Commentary on Gender Roles
in the *Wunderhorn* Songs

Among some of the earliest examples of Mahler's *Wunderhorn* lieder are stories of young people behaving inappropriately and suffering the consequences. While it may seem unusual for a bachelor in his twenties to be drawn to these kinds of stories, a few potential factors make these songs easier to explain. First, and perhaps most importantly, the poems found in *Des Knaben Wunderhorn: Alte deutsche Lieder* stem from a tradition where folk songs and fairy stories have a long-regarded history of teaching lessons to the young in the guise of entertainment. Second, the earliest examples of Mahler's settings of these poems were dedicated to the children of his patrons, Captain Karl von Weber and his wife Marion, with whom the composer was having an affair. One might infer that the moral lessons embedded in the *Wunderhorn* poems may have seemed to Mahler an appropriate vehicle for guiding the lives of his potential stepchildren should his lover decide to leave her husband. Third, circumstances with his own family would soon require him to take on the guardianship of several young people.

As stated in Chapter 1, it is unclear whether Mahler was actively aware of the long-standing history of stories like those told by the *Wunderhorn* poems as didactic tools. What we can observe, however, is that he wrote multiple songs that point very clearly to the consequences for young women who fail to behave properly in society, and that those songs were composed at times in his personal life when passing this message on to

117

118   HIDDEN TREASURES

young girls, whether that be the Weber girls or his own sisters, would have been important. So whether or not his intention was explicitly to be instructive with these songs, their very nature would have made them so, assuming their targeted audiences chose to listen and heed the warnings these songs provide.

The Weber Family

As discussed in Chapter 3, while working on the sketches for Carl Maria von Weber's opera *Die drei Pintos*, Mahler had occasion to spend a great deal of time in the home of the late composer's grandson, Captain Karl von Weber, and became quite close with his children, Katharina, age nine, Adolf, eight, and Marion, six. As his relationship with the family deepened and his work on the opera intensified, Mahler began an affair with the children's mother, Marion. The intimacy between the lovers grew to the point that eventually the captain became aware, and Mahler soon left town, with the understanding that Marion would leave her husband and run away with him. Alas, she remained behind, and the composer was left in a state of "painful agitation and expectation," hoping she would appear, and eventually he developed a "restless, depressed state of mind."[1] Nonetheless, the earliest *Wunderhorn* settings were composed during the happy time before the lovers were separated and were, in fact, dedicated to the Weber children. With this in mind, "Starke Einbildungskraft" may very well have been composed for the express purpose of demonstrating to young Katharina and Marion Weber important lessons about the roles of women and girls in society and how they should conduct themselves.

"Starke Einbildungskraft"

Among Mahler's first *Wunderhorn* settings, "Starke Einbildungskraft" (literally, "Vivid Imagination") tells the story of a young woman seeking a marriage proposal. She asks her sweetheart, "You said that you would take me as soon as summer came. Summer is here, but you have not yet taken me. Take me! Won't you take me?" The young man responds, "Why should I take you when I already have you? When I think of

Gender Roles in the *Wunderhorn* Songs   119

Table 5.1: Text comparison for "Starke Einbildungskraft"

Starke Einbildungskraft (Boxberger)	Starke Einbildungskraft (Mahler)	Vivid Imagination
Mädchen	*Mädchen*	*Maiden*
Hast gesagt, Du willst mich nehmen,	Hast gesagt, du willst mich nehmen,	You said that you would take me
Sobald der Sommer kommt.	sobald der Sommer kommt!	As soon as summer came!
Der Sommer ist gekommen,	Der Sommer ist gekommen,	Summer is here,
Du hast mich nicht genommen;	ja kommen,	Yes, here,
Geh, Bubele, geh, nehm mich!	du hast mich nicht genommen, ja nommen!	And you have not taken me, yes taken me!
Gelt, ja, Du nimmst mich noch?	Geh', Büble, geh'! Geh', nehm' mich!	Go on, sweet boy, go on, go on, take me!
	Geh', Büble, geh'! Geh' nehm' mich!	Go on, sweet boy, go on, go on, take me!
	Gelt ja? Gelt ja? Gelt ja, du nimmst mich noch?	Are you? Are you? Are you? Are you still taking me?
Bube	*Bube*	*Boy*
Wie soll ich Dich denn nehmen,	Wie soll ich dich denn nehmen,	Why should I take you, When I already have you?
Und wenn ich Dich schon hab?	die weil ich dich schon hab'?	When I think about you,
Denn wenn ich halt an Dich gedenk,	Und wenn ich halt an dich gedenk',	When I think of you,
Denn wenn ich halt an Dich gedenk,	und wenn ich halt an dich gedenk',	It seems to me, it seems to me, to me,
So mein ich, so mein ich,	so mein' ich, so mein' ich, so mein'	That I have had you the whole time.
Ich mein, ich wär bei Dir.	ich alleweile: ich wär' schon bei dir.	

you it seems that I have had you the whole time." The text provides a moral lesson in the form of a joke. The humor of the situation stems from the use of the verb *nehmen*, meaning "to take." Just as in English, the German verb can mean "to take in marriage," as used by the young woman, or "to take to bed," as used by the young man.[2] The connection between jokes and sexuality was familiar in Viennese culture of the time, as noted in this statement from philosopher Otto Weininger: "Behold the parallelism between humor and eroticism. Both are born of inhibition."[3] We find amusement in the young man's adoption of the word *nehmen* and his quick ability to transform its meaning into something completely different from the girl's. Her insistent repetition of the word *nehmen* also adds to the humor of the situation. The maiden uses the verb no fewer than four times in only six lines of text. On the other hand, the young man uses it only once, but in his hands, the implication changes instantly. This shift in meaning forms the essence of the joke. If the young man were to reply to his sweetheart's requests for a marriage proposal by saying, for example, "We have slept together so often, I do not feel it is in my interest to marry you," the intent would remain, but the cleverness of his message would have been lost. His quick-witted reply would have turned nasty and hurtful, and the song would lose its gentle lesson to young women who would engage in premarital relations first and worry about their reputations later.

Mahler maintained the *Volkston* character of the poem in what is essentially a strophic setting in B-flat major, although differences between the stanzas occur, beginning with the third phrase of each verse: the extended pleading of the maiden in the first verse is shortened by two measures by way of varied levels of textual repetition (see Examples 5.1 and 5.2).[4] The expansion of the music in her verse demonstrates the maiden's desire to cling to what is obviously a relationship with no future, while the young man's rushed, abrupt reply,

Example 5.1: "Starke Einbildungskraft," mm. 4–7

Example 5.2: "Starke Einbildungskraft," mm. 13–16

which follows the maiden with only an eighth-note pause, exemplifies his desire to move on quickly, as if he had been waiting for some time for this conversation to occur and had already prepared his argument, allowing him to make a rapid exit. The young man's melody also features a slightly higher tessitura (as seen on his word "dich" in Example 5.2) and somewhat thicker accompaniment, demonstrating his annoyance with his situation. Mahler also creates a much more stagnant melody than that heard in the original folk melody (see Example 5.3). Mahler's melody more accurately intimates the monotony of a romance that has worn out its welcome. Very similar to the original melody, however, is the melodic line of Mahler's piano introduction (see Example 5.4). The dotted rhythms, the simple I–IV–V chord progressions, and the lilting

Example 5.3: "Starke Einbildungskraft," folk melody

Example 5.4: "Starke Einbildungskraft," Mahler's piano introduction

dance-like tempos also serve to create very similar sonic environments in these two settings of the same text. Another method Mahler uses to illustrate the impending conclusion of this relationship is the song's brevity; at just over one minute in length, this is the shortest of Mahler's *Wunderhorn* songs. The events play out in very short order, almost too short to allow the listener to grasp the situation before the final statement by the young man is revealed.

Mahler includes an unusual sonic effect in measure 10, between the maiden's repeated pleas of "Gelt, ja?" The effect, two accented eighth notes with descending grace notes, gives the impression of a bird call (see Example 5.5). This mimetic gesture momentarily allows the accompaniment to extend beyond its background role and participate in the story, assuming a role of commentator and stretching the dramatic mode into the epic. The inclusion of birdsong, personified by the piano, lends the support of the world of nature to the maiden's cause, as if to say, "After this much time has passed, it is only appropriate for you to be married." The transition between the verses also offers a peculiar instance; the final

Example 5.5: "Starke Einbildungskraft," mm. 9–11

GENDER ROLES IN THE *WUNDERHORN* SONGS   123

measures of the first verse seem to be setting up a modulation to the dominant, but just when that change seems about to occur, the second verse
begins back in the tonic, just as the song had begun. It seems as if, even in
the tonal center of the song, the maiden's hopes of marriage to her sweetheart are being thwarted.

Just as the maiden in this story is left abandoned and potentially unable
to resurrect her reputation after giving up her virginity, one can readily see
how such a lesson might be potentially problematic. The Webers' daughters were only nine and six years old when the song was composed. This
is certainly too young for girls to be receiving instruction on the dangers
of premarital sex, especially from a man hoping to break up their parents'
marriage. Nonetheless, it seems likely that, upon finding a poem with such
a message, Mahler may have selected it as a lyric as a way of developing a
strategy for speaking to young girls about their reputations before being
confronted with the necessity to do so in real life.

The Mahler Family

Gustav was the second of his parents' fourteen children. His elder brother
Isidor died in an unspecified accident before Gustav was born. Of his
remaining twelve siblings, only six survived past the age of three. To
compound the tragedy, Gustav's brother Ernst died at the age of thir-
teen of pericarditis, and his sister Leopoldine at age twenty-six of a brain
tumor. To say that death was a frequent visitor to the Mahler household
is clearly an understatement, and much has been written speculating on
the psychological effects that losing so many siblings may have had on the
composer's life and music.[5]

Further compounding the tragedy surrounding the family, when
the composer was only twenty-nine years old, in 1889, both of Mahler's
parents died. He was scarcely established in his own career as the director
of the Royal Hungarian Opera in Budapest, but as the oldest surviving
member of the family, Mahler suddenly found himself charged with the
upbringing and care of his four surviving younger siblings: sisters Justine
(age 21) and Emma (age 14) and brothers Otto (age 16) and Alois (age 22).
This amounted to a monumental responsibility, emotionally and finan-
cially, just as his own career began to require increasing dedication. His

124   HIDDEN TREASURES

initial strategy involved finding care for Emma and Otto, as they were still underage, and seeing to the financial security of Justine and Alois. The youngest Mahlers went into the care of family friends Friedrich and Uda Löhr in Vienna until Otto completed his schooling at the Conservatory in Vienna for the year, Alois joined the military, and Justine came to Budapest and moved in with her brother. Of his oldest sister, he wrote to a former colleague, "My sister is very ailing. She literally destroyed her nerves through terrible physical exertions at my parents' sickbeds and all the violent emotions associated with it."[6] Within a few months, Justine, Otto, and Emma had moved in together in an apartment in Vienna, funded by their oldest brother. Justine assumed the role of head of the household, for which she was remarkably ill-suited due to her youth, her weakened health, and what Natalie Bauer-Lechner called her "impetuous, passionate, and far-from systematic nature."[7] Much of what we know of the younger Mahlers and their relationship with their oldest brother stems from letters. These precious insights into the lives of the Mahler family survive solely because of the efforts of Justine. Even before her parents' deaths, she began meticulously preserving the family's correspondence, and upon her own death she passed the documents on to her son, Alfred Rosé. Upon Rosé's death, his widow donated the collection to the University of Western Ontario, where her husband had taught composition after his flight from Vienna during the rise of the Third Reich.

Mahler's letters to his siblings over the four years following the loss of their parents reveal his many obligations, familial and financial. They also include countless mandates regarding all aspects of his siblings' lives, particularly their finances—"I want the money I send to be used as I indicate, and not as the mood strikes somebody or other"[8]—and their social conduct—"I would like you to limit your dealings with… other Iglauers to the bare essentials—In any case, I absolutely forbid Emma to come into the slightest contact with absolutely anyone from there."[9] Indeed, reading some of these letters could certainly convince someone that Mahler had little patience or kindness to offer his siblings. Yet he also expresses deep concern for their well-being: "Don't give yourself over to troubling moods.—Everything will get better for you. Whatever I can do to that end, will be done."[10] That said, his relationships with each of the four younger Mahlers differed dramatically.

GENDER ROLES IN THE *WUNDERHORN* SONGS 125

The brother closest to Gustav in age, Alois, was by far the most remote in terms of their relationship, and as such he is the sibling about whom we know the least. Over time, Alois slowly drifted away from his family. He was prone to lying and running up debts which went unpaid. While records are contradictory and scarce, by 1899 he had changed his name to Hans Christian, and at some point between 1904 and 1907, he moved to the United States, reportedly to escape debt collectors.[11] He died in Chicago in 1931 of stomach cancer compounded by the same heart ailment that killed his older brother in 1911.

Youngest brother Otto's story is less mysterious but far more tragic. Like Gustav, Otto was a gifted musician, and his family arranged for him to receive the same educational opportunities as his oldest brother—he was enrolled at the Conservatory of the Gesellschaft der Musikfreunde at the time of his parents' deaths, and he continued his studies intermittently before withdrawing permanently in 1892. After that he struggled to hold a position, despite his brother's influence and connections affording him multiple opportunities. On February 6, 1895, he shot himself in the home of a family friend. Mahler spoke little about the tragedy, but in one recorded instance he told his friend, musicologist Josef Bohuslav Foerster, "I had a brother. He, too, was a musician. A composer. Very talented, far more so than I. He died young… A pity. A great pity. He killed himself in the very prime of life."[12]

Most pertinent to this discussion, however, are Mahler's sisters, Emma and Justine. The youngest of the Mahler children, Emma was born when Gustav was fifteen, after he had already left Iglau for the Conservatory in Vienna. As a result, they were never particularly close. Depictions of her character paint her as immature and starved for attention. Her brother Otto described her as "a nuisance to the whole house."[13] And, when she asked for a doll at age sixteen, Gustav wrote in a letter to Justine, "Frankly, it is quite astonishing that Emma wanted a doll… An almost grown-up girl, who is so overripe in one respect, and so childish on the other, remains a riddle to me."[14] From the privilege of perspective, it seems reasonable to surmise that her emotional growth might have been impacted by basic factors of her young life: being the youngest child in the Mahler household, where sickness and death were such common visitors, and simply being a girl in a family that largely revolved around her

126   HIDDEN TREASURES

talented brother, whom she barely knew. Compounding these issues was her sporadic education. That said, Mahler did take an active interest in her social standing and reputation. In 1893, she asked to take dancing lessons so she could go to a ball, with the mother of a friend acting as chaperone. To this, Gustav replied, "I think that it is unsuitable that you go to a ball with a stranger.... If your sister, or a woman I know cannot go with you, then I already reject this from the outset as improper... When the proper time comes, I myself will take you to balls and go into society with you."[15] Emma was seventeen years old when her brother wrote this. Is it unclear whether he was being overprotective or simply did not trust his youngest sister to behave appropriately in such an environment. In 1897, twenty-two-year-old Emma married the cellist Eduard Rosé, elder brother to her sister's future husband.

Gustav's relationship with his sister Justine, eight years his junior, is by far the closest and best documented. While much of their communication during these four key years pertains to matters of the household and the upbringing of Otto and Emma, Justine remained one of the most significant women in Gustav's life until his marriage to Alma, which preceded her own marriage to Arnold Rosé by only one day, so that neither would be left alone. Justine also determined that she and Emma would be baptized with their brother, so he wouldn't have to "jump into it on his own."[16] Gustav took great pains to guide his sister's behavior. Sometimes this was done to save her from her own feelings of inadequacy, as when he wrote, "You shouldn't torment yourself with self-reproach.... You only must see to it (and I must help you in this) that these feelings are channeled into proper paths."[17] Other admonishments pertained more to Justine's relationships and social behavior, such as, "If you would take my advice to heart, then learn over time to be modest and considerate towards others... in the end, a 'solid human being' will yet emerge from you."[18]

Justine from time to time would bristle against these constant admonishments. In 1892, she wrote to her brother, "I absolutely cannot find my life's work anymore in the domestic management of my brothers and sisters!!!... I must become independent."[19] Still, Justine was often just as protective of her brother as he was of her. Letters from Gustav are littered with stern reprimands when he learned of bad news that she had tried to keep from him in order to keep him from worrying about family matters.

GENDER ROLES IN THE *WUNDERHORN* SONGS   127

And, most notably, for fear of upsetting her brother's routine by leaving his household, she hid her romance with violinist Arnold Rosé (which, reportedly, had been ongoing since 1897) and only revealed it after she was assured that her brother would himself be happily married.[20] Justine and Arnold married the day after Gustav wed Alma Schindler on March 9, 1902.

Despite the family frictions and the challenges that acting as guardian for his siblings clearly brought upon Mahler, songs composed during the critical four years between the deaths of their parents and Emma's reaching adulthood in 1893 stem exclusively from *Des Knaben Wunderhorn*. As such, the stories the songs tell contain moral lessons, some of which may be interpreted as being aimed at Justine and Emma regarding their behavior as young women in society, particularly "Verlor'ne Müh'!"

"Verlor'ne Müh'!"

"Verlor'ne Müh'!" from 1892, like "Starke Einbildungskraft," tells a story of a young woman who behaves immodestly toward a man. In this case, the young woman does not seek a husband, but merely a sexual partner. She uses a string of lightly veiled euphemisms in attempting to seduce her uninterested target: "Should we go look at our lambs?" "Would you like a little snack from my pocket?" "Shall I give you my heart?" To each request, the answer is a resounding "No." This song neatly reverses the gender roles found in "Starke Einbildungskraft," in that now the female uses disguised speech to engage in seduction.

Before the singer has uttered a word, the instrumental introduction of "Verlor'ne Müh'!" has given the listener a great deal of information, providing the initial narration prior to the entry of the dramatic text. The opening four measures feature a sustained dominant pitch in the oboe, offset by accented notes in the horn and the triangle. These tones combine to emulate the sounding of the chimes of a clock tower and a pastoral horn. Through the use of these stereotypical instruments, we find that it is early in the day, that the story takes place in an outdoor, rural setting, and that it likely involves *völkisch* characters. The tonic chord of A major does not appear until measure seven, upon which the voice enters and the ballad at last gets fully underway. The music continues in a rhythmic

128   Hidden Treasures

Table 5.2: Text comparison for "Verlor'ne Müh'!"

Verlorene Mühe (Boxberger)	Verlor'ne Müh'! (Mahler)	Vain Effort
Sie	*Sie:*	*Her:*
Büble, wir wollen auße gehe,	Büble, wir –	Sweet boy, let's –
Wollen unsre Lämmer besehe.	Büble, wir wollen auße gehe!	Sweet boy, let's go see!
	Auße gehe!	Go see!
Komm, liebs Büberle,	Wollen wir? Wollen wir?	Do we want to? Do we want to?
Komm, ich bitt!	Unsere Lämmer besehe?	
	Komm'! Komm'!	Go see our little lambs?
	Komm', lieb's Büberle,	Come! Come!
	komm', ich bitt'!	Come, sweet boy,
		Come, please!
Er	*Er:*	*Him:*
Närrisches Dinterle,	Närrisches Dinterle,	Foolish girl,
Ich geh Dir holt nit.	ich geh dir holt nit!	I won't go with you!
Sie	*Sie:*	*Her:*
Willst vielleicht ä Bissel nasche?	Willst vielleicht?	Maybe you'd like?
	Willst vielleicht ä bissel nasche?	Maybe you'd like a little snack to nibble?
Hol Dir was aus meiner Tasche!	Bissel nasche?	A little snack to nibble?
Hol, liebs Bübele,	Willst vielleicht? (x2)	Maybe you'd like?
Hol, ich bitt!	Hol' dir was aus miener Tasch'!	Get something out of my pocket!
	Hol' dir was! (x2)	Get something!
	Hol'! Hol'! Hol' lieb's Büberle,	Get it! Get it! Get it, sweet boy!
	hol', ich bitt'!	Get it, please!
Er	*Er:*	*Him:*
Närrisches Dinterle,	Närrisches Dinterle,	Foolish girl,
Ich nasch Dir holt nit.	ich nasch' dir holt (halt) nit!	I won't eat with you!
	Nit!	I won't!
Sie		
Thut vielleicht der Durst Dich plage?		

Verlorene Mühe (Boxberger)	Verlor'ne Müh'! (Mahler)	Vain Effort
Komm, will Dich zum Brunne trage; Trink, liebs Büberle, Trink, ich bitt!		
Er Närrisches Dinterle, Es dürst mich holt nit.		

Sie
Thut vielleicht der Schlaf
    Dich drücke?
Schlaf, ich jag Dir fort die
    Mücke;
Schlaf, liebes Büberle,
Schlaf, ich bitt!		

Er Narrisches Dinterle, Mich schläfert's holt nit.		

Sie
Gelt, ich soll mein Herz Dir
    schenke,
Immer willst an mich
    gedenke?
Nimm's liebe Büberle,
Nimm's, ich bitt!
	Sie:
	Gelt, ich soll –
	gelt, ich soll mein Herz dir
	    schenke,
	Herz dir schenke!?
	Gelt, ich soll? (x2)
	Immer willst an mich
	    gedenke!?
	Immer!? Immer!? Immer!?
	Nimm's! Nimm's!
	Nimm's! Lieb's Büberle!
	Nimm's, ich bitt'!
		Her:
		Should I give –
		Should I give you my heart,
		Give you my heart?
		Should I give?
		So you will always remember
		    me?
		Always!? Always!?
		Always!?
		Take it! Take it!
		Take it, sweet boy!
		Take it, please!

Er Närrisches Dinterle, Ich mag es holt nit.	*Er:* Närrisches Dinterle, ich mag es holt nit! Nit!	*Him:* Foolish girl, I don't want it! I don't!

Example 5.6: "Verlor'ne Müh'!" mm. 11–13

pattern associated with the folk dance called the *Ländler*, which features a lilting, lyrical triple meter in which the foot is traditionally stomped on the first beat of the measure, creating a distinctive accent, akin to a rustic waltz. Mahler highlights this rhythm in measures 12–13 of the vocal line with a pattern that recurs throughout the song (see Example 5.6). The blatant use of the folk dance also adds to the pastoral setting of the song;[21] however, this dance rhythm is repeatedly distorted by the young man in the story, who takes no interest in the girl's advances. Once he has rejected her, the tempo accelerates, and the accompaniment motive heard in measures 33–40 shifts the accent ahead by an eighth beat, demonstrating how unexpected this situation was to the maiden. The young man storms off, and she is forced to scramble to come up with a new plan to win his affections (see Example 5.7). However, as soon as she is able to formulate her new tactic, the tempo returns to that of the beginning, normality is restored, and her process of wooing begins again.

Each of the maiden's three verses begins with an identical ascending passage that spans the interval of a minor tenth, and each verse is separated by a brief instrumental interlude. This repetition and the variations that follow each occurrence of the primary motive in each verse, as well as the interludes, indicate that the maiden is spacing out her approaches to the young man over time. She uses the time allotted by the interlude to plan a new strategy, but rather than returning to seek him out again immediately, she waits until the moment is right. The similarity of the music also informs

Example 5.7: "Verlor'ne Müh'!" mm. 33–40, piano arrangement

Examples 5.8a, b, and c: "Verlor'ne Müh'!" mm. 30–33, 65–68, and 102–5

us that while she believes she is trying something new with each successive verse, her tactics are all essentially the same, and each is doomed to failure. The passing of time between verses also explains the change in the young man's musical language. After her first approach, the similarity of his response to the musical language used by the maiden suggests that he is trying to be polite. The rising pitch and wider range of his later responses, however, show increasing irritation (see Examples 5.8a, b, and c). Mahler omitted two verses from the exemplar *Wunderhorn* poem. This allows the escalation of the young man's annoyance to seem more natural. We must assume, however, that the young man has been anticipating the maiden's advances, because he requires no time at all to ponder his replies. His responses begin on the downbeat of the measure immediately following her stanza in every instance. In fact, the faster rhythmic motion of the first measures of his second and third replies (as seen in Examples 5.8b and c) makes these statements seem even more rushed, as if he could not even wait for her to finish speaking before turning her down.

Mahler distorts the *Volkston* in his song through the use of extensive chromaticism in the vocal melodies (see Example 5.9). The accompaniment, at first, remains essentially consonant and supportive of the slippery melody, except during the moment when the maiden impresses upon the young man to accept her advances toward the end of her first stanza (see Example 5.10). The dissonance of this passage creates a brief

Example 5.9: "Verlor'ne Müh'!" mm. 82–86

moment of suspense and expectation as both the maiden and the listener await her intended's response to her pleas. Later verses show the maiden's increased frustration through added dissonance and nonfunctional chromatic harmony. Verse two builds tension through the repeated alternation of C major and G augmented chords, and verse three hovers for seven measures on an F major chord before finally returning to A major in measure 89, only to begin a highly dissonant passage in which the maiden makes her final plea for the young man's attention (see Example 5.11).

Example 5.10: "Verlor'ne Müh'!" mm. 26–29

Example 5.11: "Verlor'ne Müh'!" mm. 90–93

Example 5.12: Brahms: "Vergebliches Ständchen," mm. 2–6

As a partner dance, the *Ländler* has a long-standing tradition in its association with peasant courtship. The dance was utilized before Mahler in folk-inspired art songs recalling failed attempts at wooing. The most notable example is Brahms' "Vergebliches Ständchen," op. 84, no. 4 (see Example 5.12). Mahler's case is unusual, however, in that here it is a young lady trying to win over a young man. We hear the maiden's increased motivation in the second verse, which is extended through text repetition, through her change in pitch, which lowers toward the end of the verse, and then her desperation in the final verse that lowers in pitch even further as if she is trying to lower her voice to match his. Her final exclamation, marked "immer kläglicher" (more and more wretchedly), brings the drama to an almost comic level as she makes her final, somewhat pathetic, plea with words repeated to the point of absurdity. All the while, the young man's responses to the maiden consistently rise in pitch while his tone remains cool and detached as he becomes increasingly emphatic and irritated, ending finally with his sustained statement "Nit!," held on a high G sharp for over two measures, which possesses the finality to close the matter for good. We find that the modified strophic form presents a story where, despite the young lady's best efforts, circumstances change very little from beginning to end.

While the maidens in "Starke Einbildungskraft" and "Verlor'ne Müh'!" both chase after uninterested men, their motives and approaches make their circumstances completely opposite: the first seeks to salvage her reputation by marrying the man who took her virginity, while the second has no such concerns for propriety but still faces rejection. In either case,

134   HIDDEN TREASURES

the moral clearly emerges: girls who wantonly chase after young men will become the subject of mockery. In his autobiography, novelist Stefan Zweig discusses the customary sexual education of young Viennese girls at the *fin-de-siècle*:

> In the pre-Freudian era... the axiom was agreed upon that a female person could have no physical desires as long as they had not been awakened by a man, and that, obviously, was officially permitted only in marriage. But even in these moral times, in Vienna in particular, the air was full of dangerous erotic infection, and a girl of good family had to live in a completely sterilized atmosphere, from the day of her birth until the day when she left the altar on her husband's arm.... Young girls were constantly kept busy to divert their attention from any possible dangerous thoughts.... A young girl of good family was not allowed to have any idea of how the male body was formed, or to know how children came into the world, for the angel was to enter into matrimony not only physically untouched but completely "pure" spiritually as well.... And that is how the society of those days wished young girls to be, silly and untaught, well educated and innocent, curious and shy, uncertain and unpractical, and predisposed to this education without knowledge of the world from the very beginning, to be led and formed by a man in marriage without any will of their own. Custom seemed to preserve them as a symbol of its most sacred ideals, as an emblem of womanly chastity, virginity, and unworldliness.[22]

Mahler, whether aware of the instructive power of these stories or not, can be seen as using the young ladies in "Starke Einbildungskraft" and "Verlor'ne Müh'!" as subtle examples for Katharina, Marion, Justine, and Emma of the social rejection that awaits girls that succumb to such "dangerous thoughts," in an attempt to preserve their "chastity, virginity, and unworldliness."

The power of these songs to pass on lessons presents nothing new. Folk tales and fairy stories have long remained part of their respective cultures because of the lessons they convey to their audience. "Sleeping Beauty" provides a similar admonishment against a rush toward sexual maturity.[23] The wolf and the red cape in "Little Red Riding Hood" symbolize the girl's loss of virginity.[24] Mahler's choice of poems from a folk background, telling of girls who shame themselves by throwing themselves at men, allows these songs to serve the same purpose: to encourage proper behavior from the young women in his life.

CHAPTER SIX

"Highly complicated activity of the mind"

Songs with a Freudian Slant

Musicologists and psychoanalysts alike have devoted a great deal of study to the meeting between Gustav Mahler and Sigmund Freud that occurred on the afternoon of August 26, 1910 in Leiden, The Netherlands.[1] This is quite natural, given the rarity with which scholars can examine shared moments between figures of such magnitude in their respective fields. Of course, by this time, Mahler had long since finished using *Des Knaben Wunderhorn* for song texts; however, "although Mahler had had no previous contact with psychoanalysis Freud said that he had never met anyone who seemed to understand it so swiftly."[2] This may be explained by that fact that several of Mahler's acquaintances had sought treatment from Freud and discussed it with him.[3] Given this, it seems quite reasonable, and can reveal a great deal, to examine some of the *Wunderhorn* songs using Freud's theories as an interpretive window. This by no means implies that Mahler's compositions were directly influenced by or commenting on Freudian theory, but rather that examining the songs as products as their age (i.e. the dawn of psychoanalysis) can allow one to interpret these songs in new and fruitful ways. Freud's theories made up a large part of the *Zeitgeist* of *fin-de-siècle* Vienna, and as such, their influence could be felt in all areas of the arts at this time. To discount the intermingling of ideas from the arts and sciences from this unique place and time would rob scholars and listeners of a valuable hermeneutic tool.

137

138   HIDDEN TREASURES

As the home of Sigmund Freud and the birthplace of his psycho-analytic theories, *fin-de-siècle* Vienna is typically granted a certain authoritative stance with respect to its peoples' understanding of psychological processes and human feeling. But not all activities of the mind need to be analyzed on the therapist's couch. Many view simple human emotion as the heart of the artistic impulse, and how a composer simulates emotional states in music impacts not only the sound of the work, but the audience's response. The idea that music carries emotional expression independent from those who create or hear it has been debated extensively for centuries. Plato's imitation theory written in *The Republic* holds that musical sound (or any form of art, for that matter) does not carry inherent emotional factors, but merely imitates the physical expression of said emotions.[4] In Mahler's time, Eduard Hanslick argued that music cannot in and of itself express emotion: "The representation of a specific feeling or emotional state is not at all among the characteristic powers of music… Feelings are not so isolated in the mind that they have made themselves the salient feature of an art."[5] Philosopher Susanne Langer's theories seem more in line with Mahler's often-quoted statement, "If a composer could say what he had to say in words, he would not bother trying to say it in music."[6] Langer writes, "Because the forms of human feeling are more congruent with musical forms than with the forms of language, music can reveal the nature of feelings with a language and truth that language cannot approach."[7]

Many scholars, both in music and psychology, have taken Mahler's passing acquaintance with Freud to be a free ticket to attempt their own psychoanalyses on the composer.[8] This practice holds many dangers, and any indication that one can uncover the innermost secrets of a subject who is no longer alive should not be taken seriously. However, as long as it remains clearly an exercise intended to enlighten one's understanding of the work, rather than a diagnostic discussion of a dead subject's emotional state, one can generate entirely new interpretations of a work by interrogating Mahler's music using Freudian theory. As has been mentioned previously, the purpose of stories such as those found in the *Wunderhorn* is to provide lessons for young people, just as parents use fairy tales to inform their children today.[9] Creating new modes of expression for these stories provides them with a timeless quality, allowing audiences from

Songs with a Freudian Slant   139

generations living long after the tales were first told to learn lessons that universally hold true. In these analyses, this chapter will apply Freud's psychoanalytic theory to the actions and emotions of the fictional characters that populate the poems of Mahler's *Des Knaben Wunderhorn* as a way to broaden one's understanding of these works. Mahler's musical expression of emotional states of lovesickness and defense mechanisms appear in "Selbstgefühl" and "Lied des Verfolgten im Turm," while the actions of the protagonists in "Wo die schönen Trompeten blasen" and "Der Schildwache Nachtlied" arguably take place in the world of dreams.

During the period that Mahler was composing songs to the texts of *Des Knaben Wunderhorn*, Freud published his first three major works: *Studien über Hysterie* (Studies on Hysteria, 1895), *Die Traumdeutung* (The Interpretation of Dreams, 1899), and *Zur Psychopathologie des Alltagslebens* (The Psychopathology of Everyday Life, 1901). The first of these explores the idea of lovesickness as a conversion disorder and can, as such, inform our understanding of "Selbstgefühl." *Studien über Hysterie* is also one of the first works of Freud to interpret the notion of denial as a defense mechanism, which we see employed by the protagonist in "Lied des Verfolgten im Turm." Using *Die Traumdeutung* to examine "Wo die schönen Trompeten blasen" and "Der Schildwache Nachtlied" can shed a great deal of light on the actions of the characters in the stories as well.

"Selbstgefühl"

Arnim and Brentano adapted what would become Mahler's final setting of his first collection of songs based on *Des Knaben Wunderhorn* from the *fliegende Blätter* entitled "Vier schöne neue weltliche Lieder" collected by John Meier.[10] Mahler did little to manipulate his source; however, his small changes had substantial impact. Mahler utilized the opening line of each of his source stanzas, "Ich weiß nicht, wie mir ist," as a flexible refrain, which opens two of his six stanzas and closes four. The irregular repetition of phrases underlines the protagonist's confusion. This technique also contorts Mahler's rhyme scheme, lending to the instability of the environment.

The scene painted by the protagonist is one of bewilderment; he repeats that he does not know how to describe his problem, but claims

140   Hidden Treasures

Table 6.1: Text comparison for "Selbstgefühl"

Selbstgefühl (Boxberger)	Selbstgefühl (Mahler)	Feeling the Self
Ich weiß nicht, wie mir's ist. Ich bin nicht krank und bin nicht gesund; Ich bin blessirt und hab keine Wund.	Ich weiß nicht, wie mir ist! Ich bin nicht krank und nicht gesund, ich bin blessiert und hab' kein' Wund', ich weiß nicht, wie mir ist!	I don't know what's wrong with me! I am not sick, I am not healthy, I have been blessed, but I have no wound. I don't know what's wrong with me!
Ich weiß nicht, wie mir's ist. Ich thät gern essen und geschmeckt mir nichts; Ich hab ein Geld und gilt mir nichts.	Ich tät gern essen und schmeckt mir nichts, ich hab' ein Geld und gilt mir nichts, ich hab' ein Geld und gilt mir nichts, ich weiß nicht, wie mir ist!	I eat well, but I taste nothing, I have money, but I buy nothing. I have money, but I buy nothing, I don't know what's wrong with me!
Ich weiß nicht, wie mir's ist. Ich hab sogar kein Schnupftabak Und hab kein Kreuzer Geld im Sack.	Ich hab' sogar kein' Schnupftabak, und hab' kein' Kreuzer Geld im Sack, kein Geld im Sack, ich hab' sogar kein Schnupftabak und hab' kein' Kreuzer Geld im Sack, kein' Kreuzer Geld im Sack!	I even have no tobacco and I have no money in my sack. No money in my sack I even have no tobacco and have no money in my sack. No money in my sack!
Ich weiß nicht, wie mir's ist. Heirathen thät ich auch schon gern, Kann aber Kinderschrein nicht hörn.	Ich weiß nicht wie mir ist, Wie mir ist! Heiraten tät' ich auch schon gern, kann aber Kinderschrei'n nicht hör'n, Kinderschrei'n nicht hör'n! Ich weiß nicht, wie mir ist!	I don't know what's wrong with me! I'd like to get married, But I can't stand to hear children crying! I can't stand to hear children crying! I don't know what's wrong with me!

Table 6.1: continued

Selbstgefühl (Boxberger)	Selbstgefühl (Mahler)	Feeling the Self
Ich weiß nicht, wie mir's ist. Ich hab erst heut den Doktor gefragt; der hat mir's unters Gesicht gesagt:	Ich hab' erst heut' den Doktor gefragt, der hat mir's in's Gesicht gesagt: "Ich weiß wohl, was dir ist, Was dir ist:	I went to ask a doctor this morning And he said to my face, "I know well what is wrong with you, wrong with you.
"Ich weiß wohl, was Dir ist: Ein Narr bist Du gewiß." Nun weiß ich, wie mir ist.	Ein Narr bist du gewiß!" "Nun weiß ich, wie mir ist, Nun weiß ich, wie mir ist!" "Ein Narr bis du gewiß!" "Nun weiß ich, wie mir ist, Nun weiß ich, wie mir ist!"	You are a fool!" "Now I know what is wrong with me!" "You are a fool!" "Now I know what is wrong with me!"

he has no appetite, feels worthless, has no motivation, and feels unsure about his future: all symptoms of lovesickness. At last, he visits a doctor, who tells him he is a fool. This simple answer satisfies him, as now he can at least describe his situation. He cheerfully proclaims "Nun weiß ich, wie mir ist!" (Now I know what is wrong with me!). His apparent happiness over being diagnosed as a fool serves as the final punch line, emphasizing his inanity.

If we examine the protagonist's behavior through the lens of psycho-analytic thought, this perception of silliness quickly fades away. His inability to enjoy his life would stem from lovesickness, a kind of conversion disorder, wherein the body develops physical symptoms in order to defend the mind from emotional stress. Freud and his daughter Anna were instrumental in developing the theory of defense mechanisms, but he and his partner Josef Breuer had been aware of the mind's protective instincts long before Anna identified the ten primary defense mechanisms in 1936. Breuer defined mental defense as "The voluntary suppression of painful ideas which a person feels are a threat to their enjoyment of life or their self-esteem."[11] The protagonist in "Selbstgefühl" experiences feelings that he cannot admit to himself in an effort to protect himself from the

142 HIDDEN TREASURES

potential pain of a failed relationship. He disguises his evident rejection of the possibility of pursuing the object of his affections as foolishness in an attempt to draw attention away from his own insecurities.

This odd little song perfectly portrays the protagonist's identity crisis. Within fifty-seven short measures, Mahler explores five contrasting thematic areas without ever really settling in any of them. As he reveals the young man's recent strange behaviors, the pitch center wanders through three key areas (G major, D major, and E minor), only briefly establishing any lasting tonal centers. He cannot determine the problem himself, and the rhythm contributes to his lack of identity by maintaining a consistent pulse that pushes the song relentlessly forward, almost without pause. The listener meets a protagonist who is lost and confused while his life forges relentlessly ahead, and the incessant motion of the accompaniment drags the listener right along with him.

The ascending and descending motion of the phrases of the vocal melody in the opening section resembles the act of pacing while working out a problem (see Example 6.1). Then, as is consistent with the truly perplexed, after a few steady paces a contrasting thought bursts in that throws everything off track, forcing the thinker to start again (see Example 6.2). We soon find that this effort has failed to bring resolution.

The protagonist enters into each new thematic area as if trying to take a deep breath and think rationally about his circumstances. The second area, starting at measure 16, begins a bit more thoughtfully, but by the end of the second phrase, the sensibility breaks down again in the tumbling final notes of the phrase, repeating text like an errant afterthought (see Example 6.3). Each new section begins likewise, with longer, more contemplative sustained notes that rapidly give way to a confused, irritated, or expectant series of eighth notes.

Matters come to a head at measure 35, immediately before the protagonist announces that he consulted his physician, musically enacting the existential crisis that often leads those hurting to seek professional help. Mahler represents this musically by inserting a fermata and the marking "kurzer Halt" (short pause). At last, the frenetic, relentless pace of the song has been interrupted.

Songs with a Freudian Slant 143

Example 6.1: "Selbstgefühl," mm. 1–6

Example 6.2: "Selbstgefühl," mm. 6–9

Example 6.3: "Selbstgefühl," mm. 16–20

Mahler's lyric moves almost entirely in the present tense, as the protagonist describes his confusion. The final two stanzas move briefly into a quasi-balladic mode, using both epic narration and dramatic dialogue, as we learn of the doctor visit. The protagonist simply describes the situation and his emotions in a lyrical style. Mahler's changes to the poem allow the scene to envelop the listener in the young man's mental state through subtle repetition and purposefully awkward phrasing. The audience is made to feel the man's confusion and discomfort along with him until the final comic conclusion is revealed. Mahler finally lets the audience in on the joke in the final stanzas, when we learn the doctor's diagnosis. The protagonist's contentment to finally learn he is a fool ushers in the comic conclusion, allowing the tension to resolve as the music decrescendos and finally disappears.

"Lied des Verfolgten im Turm"

Arnim and Brentano constructed this text by carefully intertwining two different folk songs: the first, from a broadside entitled "Die Gedanken sind frei!" from southern Prussia, tells of a captive soldier who vows that despite his grim circumstances, his thoughts will remain free; the second is a simple folk song about the joys of summertime.[12]

Nearly all of the *Wunderhorn* songs with military themes that Mahler composed prior to "Lied des Verfolgten im Turm" tell stories of lovers who are separated by war, and this song is no exception.[13] However, the challenges facing this couple are somewhat unusual; in this tale, only the wall of a prison tower separates the soldier and the woman.[14] The dialogue between the lovers comprises the entire text because outside narration would intrude on their implied intimacy. While the characters speak the dialogue in the present tense, the story stretches over a substantial period, long enough for the woman's cheerful optimism to transform into lonely despair. The woman's text resembles a series of lyrical interludes until her third stanza, at which time her text begins to merge with the prisoner's, allowing the lyrical and the dramatic modes to combine.

One might interpret the prisoner's repeated affirmation that his "thoughts are free" as a mantra designed to help him maintain hope and positivity while he is held captive, if it were not for the response of his beloved, who gradually gives in to the notion that his freedom is not on the horizon. As her music and text begin to reveal that life outside the tower makes the prisoner's continued incarceration and possible execution appear increasingly likely, his repeated instance that his "thoughts are free" begins to take on aspects of the defense mechanism Anna Freud defines as "The infantile ego resort[ing] to denial in order not to become aware of some painful impression without."[15]

Most of Mahler's other songs depicting a couple's conversation afford each character a distinct sonic space with a unique musical language in which he or she can express their point of view; however, due to their physical proximity, the musical environments of these lovers are not so distant, and one sound world tends to bleed into another. Mahler constructed his setting using a variation of strophic form, comprising a series of paired verses. Declamatory melodies, martial rhythms, the requisite militaristic

146 Hidden Treasures

Table 6.2: Text comparison for "Lied des Verfolgten im Turm"

Lied des Verfolgten im Thurm (Boxberger)	Lied des Verfolgten im Turm (Mahler)	Song of the Prisoner in the Tower
Der Gefangene		
Die Gedanken sind frei;	Die Gedanken sind frei,	Thoughts are free,
Wer kann sie errathen?	wer kann sie erraten;	No one can guess them,
Sie rauschen vorbei	sie rauschen vorbei	They rush by
Wie nächtliche Schatten.	wie nächtliche Schatten,	Like nighttime shadows.
Kein Mensch kann sie wissen,	kein Mensch kann sie wissen,	No man can know them,
Kein Jäger sie schießen.	kein Jäger sie schießen;	No hunter can shoot them,
Es bleibet dabei,	es bleibet dabei, (x2)	It remains thereby,
Die Gedanken sind frei.	die Gedanken sind frei!	Thoughts are free!
Das Mädchen		
Im Sommer ist gut lustig sein	Im Sommer ist gut lustig sein,	Summer is a good, happy time
Auf hohen wilden Haiden;	auf hohen, wilden Haiden.	In the high, wild meadows.
Dort findet man grün Plätzelein.	Dort findet man grün' Plätzelein,	There one finds little green places,
Mein herzverliebtes Schätzelein,	mein Herz verliebtes Schätzelein,	My loving heart, beloved,
Von Dir mag ich nicht scheiden.	von dir, von dir mag ich nicht scheiden!	Does not like being separated from you!
Der Gefangene		
Und sperrt man mich ein	Und sperrt man mich ein	One locks me in a
Im finstern Kerker,	in finstere Kerker,	dark dungeon, but
Dies alles sind nur	dies Alles sind nur, (x2)	this is only
Vergebliche Werke;	vergebliche Werke;	futile work.
Denn meine Gedanken	denn meine Gedanken	Then my thoughts
Zerreißen die Schranken	zerreißen die Schranken	tear down the
Und Mauern entzwei.	und Mauern entzwei,	dividing walls.
Die Gedanken sind frei.	die Gedanken sind frei! (x2)	Thoughts are free!

Table 6.2: continued

Lied des Verfolgten im Thurm (Boxberger)	Lied des Verfolgten im Turm (Mahler)	Song of the Prisoner in the Tower
Das Mädchen		
Im Sommer ist gut lustig sein	Im Sommer ist gut lustig sein,	Summer is a good, happy
Auf hohen wilden Bergen.	gut lustig sein	time, a good happy time
Man ist da ewig ganz allein;	auf hohen, wilden Bergen.	In the high, wild hills.
Man hört da gar kein	Man ist da ewig ganz allein	One is always here alone,
Kindergeschrei.	auf hohen, wilden Bergen,	in the high, wild hills.
Die Luft mag Einem da	man hört da gar kein	One cannot hear any
werden.	Kindergeschrei, kein	children cry.
	Kindergeschrei.	No children cry.
	Die Luft mag einem da	The wind becomes one
	werden,	there.
	ja, die Luft mag einem	
	werden.	
Der Gefangene		
So sei es, wie es will,	So sei's wie es will!	So it will be, just as it is!
Und wenn es sich schicket,	Und wenn es sich schicket,	And if it is proper,
Nur Alles in der Still!	nur Alles, Alles sei in der	It will all be in silence.
Und was mich erquicket,	Stille,	All in silence.
Mein Wunsch und Begehren,	nur All's in der Still', (x2)	My wish and desires,
Niemand kann's mir wehren.	Mein Wunsch und Begehren,	No one can hold back!
Es bleibet dabei,	Niemand kann's wehren!	It remains thereby,
Die Gedanken sind frei.	Es bleibt dabei,	Thoughts are free!
	die Gedanken sind frei, (x2)	
Das Mädchen		
Mein Schatz, Du singst so	Mein Schatz, du singst so	My dear, you sing so happily
fröhlich hier	fröhlich hier,	here,
Wie's Vöglein in dem Grase.	wie's Vögelein im Grase;	Like a bird in the grass;
Ich steh so traurig bei	ich steh' so traurig bei	I stand, so sadly by the
Kerkerthür;	Kerkertür,	dungeon door,
Wär ich doch todt, wär ich	wär ich doch tot, wär ich bei	If only I were dead! If only I
bei Dir!	dir,	were with you
Ach, muß ich denn immer	ach muß, ach muß ich immer	Ah! Must I mourn forever?
klagen?	denn klagen?	

148   HIDDEN TREASURES

Table 6.2: continued

Lied des Verfolgten im Thurm (Boxberger)	Lied des Verfolgten im Turm (Mahler)	Song of the Prisoner in the Tower
Der Gefangene		
Und weil Du so klagst,	Und weil du so klagst,	And because you mourn so
Der Lieb ich entsage,	der Lieb' ich entsage,	I renounce our love,
Und ist es gewagt,	und ist es gewagt, (x2)	and if I dare,
So kann mich nichts plagen,	so kann mich Nichts plagen!	Then nothing can plague me!
So kann ich im Herzen	So kann ich im Herzen	So I can in my heart
Stets lachen, bald scherzen.	stets lachen und scherzen;	Laugh and joke;
Es bleibet dabei,	es bleibet dabei, (x2)	It remains thereby,
Die Gedanken sind frei.	Die Gedanken sind frei! (x2)	Thoughts are free!

brass and drums, essentially diatonic harmony in D minor, and strictly duple meter define the prisoner's world (see Example 6.4). The woman's space sounds more lyrical, accompanied by soft woodwinds and strings, and moving in a meter that flexibly shifts between 6/8 and 9/8. She frequently adopts the descending chromatic scale heard in the prisoner's melody as well, as if this device were a signifier of their unity (see Example 6.5). Musical overlap occurs at the moments where the speaker changes, blurring the passage of time and narrative focus. The ends of the prisoner's passages give way prematurely to the gentler world of the woman. The first entry of the woman overlaps a trumpet fanfare played with a quick decrescendo, as if to make the military world disappear from the soldier's thoughts quickly when he hears his beloved's voice. While the text of the story indicates that the interchange takes place over a substantial period of time, the lack of distinct boundaries for each character's musical statements adds a level of continuity that belies practicality, and the temporal context blurs, leaving it difficult to determine how long the prisoner has been held in the tower. The static nature of the accompaniment provides this section with a feeling of tension, as if something is not quite right with the situation.

Mahler made a few small changes to the poem while creating his lyric, but he maintained the distinct meters and rhyme schemes of the text delivered by the two characters. Variations in the poetic rhythms of the contrasting original poems clearly delineate the statements emanating

Songs with a Freudian Slant   149

Example 6.4: "Lied des Verfolgten im Turm," mm. 99–101

from the prisoner from those of his sweetheart. The prisoner's eight-line stanzas sound completely regular, tight, and consistent, as one might expect from a proper soldier. The woman also speaks in a regular pattern in her lyrical five-line stanzas. Mahler disrupts this regularity through repetition of short phrases and contraction and expansion of words (e.g. "So sei es" becomes "So sei's," and "im Finstern" becomes "in Finstere").

Example 6.5: "Lied des Verfolgten im Turm," mm. 11–14

This allows the woman's second verse to expand dramatically, as she discusses the many wonders that the prisoner cannot experience, before she finally gives in to despair. In Mahler's hands, the prisoner's verses stay relatively regular, though several repetitions of the phrase "nur All's in der Still" (it will all be in silence), as he contemplates the silence of his prison cell, replace a line, "Und was mich erquicket," in which he claims that the quiet of his captivity has been refreshing, possibly indicating that Mahler's version of the soldier is not quite as content with his situation as he would have his beloved believe.

Mahler's use of key tells the listener a great deal about the mindsets of the characters in this story. The prisoner's verses are almost exclusively in D minor, with the exception of his penultimate verse, which changes to C major. This verse tells of the prisoner's acceptance of his situation, as he claims "So sei's, wie es will! Und wenn es sich schicket, nur Alles sei in der Stille!" (So it will be, just as it is. It will all be in silence.!). On the other hand, the woman doesn't seem to know how to deal with her feelings, as her stanzas shift from G major (measures 10–27), to B-flat major (measures 38–63), to F major (measures 77–97), drifting from key to

Example 6.6: "Lied des Verfolgten im Turm," mm. 88–95

key in hopes of finding one that will pull her closer to the prisoner's D minor, as if the eventual union of their keys might allow them to finally be together. But her melody seems unable to find the required harmonic support anywhere; eventually it loses hope in the relationship, just as the woman has (see Example 6.6).

Mahler sets each stanza of the poem separately and divides them with a descending chromatic passage in the violin, similar to that which appears throughout the prisoner's melodies. This melody simultaneously serves as a divisional device and a reminder that war still wages all around them (see Example 6.7). When the soldier returns, he brings the muted brass instruments with him. But as the song continues, the volume of the trumpets increases, suggesting that the war draws ever closer and that the soldier may be doomed to remain captive indefinitely (in fact, the details of his sentence are never revealed). Ultimately, however, he claims to remain undaunted, saying, "Thoughts are free!"

Example 6.7: "Lied des Verfolgten im Turm," mm. 25–28, violin line

The modified strophic form Mahler incorporated in "Lied des Verfolgten im Turm" emphasizes the prisoner's stoicism (even if it is only a show of strength for the sake of his beloved or indeed a denial of his true circumstances) and his refusal to allow his thoughts and emotions to become downtrodden by his captivity. The woman's much more adaptive musical language shows that she cannot share in his optimism. As the story unfolds, the woman becomes increasingly oppressed by their circumstances, and the roles are reversed, as if she has become the prisoner and her lover were instead free.

Given the unlikeliness of a young woman languishing day after day outside a prison tower without arousing suspicion from the forces holding the young man inside, it seems likely that she is merely a figment of the prisoner's imagination. Regarding her as such explains her gradual shift from encouragement to despair as his own subconscious acceptance of his fate. While he continues to claim that his "thoughts are free," deep down he seems to recognize that he will indeed never be free again, despite his mind's best efforts to protect him from that realization.

"Wo die schönen Trompeten blasen"

"Wo die schönen Trompeten blasen" tells a story of love and death in a time of war. A maiden wakes in the middle of the night to a knock on the door, and finds her sweetheart, who she believed to be away fighting, standing before her. She lets him inside, and they embrace. Suddenly, the maiden begins to cry, and the soldier consoles her, saying, "Within a year, you will be mine… I go to war on the green heath… My home of the green turf." This peculiar phrase reveals that it is not the young soldier who has appeared, but his ghost, come to inform his beloved that they will be reunited soon, as her death is also imminent. The mysterious nature of the story and Mahler's musical setting beg the question of whether this encounter was in fact real or merely occurred in the maiden's dreams.

Among the last of the *Wunderhorn* songs to be composed for 1898 publication, "Wo die schönen Trompeten blasen" displays some of Mahler's most sophisticated lieder compositional techniques, in part due to his creation of the song's text from two distinct but very similar poems, "Bildchen" and "Unbeschreibliche Freude." In addition to sharing certain phrases and ideas, each of the exemplar poems is composed of stanzas of the same length, rhythm, and rhyme scheme, but Mahler's resulting lyric uses none of these features in quite the same way; lines are mixed and matched and expanded and contracted so as to leave the song's sources practically unrecognizable. Mahler utilizes a flexible structure for the story of a young woman's late-night visit from her beloved soldier. "Wo die schönen Trompeten blasen" is made up of three basic sound worlds: the militaristic environment that begins the song, the contrasting *Ländler* passage wherein her lover announces his return, and the relaxed, duplemeter middle portion in which the woman greets her beloved. These three soundscapes are alternated in a fashion similar to a rondo form, but each recurrence of the general musical environment is so widely varied that any similarities to rondo structure ultimately collapse.

Marked "Verträumt, leise" (dreamily, quietly), the opening bars feature a muted passage in the horns played *pp*. The thirty-second-note motive in the first three measures of the passage mimetically represents a knock upon the door (see Example 6.8). The motive begins as knocking and then expands into a fanfare-like theme first heard in the oboes and clarinet.

Example 6.8: "Wo die schönen Trompeten blasen," mm. 15–20

Table 6.3: Text comparison for "Wo die schönen Trompeten blasen"

Unbeschreibliche Freude (Boxberger)	Bildchen (Boxberger)
	Auf dieser Welt hab ich keine Freud:
	Ich hab einen Schatz, und der ist weit;
	Er ist so weit, er ist nicht hier.
	Ach, wenn ich bei meim Schätzchen wär!
	Ich kann nicht sitzen und kann nicht stehn,
	Ich muß zu meinem Schätzchen gehn;
	Zu meinem Schatz da muß ich gehn,
	Und sollt ich vor dem Fenster stehn.
Wer ist denn draußen und klopfet an,	"Wer ist denn draußen, wer klopfet an,
Der mich so leise wecken kann?	Der mich so leis aufwecken kann?" –
"Das ist der Herzallerliebste Dein.	"Es ist der Herzallerliebste Dein;
Steh auf und laß mich zu Dir ein!"	Steh auf, steh auf und laß mich 'rein!" –
	"Ich steh nicht auf, laß Dich nicht 'rein,
	Bis meine Eltern zu Bette sein.
	Wenn meine Eltern zu Bette sein,
	So steh ich auf und laß Dich 'rein." –
	"Was soll ich hier nun Länger stehn?
	Ich seh die Morgenröth aufgehn,
	Die Morgenröth, zwei helle Stern;
	Bei meinem Schatz da wär ich gern."
Das Mädchen stand auf und ließ ihn ein	Da stand sie auf und ließ ihn ein;
Mit seinem schneeweißen Hemdelein,	Sie heißt ihn auch willkommen sein.
Mit seinen schneeweißen Beinen.	Sie reicht ihm die schneeweiße Hand;
Das Mädchen fing an zu weinen.	Da fängt sie auch zu weinen an.

Songs with a Freudian Slant   155

Wo die schönen Trompeten blasen (Mahler)	**Where the Shining Trumpets Blare**

Wer ist denn draußen und wer klopfet an,
der mich so leise, so leise wecken kann?
Das ist der Herzallerliebste dein,
steh' auf und laß mich zu dir ein!

Who is outside knocking
That wakes me from my sleep?
It is your beloved,
Get up and let me in!

Was soll ich hier nun länger steh'n?
Ich seh' die Morgenröt' aufgeh'n,
die Morgenröt', zwei helle Stern'.
Bei meinem Schatz da wär ich gern'!
Bei meinem Herzallerlieble!

How long should I stand here?
I see the sunrise coming,
The sunrise, two bright stars.
I want to be by my sweetheart!
By my heart's most beloved!

Das Mädchen stand auf und ließ ihn ein,
sie heißt ihn auch willkommen sein.
Willkommen trauter Knabe mein!
So lang hast du gestanden!
Sie reicht' ihm auch die schneeweise Hand.
Von ferne sang die Nachtigall,
da fängt sie auch zu weinen an!

The maiden got up and let him inside,
She also welcomed him.
Welcome my sweet boy!
You have stood there so long!
She reached out her snow-white hand.
In the distance a nightingale sang,
The maiden began to cry.

156 HIDDEN TREASURES

Table 6.3: continued

Unbeschreibliche Freude (Boxberger)	Bildchen (Boxberger)
"Ach, weine nicht, Du Liebste mein! Aufs Jahr sollt Du mein eigen sein; Mein eigen sollt Du werden, O Liebe auf grüner Erden!"	Wein nicht, wein nicht, mein Engelein! Aufs Jahr sollst Du mein eigen sein. Mein eigen sollst Du werden gewiß; Sonst Keine es auf Erden ist.
Ich wollt, daß alle Felder wären Papier Und alle Studenten schrieben hier; Sie schreiben ja hier die liebe lange Nacht, Sie schrieben uns Beiden die Liebe doch nicht ab.	
	Ich zieh in Krieg auf grüne Haid; Grüne Haid die liegt von hier so weit. Allwo die schönen Trompeten blasen, Da ist mein Haus von grünem Rasen.
	Ein Bildchen laß ich malen mir; Auf meinem Herzen trag ich's hier. Darauf sollst Du gemalet sein, Daß ich niemal vergesse Dein."

This motive tells the listener that a war is taking place, but it is far off in the distance, as are the young female protagonist's thoughts. This distance remains until measure 19, when the fanfare plays at a louder dynamic. Suddenly the war comes closer to home.

The militaristic music heard in this opening sequence then goes on to accompany the opening words, sung in a lyrical manner by the young woman. The woman's attention has been divided between her duties at home and her concern for her beloved. She acts as if stirred from a deep slumber and asks, "Wer ist denn draußen, und wer klopfet an?" (Who is outside knocking that wakes me from my sleep?), but before she can

Wo die schönen Trompeten blasen (Mahler)	Where the Shining Trumpets Blare
Ach weine nicht, du Liebste mein,	Ah! Don't cry, my love.
ach weine nicht, du Liebste mein!	Ah! Don't cry, my love!
Auf's Jahr sollst du mein Eigen sein.	Within a year, you will be mine.
Mein Eigen sollst du werden gewiß,	You will certainly be my own,
wie's Keine sonst auf Erden ist!	As no one on earth is!
O Lieb auf grüner Erden.	O love of the green earth!
Ich zieh' in Krieg auf grüne Haid;	I go to war on the green heath;
die grüne Haide, die ist so weit!	The green heath, it is so far!
Allwo dort die schönen Trompeten blasen,	Where the shining trumpets blare,
da ist mein Haus,	That is my home,
mein Haus von grünen Rasen!	My home of the green turf.

even say the words, the clarinet has answered her question with its own version of the fanfare. While these fanfares provide a glimpse into the young woman's state of mind, she does not actually hear them, owing to her preoccupation with the knocking. Her hesitation to open the door and welcome her lover inside indicates that she does not suspect that it is him waiting outside, despite the musical cues that accompany her, creating a distinction between the diegetic music that can be heard by the woman and the purely mimetic music which cannot.[16]

Only when the soldier identifies himself does the woman's militaristic music give way to the romantic *Ländler*-inspired theme that symbolizes

Example 6.9: "Wo die schönen Trompeten blasen," mm. 36–43

their love (see Example 6.9). The rustic, folk-like nature of this dance also identifies the protagonists as innocent rural people whose destinies have become entangled in political turmoil beyond their control, one of many subtle commentaries on the tragedy of war embedded in Mahler's *Wunderhorn* lieder which were examined in greater detail in Chapter 2.[17] At this crucial point, the meter changes from duple to triple, the key shifts from D minor to D major, the notes become more sustained, and the winds give way to the strings. This musical contrast emphasizes the gender reversal that points to the mental preoccupations of the protagonists. The woman, physically at home, thinks only of the soldier, and thus her musical space is filled with masculine, militaristic imagery. The soldier's concern is not

Example 6.10: "Wo die schönen Trompeten blasen," mm. 170–73

on the battlefield, but with his sweetheart, and his primary melodies take the form of the gentle, romantic *Ländler*. The narrator serves to transition the story back and forth between the disparate sonic spaces of the two protagonists, bringing back the declamatory rhythms of the opening and returning to the key of D minor, associated in this instance with militaristic music and serving as a reminder to the audience that the young man is first and foremost a soldier.

Mahler separates physical locations and past and present events through musical means, using instrumentation to create two of the song's distinct sound worlds. The winds represent the war and events that take place in some other, far-off, imagined space of the past, whereas the strings accompany events taking place in the present moment being narrated, that is, the woman's home and her conversation with the soldier.

At the end of the song, when the soldier speaks in a somewhat declamatory fashion of his military responsibilities (see Example 6.10), his sonic environment finally takes on the militaristic tropes previously only heard in the distance of the woman's thoughts and in the passages spoken by the narrator, those that one would expect to be associated with a soldier. This shift points the audience's attention to the words he speaks and lends them added significance, while at the same time subtly indicating that these thoughts dwell on remembrance of past events rather than the present moment.

In addition to his blending two separate poems from *Des Knaben Wunderhorn* to create the text for "Wo die schönen Trompeten blasen,"

Example 6.11: "Wo die schönen Trompeten blasen," mm. 5–8

Mahler also added one completely original line, which occurs after the woman has welcomed her beloved soldier into her home. The line reads "von Ferne sang die Nachtigall" (in the distance, a nightingale sang). Upon the mention of the bird's song, an oboe enters, playing not the expected call of a nightingale, but a militaristic melody first heard in measure 5 (see Example 6.11). In this unusual moment, the story is being narrated by two voices at once: the epic narrator of the text and the elusive narrative voice contained within the music, which appears in place of the silenced nightingale, and what these voices have to say is not entirely the same.[18] The nightingale song described by the narrator is overridden by the military fanfare. The woman, however, only hears the nightingale, long associated with lament, which merely warns her of an impending misfortune, but the fanfare heard by the audience transforms what she fears may occur in the future into her present reality, telling the audience that the young man who has appeared at the door is not actually the woman's lover but his ghost, come to inform her that he has died in battle and to indicate that she, too, will soon join him in death: "Within a year, you will be mine." The revenant soldier eventually confirms the tragedy by claiming that he must return to his "house of green turf," his grave. The complex exchange of recitative, lyrical singing, dialogue, and accompaniment portrays this mysterious ballad more engagingly than would be possible using any conventional song form and offers us a small glimpse of what Mahler might have been able to accomplish in a dramatic medium had he brought his youthful attempts at composing an opera to a conclusion.

The appearance of the nightingale song brings the maiden to tears, but how does it communicate the tragic truth of the soldier's death? Nightingales appear in thirty-five of the 723 *Wunderhorn* poems.[19] In most of these instances, the poems mention the bird's beautiful song. In many, the voice of the nightingale seems to possess an almost ethereal quality, as if the birds possessed the voices of the angels.[20] In "Trompeten," the nightingale song, even from the distance, has the power to make the maiden cry. She instinctively knows that the nightingale has brought the news of her lover's death on the battlefield. European folk tales and Romantic poetry have long used the nightingale to symbolize the "bringer of a gentle death" and its song to represent the damned soul.[21] Thus John Keats' "Ode to a Nightingale" refers to nightingale song as "thy sweet requiem."[22] This symbol frequently appears in the German art-song tradition as well, for example, in Brahms' "Der Tod, das ist die kühle Nacht." Mahler repeatedly wrote about nightingale song in letters to his wife Alma and to Natalie Bauer-Lechner, referring to "die Stimme des Totenvögels": "The great reverie sounds, the trumpets of the apocalypse call; in the middle of a grey silence, we hear a nightingale in the distance—a last tremulous echo of earthly life!"[23]

Freud interprets a dream of his own that is strangely similar to the story of "Trompeten," writing, "I had gone to the Brücke's laboratory at night, and, in response to a gentle knock on the door, I opened it to (the late) Professor Fleischl."[24] He goes on to explain that in the context of the dream, Professor Fleischl was not dead, and only when the dreaming Freud thought about his waking life did he remember that the figure who stood before him was not a living man but a spirit. Freud and Ernst von Fleischl-Marxow worked together at the Vienna Physiological Institute between 1876 and 1882, where they became friends. Freud explains his complicated relationship with his colleague: "I had been the first to recommend the use of cocaine, in 1885, and this recommendation had brought serious reproaches down on me. The misuse of that drug had hastened the death of a dear friend of mine. This had been in 1895."[25] The feelings of guilt that Freud felt regarding his friend's death haunted him throughout his life (he wrote of dreaming that he was Brutus to Fleischl's Caesar),[26] but through his dream, Freud was able to discover that "People of that kind [the dead] only existed as long as one liked and could be got rid of if someone else wished it."[27]

According to folklore studies, figures who come back from the dead (known as revenant visitors) seek out the living (the visited) for a number of reasons: to remove wicked spells, to uphold or oppose their partner in some quest, or, as is the case in "Trompeten," to provide information.[28] Just as Freud learned a valuable fact about dreams from his encounter with Fleischl, the maiden in "Trompeten" learned of her lover's death and her own impending demise through her ghostly visit.

162   HIDDEN TREASURES

Strangely, however, we learn indirectly that Mahler evidently did not agree with the interpretation of the song that his own textual adaptations seem to make most obvious. Bauer-Lechner wrote in her unpublished diaries regarding the premiere of the song:

> About the song "Wo die schönen Trompeten blasen," a quarrel again arose between Lipiner and Gustav: the former maintained that the soldier was dead and appears to his beloved only as a ghost—a view which the Spieglers[29] also agree with—whereas Gustav inflexibly and thoroughly asserted that he still lives and that his death comes to him only in battle. (And also, in his words, Goethe appears to be of this [Lipiner's] opinion.)[30]

The most peculiar aspect of Bauer-Lechner's memory concerns Mahler's interpretation of whether the soldier in the song is alive or a ghost. Mahler removed text from the original poetry that would support his own reported position; as such, he seems to be contradicting himself. Both original poems end with the soldier assuring the maiden that their love will endure beyond the war. Mahler's omission of these passages makes the final song text ambiguous. Had Mahler ended his song with either of these ideas, the image of a young man who visits from the battlefield and hopes to soon end his military career would emerge much more clearly. Instead, Mahler's song ends with the image of a soldier and his "house of green turf," which most people interpret as a reference to his grave.[31] Mahler plants musical and textual imagery that supports one interpretation and then suggests another while talking with friends about the song. The statement recorded by Bauer-Lechner, however, may simply serve as one of the many examples of Mahler purposely misleading others regarding the meaning of his music. In any case, Mahler has opened the door to multiple hermeneutic possibilities.

"Der Schildwache Nachtlied"

Anyone who has ever been forced to work overnight while seemingly everyone else sleeps will understand the circumstances that Mahler has illustrated musically in "Der Schildwache Nachtlied." Simply reading the poem gives no indication that the dialogue in the lyric represents anything more than two lovers having a chat during wartime. Mahler's setting, on the other hand, blurs the boundaries between the waking realm and the world of dreams. He accomplishes this by assigning each character his and her own unique musical soundscape and then gradually blending the guard's world into the maiden's, as if he were falling asleep and beginning to dream of her. Then as "real life" once again makes its presence felt, the sentry instantly jolts awake (with a sudden return to his own musical environment) to begin the cycle anew.

While the chosen poem features six stanzas of identical poetic rhythm and rhyme scheme, Mahler adapted his text to create a ballad featuring a modified strophic setting of paired verses. These stanzas alternate between two narrative sources: the guard and his lover, who appears only in his dreams. The night watchman, at first filled with dutiful enthusiasm, finds it difficult to stay awake, and he soon drifts into sweet dreams of his beloved back home, only to be instantly snapped awake by his responsibilities and forced to start over again.

Mahler narrates the story by creating two distinctive musical environments: the sentry's actual surroundings in the guard tower, created with steady 4/4 time, declamatory vocal lines, diatonic and triadic harmonies, fanfares, and drum cadences (see Example 6.12); and the

Example 6.12: "Der Schildwache Nachtlied," mm. 1–4

164 HIDDEN TREASURES

Table 6.4: Text comparison for "Der Schildwache Nachtlied"

Der Schildwache Nachtlied (Boxberger)	Der Schildwache Nachtlied (Mahler)	The Sentry's Nightsong
"Ich kann und mag nicht fröhlich sein. Wenn alle Leute schlafen, So muß ich wachen, Muß traurig sein." –	Ich kann und mag nicht fröhlich sein! Wenn alle Leute schlafen! so muß ich wachen! Ja, wachen! Muß traurig sein!	I can and may not be happy! When all the people sleep I must keep watch, yes, watch! I must be sad!
"Ach, Knabe, Du sollst nicht traurig sein! Will Deiner warten Im Rosengarten, Im grünen Klee." –	Lieb' Knabe, du mußt nicht traurig sein! Will deiner warten im Rosengarten! Im grünen Klee! (x2)	My dear boy, you must not be sad I will wait for you in the rose garden, in the green clover!
"Zum grünen Klee da komm ich nicht; Zum Waffengarten Voll Helleparten Bin ich gestellt." –	Zum grünen Klee da komm ich nicht! Zum Waffengarten! Voll Helleparten! Bin ich gestellt! (x2)	I am not coming to the green clover! To the weapons yard Full of spears I have been posted!
"Stehst Du im Feld, so helf Dir Gott! An Gottes Segen Ist Alles gelegen, Wer's glauben thut." –	Stehst du im Feld, so helf' dir Gott! An Gottes Segen ist Alles gelegen! Wer's glauben tut! (x2)	You stay in the field, so help you God! At God's blessing All is dependent! He who believes it!
"Wer's glauben thut, ist weit davon; Er ist ein König, Er ist ein Kaiser, Er führt den Krieg."	Wer's glauben tut, ist weit davon! Er ist ein König! Er ist ein Kaiser! Ein Kaiser! Er führt den Krieg!	He who believes it is far away! He is a king! He is an emperor! An emperor! He leads the war!

Table 6.4: continued

Der Schildwache Nachtlied (Boxberger)	Der Schildwache Nachtlied (Mahler)	The Sentry's Nightsong
Halt! Wer da? – Rund! Wer sang zur Stund? – Verlorne Feldwacht Sang es um Mitternacht. – Bleib mir vom Leib!	Halt! Wer da!! Rund'!? Bleib' mir vom Leib! Wer sang es hier? Wer sang zur Stund'? Verlorne Feldwacht sang es um Mitternacht! Mitternacht! Mitternacht! Feldwacht!	Stop! Who's there? Turn around! Stay where you are! Who is singing here? Who sings at this hour? The lonely watchman sings in the middle of the night!

dream world of his imagined sweetheart with its soft woodwinds and harp, legato melodies backed by lushly chromatic dissonances, flexible, meter, and slowed tempo. And as happens in real life, the waking world gradually gives way to the world of dreams, through a three-measure transition where the martial sound world dissipates into the dream soundscape (see Example 6.13). The vocal melody in this short passage, with its long pitch followed by an octave descent, could even be interpreted as the musicalization of a yawn (see Example 6.14). But in each successive verse, the watchman falls asleep only to find himself jolted awake by two abrupt notes on the timpani and low strings, as the reality of military life returns instantly. As the story progresses through successive pairs of verses, a new element appears the third time the watchman emerges from his dreams at measure 63 (see Example 6.15). The reality of the waking world abruptly returns with the same crashing timpani and low strings heard twice before, but after only three measures the key changes suddenly from B-flat major to G major, and a steady military cadence arises from the snare drum, along with a thinning of the texture and a new fanfare figure in the horns and trumpet. A change is coming that will force the sentry to question which has his greater loyalty: his sweetheart or his military cause. Ultimately, it would seem that she wins the day, as the text "Er ist ein König! Er ist ein Kaiser! Ein Kaiser! Er führt den Krieg!" (He is a king! He is an emperor! An emperor! He leads the war!) betrays his growing frustration with the war.

166   HIDDEN TREASURES

This interpretation of a night watchman repeatedly falling asleep to dream of his beloved conforms precisely to one of Freud's central theories regarding dreams, wish fulfillment:

> Dreams are not to be likened to the unregulated sounds that rise from a musical instrument struck by the blow of some external force instead of by a player's hand; they are not meaningless, they are not absurd; they do not imply that one portion of our store of ideas is asleep while another portion is beginning to awake. On the contrary, they are psychical phenomena of complete validity—fulfillments of wishes; they can be inserted into the chain of intelligible waking mental acts; they are constructed by a highly complicated activity of the mind.[32]

The sentry sits alone at his post, watching and waiting silently for the dawn. When fatigue and boredom overcome him, he drifts off to sleep. Foremost in his mind is his loneliness, so naturally, his dreaming mind turns to the person he misses most, and the sweetheart in his dream tries to tempt him into joining her for a late-night rendezvous. His dream provides him with the companionship and adventure that he so craves, and even gives him a chance to prove his loyalty to the cause and demonstrate the importance of his position by remaining at his post. Freud describes a similar dream of prolonged loneliness from a patient:

> A young woman had been cut off from society for weeks on end while she nursed her child through an infectious illness. After the child's recovery, she had a dream of being at a party at which, among others, she met Alphonse Daudet, Paul Bourget, and Marcel Prévost; they were all most affable to her and highly amusing. All of the authors resembled their portraits, except Marcel Prévost, of whom she had never seen a picture; and he looked like... the disinfection officer who had fumigated the sick-room the day before and who had been her first visitor for so long. Thus it seems possible to give a complete translation of the dream: "It's about time for something more amusing than this perpetual sick-nursing."[33]

SONGS WITH A FREUDIAN SLANT   167

Example 6.13: "Der Schildwache Nachtlied," mm. 17–21

One can imagine the young mother, passing the fretful hours while her sick child sleeps by reading one French novel after another simply to distract herself from her worries. She longs for society, excitement, and witty conversation, but for the time being, she must settle for living vicariously through her books. That the dreamed image of Marcel Prévost should bear the face of the first person she had seen in so long speaks to the depth of her isolation, much like Mahler's sentry. Both figures dream of what they want most desperately, human companionship.

Example 6.14: "Der Schildwache Nachtlied," mm. 9–12

Example 6.15: "Der Schildwache Nachtlied," mm. 66–68

170   Hidden Treasures

Mahler presented numerous musical depictions of complex human emotion among his *Wunderhorn* lieder. The fact that he found the sources for these songs in poetry at least one hundred years old with roots reaching back into German speakers' folk pasts demonstrates that the emotions he chose to represent through music are not merely products of the age renowned for the "birth of psychoanalysis" but are essential, omnipresent elements of human society. Mankind has always grappled with self-doubt, fear, despair, and misplaced loyalty, and we have always had the wisdom of past generations to help guide and instruct us in dealing with our issues. Mahler's *Wunderhorn* songs portray such emotional states that extended well beyond that single time and place. Such feelings are, in fact, a universal part of the human experience.

CHAPTER SEVEN

"The brutal bourgeoisie"
Mahler and Socioeconomic Equality

As noted in Chapter 2, throughout his adult life Mahler made very few references to his views on politics. No direct statements explicitly referring to the political matters of the day have survived after his years at the University of Vienna. It may, of course, simply be that any political discussions he had were not recorded, or perhaps he avoided discussing politics due to his often-quoted feelings of being an "outsider," leaving him disinclined to take an interest in matters of state.[1] Whatever his reasoning, his political ideals and opinions remain largely uncertain, and we might reasonably have cause to doubt whether he even gave enough thought to governmental policies and procedures to have formed opinions on them. But in contrast to this lack of verbal evidence, we do have accounts of several instances where Mahler sought to help people in financial distress and participated in socialist events. In addition, several of the *Wunderhorn* songs address economic injustice, and thus we can extrapolate from these a notion of where Mahler stood on such matters and so reach a better understanding of his relationship to his broader world. But as with so many facets of Mahler's personality, matters are not as straightforward as they seem on the surface to be.

171

172   HIDDEN TREASURES

Mahler's Youthful Political Engagement

The lack of documented evidence regarding Mahler's youthful political activities makes difficult the process of piecing together a definite chain of events and consequences that may shed light on his later views. We do, however, know where Mahler spent his time during the formative years of his university career and with whom he associated. Weaving together Mahler's history with those of his activist friends makes it possible to construct a picture of Mahler's engagement with socialist politics and Pan-Germanism during the late 1870s and early 1880s. The ideals that Mahler developed during his time at the university would continue to impact his opinions on economic justice and influence his choices of *Wunderhorn* poetry and his musical techniques over the next twenty years.

At the age of eighteen, while studying jointly at the Vienna Conservatory and the University of Vienna, Mahler became involved with a group of politically minded students known as the Pernerstorfer Circle.[2] The Circle counted among its number future politicians such as Engelbert Pernerstorfer, Victor Adler, and Heinrich Friedjung, and artists such as Richard von Kralik, Siegfried Lipiner, and Mahler's colleague at the conservatory, Hugo Wolf. Kralik reports in his unpublished essay "Geschichte und Gestalten—Victor Adler und Pernerstorfer" on a political meeting in which Mahler played piano (to the tune of "O du Deutschland, ich muss marschieren") while Adler and Friedjung led their cohorts in a rousing chorus of "Deutschland, Deutschland über alles," a remarkable emblem of Pan-Germanism and youthful optimism, to be sure.[3] Active within larger, more visible, student activist groups, such as the Leseverein der deutschen Studenten Wiens (the Reading Association of the German Students of Vienna), the Pernerstorfer Circle, inspired by the philosophical writings of Arthur Schopenhauer, Richard Wagner, and Friedrich Nietzsche, believed that a government based on the values of social equality, Pan-Germanism, and populist leadership would best serve the Austrian people. Max von Gruber, a member of the Circle, described his frustration with the existing empire:

> Inflamed... national feeling, [and] glowing hatred of the Habsburg-Lothringens overflowed into me, hatred of this

MAHLER AND SOCIOECONOMIC EQUALITY 173

dynasty which was Germany's misfortune, hatred of their state which had to be shattered if the nation were to be united... Torn loose from everything existing around me, separated from my beloved father in all these things, robbed of any support, I stood on a surface which shook volcanically. With a passionate longing for order and law I was confronted only by the chaos of a world of presumptions and realities collapsing into ruins, ordained for destruction.[4]

One might easily dismiss this extreme sentiment as youthful rebellion and adolescent angst had the Circle not produced figures such as the founder of Austria's Social Democratic party, Victor Adler, and others who devoted their careers to promoting the Circle's causes.

Student groups such as the Pernerstorfer Circle and the Leseverein had to constantly contend with the University of Vienna's requirement that all university organizations be nonpolitical in nature.[5] This rule put the very *raison d'être* of these clubs at odds with the institutions that supported them and contributed to numerous conflicts with university administration and local government. Mahler began his association with the Pernerstorfer Circle in 1878, shortly before civic authorities dissolved the Leseverein, which still counted many members from the Circle among its ranks.[6] The government's declaration that the Leseverein was "a danger to the state" only served to fan the flames of Viennese student activism, but several key members of the Circle, many of whom had since completed their student careers, abandoned their former political agitation and turned instead to various professional arenas. Mahler, however, remained intermittently enrolled at the University of Vienna, studying history, philosophy, literature, and art, with seemingly no particular practical course of study in mind.[7] His continued, if sporadic, contact with the university and the Pernerstorfer Circle allowed him to observe firsthand the creation and suppression of several other student political organizations, perhaps leading in part to his eventual ambivalence toward government which remained with him throughout his life.

Following a number of scandals in the wake of the 1873 market crash, the group turned its political position from liberalism to what Johannes Volkelt, a member of the Circle, termed "radical socialism."[8] It is vital to

174   HIDDEN TREASURES

note, however, that the socialist ideals of Karl Marx's *Communist Manifesto*, while published in 1848, had not yet taken root in Austrian thought, and as such, what precisely Volkelt and his compatriots meant by radical socialism is not entirely clear. Nonetheless the group held to these basic principles of socialism: solidarity with the worker, economic assistance for those in need, and a greater sense of equality among members of the community.

Playwright Siegfried Lipiner in particular spoke of his work being written for the common man and seemed to romanticize the suffering of those in poverty when he stated, "It must be made readily apparent to the Volk that salvation lies in suffering, not in wealth," an idea that one might apply to Mahler's treatment of characters in the songs discussed below.[9] We can observe evidence of his views on economic justice by way of the songs "Das irdische Leben" and, to a more roundabout degree, "Rheinlegendchen" and "Wer hat dies Liedlein erdacht?"

Mahler's Views on Economic Justice

People close to him have reported that Mahler expressed his views about poverty and class relations on more than one occasion, but his opinions often read as quite contradictory. As previously noted, while at university he became very interested in socialist politics and reportedly often reached out to help the poor, as we see from an instance in Berlin in March 1896, reported by Natalie Bauer-Lechner:

> Mahler was on his way over the railway viaduct that crosses the Spree from the Schöneberg Bank when he encountered a man staggering along beneath a heavy bundle... As he approached he heard the words: "God will go on helping." They were muttered... by an old man of horribly wasted countenance and wretched appearance. He looked on the verge of fainting from weakness, and could go no further... Mahler took the bundle form him, and supported him—learning from the poor man... that he had been ill in hospital for some months and had now been discharged as fit; but as he had neither shelter nor money he would have to go on the streets... He was now going with his few belongings

in search of somewhere to stay, and of some employment by which he might sustain the life that had been preserved for him. Mahler, terribly shaken by the sight and the story of the unfortunate man, did for him and gave him what he could on the spur of the moment. He was deeply moved and grief-stricken about it, however, and took it so much to heart that he arrived home in a state of complete distraction, lay down upon the sofa and began to weep bitterly—he whom I had never seen weep.[10]

Later that day, Mahler conducted a poorly received performance of his First Symphony and his *Lieder eines fahrenden Gesellen*, pieces of a tragic nature, which further darkened his mood and intensified his sadness.[11]

In addition, Alma Mahler reveals one of the rare recorded examples of her husband's active political engagement when she describes his participation in a May Day demonstration: "[Mahler joined] a procession of working-men in the Ring [that he] even accompanied for some distance. They had all looked at him in so brotherly a way—they *were* his brothers—and they were the future!"[12] His support of the worker also becomes evident in Mahler's many battles with opera management to secure decent wages for his musicians and technical crews.[13]

Yet while capable of these examples of compassion and generosity, Mahler could also express rather callous opinions about the very people he strove to assist. Commenting on a well-known anecdote known as "Der Müller von Sanssouci" about Frederick the Great, whose summer retreats were disrupted by the sound of a nearby windmill, Mahler told Bauer-Lechner:

It's all well and good that the peasant's rights are protected in spite of the King, but there's another side to the story. Let the miller and his mill be protected on their own ground—if only the mill-wheels didn't clatter so, thereby overstepping their boundaries most shamelessly and creating immeasurable havoc in the territory of someone else's mind.[14]

This attitude seemingly stems more from Mahler's intolerance of noise while composing than from a lack of empathy for the peasant class, but

176   Hidden Treasures

it nevertheless complicates the picture of Mahler's attitudes toward the poor and those who are forced to perform manual labor to make a living. His occasionally thoughtless views also appeared in a letter written to his sister Justine in order to reassure her that he would not become ill during the 1892 cholera epidemic in Hamburg:

> Don't forget that the epidemic strikes mainly that portion of the populace that *does not have the intelligence and the means to protect themselves from it.* Whoever lives healthily and openly, keeps on a strict diet, and *has enough money to enjoy only the best and the purest* has nothing to fear. The inhabitants of the stinking "old city," full of narrow streets and bad sewers, near the harbor are affected by the cholera, thus, about half an hour away from my house, which lies on the healthiest part of town.[15]

Mahler's implication that the poor were unintelligent and unhealthy, as contrasted to those with "enough money to enjoy only the best and the purest," suggests that his views on poverty were not as idealistic and straightforward as they might seem. While such an idea was in keeping with common socialist beliefs of the day, that the uneducated lacked the financial means and knowledge to obtain proper nutrition, thus leading to their poor health (a situation that socialists hoped to remedy), one does detect a note of superiority in Mahler's words. Ironically, Mahler actually contracted cholera in January of the following year, and he was said to have "floated between life and death for days" before quickly recovering to conduct his First Symphony with the Hamburg Philharmonic Society on the twenty-seventh of that month.[16]

Mahler's Economic Status

Mahler grew up in a strictly petit bourgeois home; the Mahlers were comfortable but certainly not wealthy. His father made and sold liquor and ran a small pub and inn in Iglau.[17] Financial success, however, was not necessarily the primary goal for families like Mahler's. In his memoir *The World of Yesterday*, Jewish and Viennese author Stefan Zweig describes that the true purpose of the Jewish desire for wealth in Habsburg Austria had little to do with possessions and power, but instead gave the successful Jew the necessary tools for increasing the intellect.[18] This attitude explains precisely what inspired Mahler's parents to send their oldest surviving son to the Conservatory in Vienna at the age of fifteen. This effort posed somewhat of a financial burden for the family; Mahler had to petition for decreased tuition fees during his second and third years and had to supplement the funds sent by his parents by teaching piano lessons, but clearly the sacrifice paid dividends.[19] Because of these early struggles, Mahler always maintained a keen awareness of his financial situation and that of his family, which, after the deaths of their parents, he left in the hands of Justine. He frequently wrote to her about the family's budget, and often struggled to find a balance in his siblings' finances. Sometimes they spent too little:

> Just tell yourself cheerfully what's what, and consider how one can manage with what one has, how to establish a limit—or more precisely stay within the limits of one's circumstances—without gnawing hunger pangs, or becoming mindless for lack of spiritual utterances, or without declining into the brutal bourgeoisie by oppressing all the serving and working classes.[20]

At other times, they spent too much:

> About every six weeks I receive notice that from now on I should increase your allowance by sum a or b, which naturally decreases my own. I never say a word on the assumption that everything has a limit, [but] now the matter is getting a bit too obvious. Can you all subtract?—then kindly take the amount of my monthly income and subtract what on average I have to send you.... Perhaps then you will find a way to get along on what we have agreed upon together.[21]

While Mahler's financial status at the time placed him firmly within the realm of the bourgeoisie, he rebelled against the social climbing, rudeness, and lack of sophistication with which the class was commonly associated. As the economic standing of wider populations began to shift

178   HIDDEN TREASURES

with the Industrial Revolution and the granting of full citizenship rights in 1867, increasing numbers of Austrian Jews entered the middle class, and tensions between this population and non-Jews simultaneously began to rise. Mahler saw the results of this clash during his years at university, as the ideals of the Pernerstorfer Circle began to shift into racist bigotry. One might even view Mahler's distaste for the bourgeoisie as another form of "Jewish self-hatred," the self-discrimination of assimilated Jewish populations against the newcomers who threatened to disrupt the social acceptance they had worked so hard to gain for generations.[22] Regardless, Mahler viewed himself as a man of higher sensibility than those he disparaged.

"Das irdische Leben"

Issues of economic disparity can clearly be identified in Mahler's *Wunderhorn* song "Das irdische Leben," which tells the tragically ironic story of an impoverished child who starves to death while waiting for her mother to finish baking bread to feed her. Mahler described to Bauer-Lechner his attraction to this poem, originally entitled "Verspätung":

> The text only suggests the deeper meaning, the treasure that must be searched for. Thus, I picture as a symbol of human life the child's cry for bread and the mother's attempt to console [her] with promises. I named the song "Das irdische Leben" for precisely that reason. What I wished to express is that the necessities for one's physical and spiritual growth are long delayed, and finally come too late, as they do for the dead child.[23]

Mahler claims here that life denies humanity not only bread and other necessities of physical life, but the metaphysical nutrients necessary for spiritual development. Despite each individual's cries for help, we each must "only wait, only wait, my dear child" (as the mother tells the child) to achieve our own spiritual potential, and only in death are we truly complete.

The *Wunderhorn* poem "Verspätung" was first printed in Leo Freiherrn von Seckendorf's *Musenalmanach für das Jahr 1808*, shortly before

MAHLER AND SOCIOECONOMIC EQUALITY   179

Table 7.1: Text comparison for "Das irdische Leben"

Verspätung (Boxberger)	Das irdische Leben (Mahler)	The Earthly Life
Mutter, ach Mutter, es hungert mich! Gieb mir Brod, sonst sterbe ich. – "Warte nur, mein liebes Kind! Morgen wollen wir säen geschwind."		
Und als das Korn gesäet war, Rief das Kind noch immerdar: Mutter, ach Mutter, es hungert mich! Gieb mir Brod, sonst sterbe ich. – "Warte nur, mein liebes Kind! Morgen wollen wir ernten geschwind."	"Mutter, ach Mutter, es hungert mich! Gieb mir Brod, sonst sterbe ich!" "Warte nur! Warte nur, mein liebes Kind! Morgen wollen wir ernten geschwind!"	"Mother, oh Mother, I am hungry!" Give me bread, so I don't die! "Wait now, wait now, my dear child! Tomorrow we will quickly harvest!"
Und als das Korn geerntet war, Rief das Kind noch immerdar: Mutter, ach Mutter, es hungert mich! Gieb mir Brod, sonst sterbe ich. – "Warte nur, mein liebes Kind! Morgen wollen wir dreschen geschwind."	Und als das Korn geerntet war, rief das Kind noch immerdar: "Mutter, ach Mutter, es hungert mich! Gieb mir Brod, sonst sterbe ich!" "Warte nur! Warte nur, mein liebes Kind! Morgen wollen wir dreschen geschwind!"	And once the corn was harvested, the child cried again: "Mother, oh Mother, I am hungry!" Give me bread, so I don't die! "Wait now, wait now, my dear child! Tomorrow we will quickly thresh!"
Und als das Korn gedroschen war, Rief das Kind noch immerdar:	Und als das Korn gedroschen war, rief das Kind noch immerdar:	And once the corn was threshed, the child cried again:

180 Hidden Treasures

Table 7.1: continued

Verspätung (Boxberger)	Das irdische Leben (Mahler)	The Earthly Life
Mutter, ach Mutter, es hungert mich!	"Mutter, ach Mutter, es hungert mich!	"Mother, oh Mother, I am hungry!"
Gieb mir Brod, sonst sterbe ich. –	Gieb mir Brod, sonst sterbe ich!"	Give me bread, so I don't die!
"Warte nur, mein liebes Kind!	"Warte nur! Warte nur, mein liebes Kind!	"Wait now, wait now, my dear child!
Morgen wollen wir mahlen geschwind."	Morgen wollen wir backen geschwind!"	Tomorrow we will quickly bake"
Und als das Korn gemahlen war,		
Rief das Kind noch immerdar:		
Mutter, ach Mutter, es hungert mich!		
Gieb mir Brod, sonst sterbe ich. –		
"Warte nur, mein liebes Kind!		
Morgen wollen wir backen geschwind."		
Und als das Brod gebacken war,	Und als das Brot gebacken war,	And once the bread was baked,
Lag das Kind schon auf der Bahr.	lag das Kind auf der Totenbahr!	The child lay dead on the bier!

it appeared in Arnim and Brentano's anthology, and stemmed from a children's game song collected near the Erzgebirge mountain range.[24] In the instances of the most repetitive *Wunderhorn* texts, such as "Das irdische Leben," Mahler removed several poetic stanzas to reduce monotony and propel the story forward more quickly. Mahler told Bauer-Lechner of his dislike for redundancy: "Repetition is a lie. A work of art must evolve perpetually, like life. If it doesn't, hypocrisy and theatricality set in."[25] This aversion to redundant material can also in part explain why Mahler avoids purely strophic musical forms.

This epic tale portrayed by a narrator includes dramatic dialogue between the mother and her child. As each step of the bread preparation is completed, the narrator sets up another interchange between the child and her mother: "And when the corn was harvested, the child cried again…" The temporal proximity of the events described in Mahler's story creates a more cohesive narrative trajectory by way of the deleted stanzas. A listener can possibly imagine a mother ignoring her child's repeated pleas for food during the time it takes to harvest, mill, and bake grain into bread. This situation would not be possible for the time between sowing and harvesting the grain. It also heightens the tension as the audience speculates as to whether the child will receive her bread or starve while waiting.

Mahler's alterations to the text do not change the poetic meter or the rhyme scheme. The speaker changes in "Das irdische Leben" with every two lines of text. The mother and child address each other, and the narrator addresses the audience. The constant shifting of narrative voice feels as unsettling as the subject matter itself. Quite reminiscent of Goethe's "Der Erlkönig," the continual change of person examines the tragic circumstances from three points of view, repeatedly ratcheting up the tension until the inevitable conclusion.

Mahler's use of formal structure to help convey his story finds its ideal representative in "Das irdische Leben." Essentially strophic in form, Mahler uses subtle changes in pitch, harmony, and phrasing to portray the growing tension of the situation. The *moto perpetuo* heard in the accompaniment maintains a certain temporal stasis throughout the song (see Example 7.1). This motion represents the mother's gristmill constantly turning in order to complete the task of baking bread.[26] One might also view the constant circular motion as a metaphor for the monotony and cyclical nature of peasant life in which any accomplishment is overshadowed by

Example 7.1: "Das irdische Leben," mm. 1–3

182   HIDDEN TREASURES

the immediate need to begin work anew. Mahler told Bauer-Lechner of his own views of the song:

> I believe that [the cruelty of life] is characteristically and fright-eningly expressed in the uncanny notes of the accompaniment, which bluster past as in a storm; in the child's anguished cry of fear, and the slow, monotonous responses of the mother—of fate, which is in no particular hurry to satisfy our cries for bread.[27]

The only breaks in the E-flat minor *moto perpetuo* (not including measures 27–32, which will be explained shortly) occur in the final three measures, when it is too late. But the child is not the only one made to wait for suste-nance. In the first three verses, Mahler separates the narrator's transitional passage from the preceding line of the mother by six measures. In the final verse, that six-measure interlude is extended to sixteen measures. Even the listener is forced to wait for satisfaction. Theodor Adorno wrote of the universality of this song:

> ["Das irdische Leben"] look[s] on the dead as children. The hope of the unrealized, which settles like a ray of holiness about those who die early, is not extinguished even for grown-ups. Mahler's music brings food to the mouth that is no more, watches over the sleep of those who shall never wake.[28]

The changing vocal lines of each of the three speakers in the story demon-strate the heightening drama of the ballad. As the child's hunger becomes increasingly critical, the melodies of both the child and the narrator rise in pitch and increase in range (see Examples 7.2a and b), while that of the mother remains essentially the same. One could conceivably inter-pret this in one of two ways: either the mother is trying to placate her daughter with her calming lack of emotion, or in her haste to complete the task of baking, she has ironically neglected to notice the severity of her child's need for food. Mahler's previously mentioned statements to Bauer-Lechner seem to indicate the latter.

Harmonic qualities also add to the frenetic nature of this situation. The only definitive cadence that occurs in the entire song appears at the

Example 7.2a and b: "Das irdische Leben," mm. 7–14 and 75–82

final pitch; only after the child has died can her mother cease her endless work (see Example 7.3). Each speaker in the story has her own pitch center: the child is the only figure who sings over the tonic chord, the mother maintains an unceasing instability by singing around the dominant, and the narrator ratchets up the tension with each successive verse with increasing amounts of chromaticism.

Mahler uses the unique musical language of the child to reveal the story's tragic outcome in the final verse. The opening line of this verse features a melody identical to that sung by the child in the beginning of the song, only now it is the narrator who speaks, telling us that the bread

Example 7.3: "Das irdische Leben," mm. 132–35

Example 7.4: Schubert: "Erlkönig," mm.1–3

is finally ready, but it is too late. The child can no longer deliver the melody herself, and once again, it is not her mother that comes to her aid, but the narrator. The shift in narrative point of view leaves the listener with an uncanny feeling, emphasizing the tragedy of what has occurred.

Similarities abound between "Das irdische Leben" and another ballad portraying the death of a child, Schubert's "Erlkönig," based on a *Kunstballade* by Goethe. Mahler adopts several techniques used by Schubert to convey his story. Both songs use modified strophic form in which the voices of the dying children continually rise in pitch to reflect the increasing drama while the parents' melodies remain relatively stable as they concentrate on the task at hand. Schubert also uses a *moto perpetuo* in "Erlkönig" that represents the sound of the father's horse galloping through the night (see Example 7.4). Crucial differences between the songs stem from the amount of time the stories encompass: Mahler's story plays out over several days, whereas Schubert's child meets his end within hours. But in both cases, the temporal qualities of the stories are substantial enough and the events heartrending enough to ensure that the listener will become sufficiently engrossed in the drama to attempt to speculate on whether the tales will end happily or in tragedy. The participation of the third-person narrator differs in these ballads as well: Schubert's narrator merely sets the scene in the beginning and delivers the grim conclusion at the end, but Mahler's narrator propels the story forward throughout. Both stories present a similar moral lesson: parents must beware becoming so caught up in the task of caring for their children that they forget to listen and lose what matters the most.

The lyrics tell us that the time that elapses from the beginning to the end of "Das irdische Leben" fills that which would occur between the harvesting of grain until the baking of bread. The frantic but lyrical

Example 7.5: "Das irdische Leben," mm. 27–32

speech of the child and the flat, declamatory statements from her mother are necessarily trapped in real time, but the intrusion of an instrumental interlude (first heard in measures 27–32) allows time to accelerate to the next phase in the bread-making process in each successive verse (see Example 7.5). This segment provides the only moment prior to the child's death at the end where the *moto perpetuo* ceases to be a constant presence. This allows time to pass at a rate independent from that of the dramatic action. No longer confined by the regular motion of the gristmill, the story can propel to the next phase of baking. The lyrical phrases presented by the third-person narrator also help to move time forward and inform us that the previous task has been completed—"und als das Korn [geerntet] war, rief das Kind noch immerdar"—but the child has still not been fed. An interlude also separates the child's request for food and her mother's admonishment to wait, but the *marcato* markings over these pitches and the return of the *moto perpetuo* motive in the bass suggest a sense of agitation and impatience on the part of both the child and the mother that would not allow any further time to pass.[29] These interludes provide the opportunity for Mahler to introduce another narrative voice in the form of his accompaniment, shown in Example 7.6 in piano reduction.

Example 7.6: "Das irdische Leben," mm. 15–18, piano arrangement

186   HIDDEN TREASURES

The short melodic statements surround every instance of the mother's response to her child, and they serve to comment both on the child's cries and the mother's replies, seemingly to imply a sense of frustration that the text does not directly indicate, as if a distant, not-entirely-human voice were trying desperately to tell the mother that she must hurry to feed her starving child.

Of course, on the surface, this song is simply a commentary on the particular struggles of the poor and the tragic effects of society's blindness to their suffering. Audiences can easily identify with the hardships of both mother and child, whether they view the child as starved for nourishment or spiritual sustenance. Mahler's message is twofold: viewing the song and its surface meaning encourages audiences to recognize the plights of the poor and to give aid whenever possible. The deeper message, revealed in his comments to Bauer-Lechner, indicates that we are all starving children, seeking enlightenment, and that only together can we truly begin to reach our full potential.

"Rheinlegendchen"

A second song setting which could potentially be explored as a commentary on economic justice is "Rheinlegendchen." This ballad tells the story of a young man who makes a living farming while his beloved has had to leave to accept a position serving in the king's distant court. Naturally, being kept apart has impacted their relationship, and so the farmer imagines how a series of drastic measures and unlikely circumstances might allow him to reunite with his love. If he cast his most valuable possession, a little gold ring, into the river, it would flow into a larger body of water. There it would be eaten by a fish, who would then be caught and served to the king. The king, upon finding the ring in his dinner, would give it to his servant and grant her leave to return it to its rightful owner.

Frau Auguste Pattberg shared this folk song, common to the areas of Swabia, Nassau, the Mosel River, and the Rhine, with Arnim and Brentano for their collection. Bode and Reiser have both determined that the poem had already been edited by her hands before it reached them, as evidenced by the inconsistent poetic language between the first two

Table 7.2: Text comparison for "Rheinlegendchen"

Rheinischer Bundesring (Boxberger)	Rheinlegendchen (Mahler)	Little Legend of the Rhine
Bald gras ich am Neckar, Bald gras ich am Rhein; Bald hab ich ein Schätzel, Bald bin ich allein.	Bald gras' ich am Neckar, bald gras' ich am Rhein; bald hab' ich ein Schätzel, bald bin ich allein!	Sometimes I mow by the Neckar, Sometimes by the Rhine; Sometimes I have my sweetheart, Sometimes I'm alone!
Was hilft mir das Grasen, Wann die Sichel nicht schneidt? Was hilft mir ein Schätzel, Wenn's bei mir nicht bleibt?	Was hilft mir das Grasen, wenn d'Sichel nicht schneid't; was hilft mir ein Schätzel, wenn's bei mir nicht bleibt!	What's the use of grazing If the sickle doesn't cut? What use is a sweetheart, If she doesn't stay with me?
So soll ich dann grasen Am Neckar, am Rhein, So werf ich mein goldiges Ringlein hinein.	So soll ich denn grasen am Neckar, am Rhein; so werf' ich mein goldenes Ringlein hinein!	So I should then mow By the Neckar and the Rhine; So I throw my little golden ring into the water!
Es fließet im Neckar Und fließet im Rhein, Soll schwimmen hinunter Ins tiefe Meer nein.	Es fließet im Neckar und fließet im Rhein, soll schwimmen hinunter in's Meer tief hinein!	It floats in the Neckar And floats in the Rhine, It flows down under Until it gets to the deep sea!
Und schwimmt es, das Ringlein, So frißt es ein Fisch; Das Fischlein soll kommen Auf's König sein Tisch.	Und schwimmt es, das Ringlein, so frißt es ein Fisch! Das Fischlein soll kommen auf's König's sein Tisch!	And the little ring flows, And is eaten by a fish! And the little fish shall end up On the king's plate!
Der König thät fragen, Wem's Ringlein soll sein? Da thät mein Schatz sagen: Das Ringlein g'hört mein.	Der König tät fragen, wem's Ringlein sollt' sein? Da tät mein Schatz sagen: "Das Ringlein g'hört mein!"	The king will ask, "Whose ring is this?" And my sweetheart will say, "The ring belongs to me!"

188 HIDDEN TREASURES

Table 7.2: continued

Rheinischer Bundesring (Boxberger)	Rheinlegendchen (Mahler)	Little Legend of the Rhine
Mein Schätzlein thät springen	Mein Schätzlein tät springen	My sweetheart will run
Berg auf und Berg ein,	Berg auf und Berg ein,	Up and down the hills,
That mir wiedrum bringen	tät mir wied'rum bringen	Until she can bring back
Das Goldringlein fein.	das Goldringlein fein!	The gold ring that is fine!
	(mein!)	(mine!)
Kannst grasen am Neckar,	Kannst grasen am Neckar,	You can mow by the Neckar
Kannst grasen am Rhein;	kannst grasen am Rhein!	You can mow by the Rhine
Wirf Du mir nur immer	Wirf du mir nur immer	As long as you always
Dein Ringlein hinein!	dein Ringlein hinein!	Throw your little ring in!

and the remaining stanzas.[30] The protagonist directly narrates the story in "Rheinlegendchen." He opens and closes the story by speaking of his current circumstances, which creates a kind of narrative frame in which he places the imagined chain of events that he believes will result in a reunion (albeit a temporary one) with his sweetheart. Within the imagined story, a brief moment of narrated dialogue ("Der König tät fragen," "Da tät mein Schatz sagen") between the king and the sweetheart occurs, but they are kept firmly within the mode of the narration.

Mahler makes only a few minor adjustments to the text (primarily the use of contractions and shifting accents) in order to instill a more consistent meter. Both the original poem and Mahler's song text use an essentially ABAB rhyme scheme. The first three verses do more to set the scene than to progress the action of the song, until the final lines of the third, in which the mower throws his ring into the river. At this point, the story changes from a relaying of actual circumstance and events to an imagined story of the path the ring will have to travel in order to reach the beloved; in a sense, the narrator speculates the outcome of his own story. The mower distinguishes this section from real-life events through the use of the subjunctive, and it is not until his beloved has returned the ring that he returns to the present tense. Throughout the ring's journey, the listener can speculate along with him: where will the ring turn up?

Example 7.7: "Rheinlegendchen," mm. 10–14

How will it reach his beloved? Will she be able to return? Of course, any number of potential outcomes could occur, and since the entire scene is imaginary, how or if these lovers will be reunited is unclear, but if only for the moment, "Rheinlegendchen" offers the listener a bit of whimsical fantasy. The moral of the story tells us that if someone is only willing to take a chance and believe, the most extraordinary things can happen, but it also points to the extreme measures that the poor must take in order to preserve their love.

Upon first hearing, "Rheinlegendchen" strikes the listener as a simple, dance-based, folk-inspired song; however, great complexity is hidden below the surface.[31] The orchestral introduction begins to display the inherent tensions that plague the protagonist from the outset. Through the opening pitch, a single pitch from the horn held for eight measures, we quickly learn of the pastoral setting of the story. The dance that was once an enjoyed leisure activity for the separated couple has become distorted and nonfunctional, as demonstrated by dramatic ritardandos in measures 2 and 15–16, while strong accents on the first beats of measures 3–9 try valiantly to restore the offset rhythm. A sixteenth-note melody passed between the flute, clarinet, and oboe also establishes a pastoral topos through its emulation of birdsong (see Example 7.7). When the voice of the protagonist enters in measure 16, the vocal line is considerably more erratic than one would expect in a folk song.[32] Large leaps of major and minor sevenths betray the complexity of an artistic rather than a

Example 7.8: "Rheinlegendchen," mm. 18–24

folk nature. The singer is also made to offset the rhythm through large ascending intervals that naturally accent the second beat of the measure rather than the first, and further contend with snaking, chromatic melodies that belie the folk nature of the song (see Example 7.8).

The ternary form Mahler chooses to set the poem creates distinct geographical spaces for the characters, designed to emphasize the distance between them.[33] The music of the male protagonist, who remains between the Neckar and the Rhine, dwells strictly in a major key, but while he imagines his ring traveling through the rivers to the sea, from the fish to the king's table, and finally to his beloved, the music changes drastically. As soon as the ring reaches the sea, the key changes to minor, and the rhythmic and melodic qualities that established the farmer's home disappear and are replaced with a slower tempo and more sustained pitches and pedal tones. This new section creates an entirely new soundscape used to indicate events taking place off in the distance (even though those events are confined to the imagination of the young man). The musical landscape created by the opening section does not recur until he imagines his beloved, having identified the ring that the king has found inside his dinner, beginning her trip home. Once she returns, the dance rhythm can freely move forward without distortion or interference, as will their love.

The fact that so many of the events portrayed in "Rheinlegendchen" do not actually occur outside of the young man's imagination blurs the temporal qualities of the song. This does not, however, diminish the potential for the listener to become caught up in the fantastic story and to hope that the ring's miraculous voyage will result in the couple's eventual reunion. While the entire story of "Rheinlegendchen" is narrated by the young man, Mahler allows the change in musical material to separate real time and space from that of fantasy. This transforms a potentially sad story about separated lovers into a romantic tale filled with innocent whimsy.

The Neckar and Rhine rivers meet near Mannheim, and the Rhine then flows north-west to the North Sea at Rotterdam. If one follows the path of the Rhine from Mannheim, the nearest location boasting both a castle and a sizeable body of water to merit the use of the German word "See," meaning sea or lake, is Eltville, home to an electoral castle, roughly 100 km northwest of Mannheim. If one were to presume that this was the farmer's sweetheart's place of work, the distance that she would have to travel to find gainful employment serves as another marker of economic injustice.

The fanciful nature of the mower's scheme demonstrates the depth of his love, and the fact that he would even entertain the idea of sacrificing an item of such value as a golden ring serves as a testament to his faithfulness and longing. However, that he should be forced to do so also points to the desperation of a couple forced apart by their need to work and the elaborate lengths that they would go to just to steal a short period of time together.

"Wer hat dies Liedlein erdacht?"

This final example actually demonstrates Mahler's views on economic justice more acutely by way of the text he omits rather than the text he chooses. Mahler cobbled together the lyrics for his song "Wer hat dies Liedlein erdacht?" from two separate poems from *Des Knaben Wunderhorn*. His first and final verses were adapted from a poem with the same title as the song, while the central verse is a modification of a portion of another poem called "Wers Lieben erdacht."

Despite the similarities in their titles, Mahler's two source poems are quite different. The first poem tells of a lovely young woman, her dowry of a thousand thalers, and her potential husband being asked to forsake wine in order to win her hand, which, the closing stanza seems to indicate, the protagonist finds to be ridiculous. The second poem features a young man attempting to seduce a young lady by speaking of her beauty's power to heal the sick and raise the dead. She responds by saying, "My mother has only one black and brown cow. Who is going to milk it if I marry?," a clever way of refusing his advances by hiding behind a veil of innocence. From this second poem, Mahler only borrows the passage about the powers of the young woman's beauty, ignoring the context of the seduction and the young woman's refusal.

192   HIDDEN TREASURES

Table 7.3: Text comparison for "Wer hat dies Liedlein erdacht?"

Wer hat dies Liedlein erdacht? (Boxberger)	Wers Lieben erdacht (Boxberger)
Dort oben in dem hohen Haus	*Knabe*
Da guckt ein wacker Mädel raus.	Zum Sterben bin ich
Es ist nicht dort daheime;	Verliebet in Dich;
Es ist des Wirths sein Töchterlein,	Deine schwarzbraune Aeugelein
Es wohnt auf grüner Haide.	Verfuhren ja mich. :I:
Und wer das Mädel haben will,	Bist hier oder bist dort
Muß tausend Thaler finden	Oder sonst an eim Ort,
Und muß sich auch verschwören,	Wollt wünsche, könnt rede
Nie mehr zu Wein zu gehn,	Mit Dir ein paar Wort. :I:
Des Vaters Gut verzehren.	
	Wollt wünsche, es wär Nacht,
Wer hat denn das schöne Liedel	Mein Bettlein wär gemacht;
Es haben's drei Gäns' übers Wasser	Ich wollt mich drein legen,
gebracht,	Feins Liebchen darneben,
Zwei graue und eine weiße;	Wollt's herzen, daß's lacht.
Und wer das Liedlein nicht singen kann,	
Dem wollen sie es pfeifen.	Mein Herz ist verwundt,
	Komm, Schätzel, mach's gesund;
	Erlaub mir zu küssen
	Dein purpurrothen Mund! :I:
	Dein purpurrothen Mund
	Macht Herzen gesund,
	Macht Jugend verständig,
	Macht Todte lebendig,
	Macht Kranke gesund.
	Mädchen
	Meine Mutter hat nur
	eine schwarzbraune Kuh;
	Wer wird sie denn melken,
	Wenn ich heurathen thu? :I:
	Sänger
	Der dies Liedchen gemacht,
	Hat's Lieben erdacht;
	Drum wünsch ich mein feins Liebchen
	Viel tausend gute Nacht. :I:

MAHLER AND SOCIOECONOMIC EQUALITY 193

Wer hat dies Liedlein erdacht?! (Mahler)	Who Thought Up This Little Song?
Dort oben am Berg in dem hohen Haus!	There in the high-up house!
In dem Haus!	In the house!
Da gucket ein fein's, lieb's Mädel heraus.	A lovely little girl looks out the window.
Es ist nicht dort daheime! (x2)	She does not live there,
Es ist des Wirt's sein Töchterlein!	She does not live there.
Es wohnet auf grüner Haide!	She is the little daughter of the innkeeper,
	And she lives on the green meadow.
Mein Herzle is' wund!	My heart is wounded!
Komm, Schätzle, mach's g'sund!	Come, dearest, make it well!
Dein' schwarzbraune Äuglein,	Your dark brown eyes
die hab'n mich verwund't!	Have left me wounded!
Dein rosiger Mund	Your rose-colored mouth
macht Herzen gesund.	Makes hearts healthy,
Macht Jugend verständig,	Makes youth wise,
macht Tote lebendig,	Makes the dead live,
macht Kranke gesund,	Makes the sick healthy, makes the sick
macht Kranke gesund, ja gesund.	healthy, yes, healthy!
Wer hat denn das schön schöne Liedlein erdacht?	Who thought up this little song?
Es haben's drei Gäns übers Wasser gebracht,	It has brought three geese over the water,
Zwei graue und eine weiße! (x2)	Two gray and one white!
Und wer das Liedlein nicht singen kann,	And whoever cannot sing this little song,
dem wollen sie es pfeifen!	They will whistle it!
Ja!	Yes!

194   HIDDEN TREASURES

At first blush, both poems strike the reader as somewhat absurd, and Mahler's selection of stanzas from each of the source poems does little to clarify the meaning of his text. In his version, we learn of a lovely girl who spends a lot of time in a fine house on the hill, but, as the daughter of the innkeeper, her actual home lies in the valley. Her beauty has the power to both wound the heart and heal it again. Then the song's lyrics turn inward and become self-referential, noting that the song itself has lured three geese, and that even those who cannot sing it can surely whistle it. While Mahler's letters to Bauer-Lechner, his sisters, and others sometimes refer to specific songs and what drew him to their texts, we have no such evidence for this song, and one cannot help but wonder what drew the composer to create this strange, nonsensical situation and what it might have meant for him.

However, the omitted text that concerns us here, as we examine this song as evidence of Mahler's views on utopian socialism, pertains to the young woman's thousand-thaler dowry. Removing this aspect from the scenario described in this song focuses the listener's attention on the romance between the two lovers and their *völkisch* charm. As mentioned previously, Mahler's notion of pure, untarnished, unbigoted "Germanness" rested in the idea of the *Volk*, and that for this population, according to his friend Siegfried Lipiner, "Salvation lies in suffering, not in wealth."[34] As such, eliminating the mention of the young woman's dowry and emphasizing her separation from the wealthy guests of her father's inn creates a narrative that emphasizes the couple's love despite their lack of money.

Mahler uses musical techniques to create the illusion of distance between the lovers and those at the inn as well. Two lengthy melismatic passages, one in measures 35–46 and the other in measures 88–98 (see Example 7.9), feature leaps of up to a perfect fourth at the beginning of passages, emulating, to a degree, what one might hear in a yodel. These same motives occur in the orchestration, played by clarinets and oboes and punctuated by the triangle, furthering the pastoral sound. The yodel can be inferred as the young man calling to his beloved while she is up the hill in the inn.

A ternary form separates the texts and their origins. The opening and closing sections, drawn from the poem "Wer hat dies Liedlein erdacht?," with its tempo marking "Mit heiterem Behagen" (comfortably cheerful),

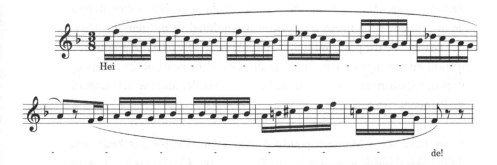

Example 7.9: "Wer hat dies Liedlein erdacht?" mm. 35–46, vocal line

lies solidly in F major and features the hallmark rhythmic features of a *Ländler*. Beginning in measure 46, the B section is marked "Gemächlich" (leisurely) and rapidly destabilizes the tonality through a whirlwind of chromaticism before landing squarely back in F major for the return of the A section in measure 68 (see Example 7.10). The young woman's beauty and her position as the daughter of the innkeeper, as well as the song's power to attract the attention of the three geese, create a stability that helps to ground the unbelievable capability of the woman's dark brown eyes and rosy mouth to heal the sick, educate the young, and even raise the dead.

Ultimately, this example points out the most problematic aspect of Mahler's views on economic equality. Leaving out mention of the young woman's dowry denies the couple the opportunity to escape their humble surroundings. While utopian socialism is based on the desire to create a

Example 7.10: "Wer hat dies Liedlein erdacht?" mm. 46–53, piano reduction

196 HIDDEN TREASURES

world that cares for the poor and takes away the hardships inherent to a life in poverty, once those very people are uplifted from their struggles, they cease to be the pure, authentic *Volk* whose simple lives are untouched by modern, corrupt society. This paradox lies at the heart of the failure of utopian socialism and its role in the beliefs of Mahler and the aesthetes of the Pernerstorfer Circle.

As we have seen, Mahler's youthful enthusiasm for the aesthetic and philosophical ideals espoused by the Pernerstorfer Circle exposed him to political ideals that resonate throughout his *Wunderhorn* songs. Roughly half of these songs can be interpreted as having political undertones, whether they pertain to poverty and economic justice or to wartime violence, as we examined more closely in Chapter 2. This is remarkable, given that nearly twenty years elapsed between his resignation from the Circle and his final *Wunderhorn* setting. Despite his lack of later active civic engagement, his dealings with politics at the university and the values this experience instilled in him regarding Pan-Germanism and social injustice clearly made an indelible mark on Mahler that he expressed musically time and time again over the years to come.

CHAPTER EIGHT

"The misery of a pioneer"
Mahler's Responses to Critics and Audiences

Throughout the fourteen years during which Mahler was engrossed in the poetry of *Des Knaben Wunderhorn*, he struggled for acceptance of his compositions, while moving from one conducting position to another. Even after he finally settled (albeit briefly) at the Hofoper in Vienna, in what he believed would be the culmination of his career, the composer still maintained an ambivalent relationship with his critics and audiences. The most brutal attacks he endured came from opponents who commented on his compositions—not just the songs, but the symphonies as well—though his conducting style was not above criticism either. His negative critics tended to fall into two camps: those who disliked Mahler's work due to its unapologetic modernity, and those whose disdain stemmed not from the music itself, but simply from the fact that Mahler was Jewish, as discussed in Chapter 4. Mahler occasionally chose to confront his critics in songs. Three of the *Wunderhorn* lieder tell stories dealing with unfair criticism: "Lob des hohen Verstandes" addresses those critics who took issue with Mahler's Secessionist, proto-modernist tendencies; in "Ablösung im Sommer," his gaze turns to ignorant audiences and their fleeting loyalties; and "Des Antonius von Padua Fischpredigt" examines how ignorance and bigotry can cloud the critical judgment of both audiences and critics.

197

198   HIDDEN TREASURES

Mahler the Modernist

Mahler recognized that his compositional style marked a departure from earlier conventions. Of his songs, he told Bauer-Lechner:

> I have come to recognize a perpetual evolution of the song's content... as the true principle of music.... For music is governed by the law of eternal evolution, eternal development—just as the world, even in one and the same spot, is always changing, eternally fresh and new. But of course the development must be progressive, or I don't give a damn for it![1]

Due to his complex harmonic language and compositional techniques that ushered in the era of modernism, many older critics and audiences in particular simply did not understand Mahler's music, and, due to their confusion, they accused the composer of creating incomprehensible noise, a common response when innovative artistic movements begin to emerge. The Viennese author Stefan Zweig, who was only a generation younger than Mahler, describes the conflict between generations of Viennese patrons of the arts at the *fin-de-siècle*:

> Suddenly the old, comfortable order was disturbed, its former and infallible norms of the "aesthetically beautiful" (Hanslick) were questioned, and while the official critics of our correct bourgeois newspapers were dismayed by the often daring experiments and sought to dam the irresistible stream with such epithets as "decadent" and "anarchistic," we young ones threw ourselves enthusiastically into the surf where it foamed at its wildest.[2]

Unfortunately, the younger generation held little power over the tastes of the people at large. That honor fell to the *feuilletonists*, writers of short essays discussing the arts that typically appeared on the lower front page of important newspapers, such as the *Neue Freie Presse*, *Die Zeit*, and the *Wiener Allgemeine Zeitung*. These *feuilletons* were powerful instruments for swaying the cultural tastes of the people. "Their yes or no in Vienna decided the success of a work, a play, or a book, and with it that of the

Mahler's Responses to Critics and Audiences   199

author. Each of these essays was the talk of the day in intellectual circles."[3] Established figures in the Viennese cultural scene typically wrote the *feuilletons*, and most of them were primarily among the conservative voices calling modern works, such as those of Mahler, "decadent" and "anarchistic," simply because they did not fully understand what the younger generation of artists was trying to express. In the spring of 1901, in a letter to his long-time friend the musicologist Guido Adler, Mahler complained of the press's unwillingness to make the effort to understand his music:

> It's not just a question of conquering a summit previously unknown, but of tracing, step by step, a new pathway to it, whereas the audience and *the "judges" come rushing in all of a sudden and want to see everything immediately, without realizing that their shortsightedness prevents them from seeing anything more than the nearest bush*... They then utter harsh criticism, nothing satisfies them, everything must be otherwise; although it might never even have occurred to them that such a path is possible, they are determined to make us responsible for the fact that nature is thus and not otherwise.[4]

Mahler's music demanded time, energy, and thoughtful contemplation from its listeners, and this was something these conservative critics were not willing to give. In his letters, Mahler expressed his frustrations, often referring to "the stupidity of the critics," his "very mean-spirited opponents," and their "shallowness and incomprehension."[5] In spring 1896, he told Bauer-Lechner about a realization that his music was not connecting with audiences, critics, or even the performers who played in his orchestra:

> I shall not live to see my cause triumph! Everything I write is too strange and new to my listeners, who cannot establish contact with me. People have not yet accepted my language. They have no notion of what I am saying or what I mean, and so it all seems senseless and unintelligible to them. Why do I have to suffer all this? Why must I take this fearful martyrdom upon myself? I was overwhelmed with boundless grief, not only for myself, but for all those who were nailed to the cross before me, because they

200   HIDDEN TREASURES

wanted to give their best to the world, and for all those who will suffer the same fate after me.[6]

One might conceivably argue that Mahler's reaction was a bit melodramatic, but in any case, it does reveal his concerns about writing music that he perceives to be ahead of its time and his desire to continue to offer his "best to the world," in spite of a lack of understanding and appreciation.

Mahler had good reason to be discouraged. Critics as highly regarded as Eduard Hanslick struggled to understand some of Mahler's compositional practices, as seen in this review of the premiere of several *Wunderhorn* lieder:

> In the middle of the program stood a novelty, yielding the curiosity of the public, and leaving them particularly excited: Five Songs with Orchestral Accompaniment by G. Mahler, sung by Miss Selma Kurz. The songs were selections from *Des Knaben Wunderhorn* and from the cycle *Lieder eines fahrenden Gesellen*, for which the composer wrote the texts himself. Director Mahler already has shown a humble, touching modesty in keeping his own works to himself in Vienna, despite his success in premiering them in other cities. We expect the new and the strange: in his Second Symphony (which I know, unfortunately, only from reports), he created an entirely new style, with enormous expansion of form and means of representation. In his songs yesterday, we heard an enemy of the typical and conventional, new, without connecting a disparaging criticism to the term "enemy." These new "songs" are difficult to classify: neither lied nor aria, nor dramatic scene, but having something of all of these. The form in these songs is reminiscent of the orchestral songs of Berlioz: "La captive," "Le chasseur danois," "Le pâtre breton." Mahler has drawn the majority of his texts from the folk-song collection *Des Knaben Wunderhorn*. Its contents are so strangely beautiful that Goethe's earlier admiration for it led to an upswing in German lyric poetry. Goethe famously praised the work of Arnim and Brentano, noting the "woodcutting manner" of folk songs, and claiming there should be a place for this book "at the window,

Mahler's Responses to Critics and Audiences 201

by the mirror, or wherever the music and cookbooks are kept." Mahler, as the leader of the modernist movement, tends, as is often the case, to flee to the extremes, in naivety, in the familiarity, the rarity, the unstructured language of old folk songs. He does not, however, treat them in the lowbrow, simple nature of earlier composers. The singer is supported by a sumptuous accompaniment, with richly spirited motion and sharp modulation. An orchestra plays this accompaniment, not the piano. Indeed, for folk song, it is an unusually rich and refined ensemble: three flutes, piccolo, three clarinets, bass clarinet, English horn, four horns, two harps. One cannot deny the contradiction, the conflict between the term "folk song" and this ornate, exceptionally rich orchestral setting.[7]

Hanslick uses a portion of this review as a platform to address an important debate brewing among composers, critics, and music scholars of the time regarding the genre classification of the orchestral song. Traditional figures, such as Hanslick, Rudolf Louis, and Siegmund von Hausegger, felt that the use of the traditional German term *Lied* implied certain characteristics: piano accompaniment, simple poetry, and an intimate performance context, typically the home. These were not compatible with orchestral setting. Orchestrating songs required larger performance spaces and, of course, many more people, instantly destroying the intimacy inherent in the salon. Composers like Mahler felt that fusing the lied with an orchestral accompaniment allowed for greater expressive potential but still sought to maintain the connection to musical and literary tradition by preserving the label of "lied," particularly given that the texts found in *Des Knaben Wunderhorn* predominantly started out as folk-song lyrics.[8] Comparing his *Wunderhorn* settings to the works of ballad composer Carl Loewe, he stated, "He didn't achieve the utmost in [his songs]. He settled for the piano, whereas a large-scale composition that plumbs the depth of the subject, unconditionally demands the orchestra."[9] Hanslick's argument lies not with the music itself, in fact he seems to appreciate Mahler's skills, but the critic takes issue with the composer's use of a genre classification that was commonly perceived as a setting of simple, traditional poetry in combination with an uncharacteristically elaborate and modern musical

202   HIDDEN TREASURES

setting. What emerges is what Mahler would have viewed as a misunderstanding of the nature of these songs, with Hanslick calling them "new and strange," "an enemy of the typical and conventional," and noting their "contradiction" and "conflict." Indeed, Mahler seems to have expected this kind of reaction, as he told Bauer-Lechner about one of his *Wunderhorn* songs that "In spite of all its simplicity and folklike quality, the whole thing is extremely original, especially in its harmonization, so that people will not know what to make of it, and will call it mannered."[10] In *On the Musically Beautiful*, Hanslick wrote, "With every artistic pleasure, there is an indispensable intellectual aspect."[11] Nonetheless, Hanslick seems to "not know what to make of" the songs. Eventually the critic's perplexity gives way to a kind of resignation, as he goes on to write in his review:

> Mahler has executed this piece with extraordinary refinement and masterly technique. Now, at the beginning of a new century, it is advisable to often repeat the novelties of the musical "Secession" (Mahler, Richard Strauss, Hugo Wolf, etc.): it is very possible that the future belongs to them.[12]

The famed critic reluctantly hands over the reins of Vienna's musical future to a style that he no longer fully understands. Merely six years earlier, however, he had declared himself a champion of new music:

> Indeed our age... cannot do without the new, through which our blood courses. Poems and musical works of the classical periods of art might still live on in the bright light of day, but only modern music reveals those colors that correspond to the magical light of sunrise and sunset. I consider it the critic's responsibility to avoid discouraging productivity, to acknowledge those works of our time that are truly felt and unaffectedly entertaining, and not to disparage such works contemptuously in favor of a vanishing "golden age."[13]

Hanslick's lack of appreciation of Mahler's new style betrays his advancing age, and the accompanying unease that he and many others among the Viennese elite felt regarding the future of the city's role as a musical center seems to be at the heart of much of the backlash against the approach of modernism in general and Mahler in the specific. The long-standing musical traditions of Vienna were moving in a new direction, and many Viennese, renowned for their discernment, feared that these radical changes might damage the city's treasured reputation as a musical capital.

But Mahler had been contending with this type of criticism long before he arrived in Vienna in 1897. On December 12, 1892, the Berlin Philharmonic performed "Der Schildwache Nachtlied" and "Verlor'ne Müh'!" with contralto Amalie Joachim. Critic Arno Kleffel of the *Neue Berliner Musikzeitung* failed to even acknowledge the musical qualities of Mahler's work:

> Never before have I heard anything so unsatisfactory, so distorted, so sad as these two songs... A wasteland, nothing but mannered, insignificant phrases, not a single blossom or green leaf. Judging by the depression that reigned afterward in the auditorium, it was easy to deduce that the public is unwilling to accept such tasteless gifts.[14]

Kleffel was so mystified by these songs that he would not even begin to appreciate their value. Mahler did not attend this performance, as he was conducting in Hamburg the same evening. He later received a copy of Kleffel's review, which he then passed along with another to his siblings, writing, "Now, dear children, to amuse you I send you... two little accounts by the Minoses of Berlin," referring to Minos, one of the cruel judges of the underworld found in Greek mythology.[15] In this case, Mahler's response shows not frustration or despair but rather amusement, for if he were instead disheartened by that particular review it is doubtful he would have sent it on to his family and poked fun at the writers. Mahler recognized and often acknowledged that his music said something new that an uninformed audience simply would not be able to grasp, and as we shall see, sometimes he mocked their ignorance.

Alas, it was not only critics and audiences who struggled to understand Mahler's music. In autumn 1892, Amalie Joachim suggested to the famed conductor Hans von Bülow that he include some of Mahler's *Wunderhorn* lieder in the program for an upcoming performance in Hamburg. Mahler

204 HIDDEN TREASURES

anxiously sent him the music, hoping that working with such an esteemed figure would help cement his reputation as a composer. Instead, Mahler received a letter on October 25 stating:

> My numerous attempts (not superficial) to comprehend, and to feel, the special style of the songs that you so kindly sent me have turned out to be so futile that, with regard to the composer as well as the performer, I feel unable to accept the responsibility of their performance at the 7 November concert.[16]

If Bülow was unable to "comprehend" and "feel" the songs from studying the scores, it is no wonder that so many lesser musical figures struggled to understand them after only hearing a single performance.

Mahler's contemporaries recognized his music had a style that went beyond those of his predecessors; he was blatantly called a modernist (though whether that term was used approvingly or disparagingly tended to vary) in reviews and discussions of his work. On November 20, 1900, the day after Mahler conducted his First Symphony at the Vienna Philharmonic, a *feuilleton* by Max Burckhard discussing modernism in music appeared in the *Neue Freie Presse*. Burckhard equates musical modernity with the use of military music, church music, patriotic national music, and dance music. The appearance of these precise styles of music in Mahler's First Symphony indicates that Burckhard likely wrote his essay in response to the performance, though neither Mahler nor the symphony are mentioned by name. Indirectly speaking, this review reveals that at least some looked at Mahler's modernism in a fashion that attempted to understand the composer's approach.[17]

Burckhard also describes modernism as a movement that distances itself from the beauty of sound and leans toward the sounds of nature. This observation points to the strong contrast between Mahler's musical philosophy and more conservative ideals. In 1897, Mahler told Bauer-Lechner:

> We probably derive all our basic rhythms and themes from nature, which offers them to us, pregnant with meaning, in every animal noise. Indeed, Man, and the artist in particular, takes all his materials and all his forms from the world around him—transforming

and expanding them, of course. He may find himself in a harmonious and happy relationship with Nature, or alternatively in painful and hostile opposition to her.[18]

By way of contrast, Hanslick devotes an entire chapter of *On the Musically Beautiful* to "The Relation of Music to Nature," in which he writes, "In music, everything must be commensurable, while in the sounds of nature, nothing is so, these two realms of sound remain almost completely irreconcilable."[19] The incredible discrepancy between Mahler's statement and Hanslick's views on the relationship of nature and music demonstrates the gulf between the different generations' notions of the very essence of musical expression.

Negative criticism sometimes also carried an undertone of anti-Semitism. Musical language began to radically shift around the same time as the revolutions of 1848, and people's lives were disrupted by what largely began with a movement for "Jewish emancipation," essentially a call for equal civic and political rights and an end to legalized discrimination. As such, Jews were frequently blamed for all changes in the cultural landscape, including increasingly modernist music, which had coincided with the end of the peaceful age of the past.[20] Given these connections, one might accuse all critics who attacked Mahler's modernism as demonstrating a subtle brand of anti-Semitism. For some, this may have in fact been the case, while for others, modern music simply did not "make sense," particularly to those who did not allow for the time and energy needed to fully understand it. Still other critics were simply proud to let their views on "the pernicious influence of the Jewry" be clearly known and to denounce Maher's music purely on that basis.[21]

"Lob des hohen Verstandes"

Composed in late June 1896, Mahler's "Lob des hohen Verstandes" serves to address his relationship to critics who failed to grasp his modernist style, through both the choice of text and features of the music itself. The ballad tells of a cuckoo that challenges a nightingale to a singing contest. Since the nightingale is renowned for the beauty of her song and the cuckoo's call is associated with humor and even insanity, one would assume

206 HIDDEN TREASURES

Table 8.1: Text comparison for "Lob des hohen Verstandes"

Wettstreit des Kuckuks mit der Nachtigall (Boxberger)	Lob des hohen Verstandes (Mahler)	In Praise of a Higher Intellect
Einsmals in einem tiefen Thal Der Kuckuk und die Nachtigall Thäten ein Wett anschlagen, Zu singen um das Meisterstück: "Gewinn es Kunst, gewinn es Glück, Dank soll er davon tragen."	Einstmals in einem tiefen Tal Kukuk und Nachtigall täten ein' Wett' anschlagen: Zu singen um das Meisterstück, gewinn' es Kunst, gewinn' es Glück: Dank soll er davon tragen.	One day in the deep woods A cuckoo and a nightingale Made a wager To see who was the better singer. Whether the winner has art or luck, He will receive thanks!
Der Kuckuk sprach: "So dir's gefällt, Ich hab zur Sach ein Richter wählt," Und thät den Esel nennen. "Denn weil er hat zwei Ohren groß, So kann er hören desto baß, Und was recht ist, erkennen."	Der Kukuk sprach: "So dir's gefällt, hab' ich den Richter wählt." Und tät gleich den Esel ernennen. "Denn weil er hat zwei Ohren groß, Ohren groß, Ohren groß, so kann er hören desto bos! Und was recht ist, kennen!"	The cuckoo said, "If it pleases you, I have a judge." And he named the donkey. "Because he has two large ears, Two large ears, He can hear the best, and can tell us what is correct."
Sie flogen vor den Richter bald. Wie ihm die Sache ward erzählt, Schuf er, sie sollten singen. Die Nachtigall sang lieblich aus; Der Esel sprach: "Du machst mir's kraus, Ich kann's in Kopf nicht bringen."	Sie flogen vor den Richter bald. Wie dem die Sache ward erzählt, schuf er, sie sollten singen. Die Nachtigall sang lieblich aus! Der Esel sprach: "Du machst mir's kraus! Du machst mir's kraus! Ija! Ija! Ich kann's in Kopf nicht bringen!"	They then flew to the judge, When they explained the matter to him, he had them sing. The nightingale sang beautifully! The donkey said, "You're confusing me! You're confusing me! Hee haw! Hee haw! I cannot get it into my head."

MAHLER'S RESPONSES TO CRITICS AND AUDIENCES   207

Table 8.1: continued

Wettstreit des Kuckuks mit der Nachtigall (Boxberger)	Lob des hohen Verstandes (Mahler)	In Praise of a Higher Intellect
Der Kuckuk drauf anfing geschwind:	Der Kukuk drauf fing an geschwind	The cuckoo then began his song,
Kuckuk! Sein sang durch Terz, Quart, Quint	sein Sang durch Terz und Quart und Quint.	He sang in thirds and fourths and fifths.
Und thät die Noten brechen;	Dem Esel g'fiels, er sprach nur:	The judge liked it, and said
Er lacht auch drein nach seiner Art.	"Wart! Wart! Wart!	"Wait! Wait! Wait!
Dem Esel gefiel's, er sagt: "Nun wart,	Dein Urteil will ich sprechen, ja sprechen.	I will tell you my judgement, yes, tell you."
Ein Urtheil will ich sprechen:		
Wohl sungen hast Du, Nachtigall;	Wohl sungen hast du, Nachtigall!	"You have sung well, nightingale,
Aber, Kuckuk, Du singst gut Choral	Aber Kukuk, singst gut Choral! Gut Choral,	but the cuckoo sings a good chorale, good chorale,
Und hältst den Takt fein innen.	Und hältst den Takt fein innen, fein innen!	and he keeps well in time, in time.
Das sprech ich nach mein hohn Verstand,	Das sprech' ich nach mein' hoh'n Verstand!	I say this according to my higher intellect,
Und kostet's gleich ein ganzes Land,	Hoh'n Verstand! Hoh'n Verstand!	higher intellect, higher intellect,
So laß ich Dich's gewinnen."	Und kost' es gleich ein ganzes Land,	And thought it may cost me my whole land,
	so laß ich's dich gewinnen, gewinnen!"	I make you the winner, the winner."
	Kukuk! Kukuk! Ija!	Cuckoo, cuckoo, hee haw!

from the outset that the former would easily win. However, the cuckoo suggests that they seek out the donkey to serve as judge: "because he has two big ears, he can hear the best." The donkey, a creature not normally known for its intelligence and discernment, simply cannot comprehend the intricacies of the nightingale's song (he exclaims, "You're confusing me! I cannot get it into my head!"), and so he declares the cuckoo the victor, claiming he sings "a good chorale and keeps well in time." In this

208   HIDDEN TREASURES

tale, the judge's stupidity has cost the nightingale her rightful victory, and we learn that ignorance can sometimes rob the more worthy competitor of her proper spoils.

Mahler's source poem, "Wettstreits des Kukuks mit der Nachtigall," first appeared in print in Nuremberg in Bernhard Joseph Docen's 1807 publication, *Docens Miscellaneen zur Geschichte der teutschen Literatur*, bearing the inscription "1580." Portions of the folk song also appeared in Johann Gottfried Herder's 1778 collection simply titled *Volkslieder* (unbeknownst to Docen).[22] In this seemingly innocent tale of a singing contest between a cuckoo and a nightingale, Mahler found a "priceless piece of satire on criticism."[23]

Mahler alters the poem in minor ways to create his song text. He preserves the rhythm and rhyme scheme and improves the rhyme by changing "desto baß" to "desto bos" to rhyme with "Ohren groß." He omits two brief lines describing the cuckoo's contest performance, "Und thät die Noten brechen; er lacht auch drein nach seiner Art" (He arpeggiated the notes, and he laughed, in accordance with his kind). It appears, though, that Mahler did not initially plan to omit the text: the two missing lines appear (as one of the few spots that is fully composed with accompaniment) in a sketch that maps out the vocal melody and small bits of accompaniment. [24]

A narrator presents the majority of "Lob des hohen Verstandes," leaving only four instances of dialogue, two each for the cuckoo and the donkey. Narration allows the time during which the birds fly to find the donkey to pass in an instant, propelling the story forward and increasing the listener's desire to speculate. Mahler's manipulation does not disrupt this narrative flow. Barring repeated phrases and the aforementioned omitted sentences, Mahler's story progresses at roughly the same rate as the poem.

Mahler does, however, manipulate the dramatic qualities of the poem. In the first stanza, the poem shows quotation marks around the words "Gewinn' es Kunst, gewinn' es Glück, Dank soll er davon tragen" (Whether the winner has art or luck, he will receive thanks), indicating them as part of the cuckoo's coaxing the nightingale into the contest. Mahler assigns those words to the narrator. He also blurs the line between narrator and characters at the very end. The final statement, "Kukuk! Kukuk! Ija!,"

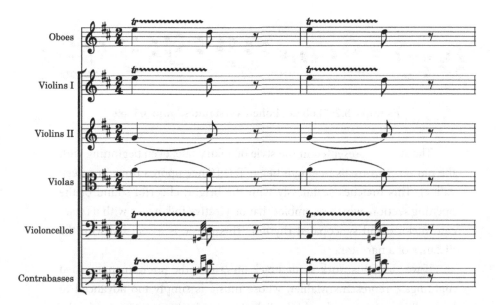

Example 8.1: "Lob des hohen Verstandes," mm. 25–26

should come from the cuckoo and the donkey, but the lack of quotation marks in the song text renders it ambiguous.

The poem features a somewhat regular rhythmic pattern, which Mahler follows at the beginning of the song. This does not remain the case, however. Beginning with the first hint that something droll and humorous is taking place—the cuckoo's comment that the donkey's large ears allow him to hear the best, making him the prime candidate to serve as judge—Mahler begins to unravel the rhythmic regularity, using repetition and animal sounds. The more outrageous the story becomes, the more peculiarly the stanzaic rhythm follows. Mahler morphs the poem's regular six-line stanzas into verses of seven, nine, four, and eight lines each.

Clearly Mahler recognized the humorous qualities of the song. He told Bauer-Lechner in the summer of 1898, "You will laugh when you hear it," and small musical cues inform the audience of the song's jocular nature. Those who see it performed live will witness the performance direction at measure 12 requiring the clarinets to point their bells upward ("Schalltrichter in die Höhe!"), and even listeners to recordings will hear the exaggerated trills which occur in measures 25–26 and 52 (see Example 8.1).

Example 8.2: "Lob des hohen Verstandes," mm. 65–69

The story is presented in the style of a fairy tale, even beginning with the phrase "Einstmals in einem tiefen Tal" (Once upon a time, in a deep valley). This matches seamlessly with the bright, cheerful sound of the opening section, which resembles that of a festive folk dance with its staccato melody and syncopated rhythm. This music is associated with the distance of a narrator.

If we view this work as an attack on critics, the poor, unappreciated nightingale represents Mahler, whose music is simply too advanced to be readily understood by the foolish (i.e. the donkey). Interestingly, the nightingale never speaks directly in the song. An imitation of nightingale song can be heard in the accompaniment only as the musical language begins to change and the singing contest begins.[25] She is essentially robbed of her voice's agency by the circumstances in which she has found herself.

The nightingale's contest entry, played by the flutes, appears in Example 8.2. At the same time, the nightingale's own silence in the face of the donkey's foolishness and the cuckoo's prank demonstrates her stoicism and nobility. In much the same way, Mahler did not outwardly address his critics but instead wrote about his critical defeats in letters home and in carefully concealed musical comments, such as this song.

We know that Mahler viewed the donkey as a symbol of critical ignorance by his own statement, made soon after the composition of "Lob des hohen Verstandes," regarding critics of the "Blumenstuck" movement of his Second Symphony (among his most accessible symphonic writing): "They have devoured it *as donkeys eat hay*, without even guessing at its real meaning and true form."[26] In literature, "The donkey is a symbol of bad principles. He is the 'bad horse,' stubborn, dumb, and lazy,"[27] precisely how Mahler perceived many of his critics. The cheerful dance tune that Mahler chose to accompany his tale ironically serves

Example 8.3: "Lob des hohen Verstandes," mm. 86–90

to underline the same principle; those who simply enjoy the work as a pretty folk song with funny animal sounds have entirely missed the point.

Mahler also used this song to take a poke at some of his more critically successful composer colleagues. The melody sung during the cuckoo's presentation for the singing contest actually imitates a donkey call, rather than a typical cuckoo song, which, just like the nightingale song, appears at first only in the accompaniment. (see Example 8.3). The cuckoo's natural call does not appear in the vocal melody until the final line of the song, after he has been declared the victor. In other words, the cuckoo compromises his own natural sound to appeal to the donkey in order to win the contest. Through this melodic setting, Mahler subtly calls to task composers who would manipulate their own musical styles in order to garner favor with the critics. In the French literary tradition, the cuckoo is associated with feelings of jealousy, such as what a mediocre composer might feel toward Mahler's innovative works.[28] And by placing his competition in the role of the conniving cuckoo, Mahler has taken the opportunity to subtly accuse his competitors of betraying their own creative expression in exchange for critical and commercial success.

Mahler's use of the accompaniment, rather than the vocalist, to serve as the birds' voices has a disorienting effect. One would expect the nightingale's words to sound beautiful and the cuckoo song to sound characteristically silly, but neither bird's contest entry fulfills that expectation. Denying the listener the satisfaction of fulfillment adds to the absurdity of the situation and lends to the true meaning of the song.

212   HIDDEN TREASURES

Of course, Mahler did not want to make the ballad's message *too* clear, as after all, he ultimately did want the song to be commercially and critically successful. Initially, he titled the song "Lob der Kritik" (In Praise of Criticism), but he later changed it to "Lob des hohen Verstandes" (In Praise of a Higher Intellect), lessening its harshness. While perhaps even more bitterly ironic, the change made the message a good deal subtler.

"Ablösung im Sommer"

A very similar song, "Ablösung im Sommer," also featuring a cuckoo and a nightingale, addressed Mahler's audience rather than the press. The famously decadent society of *fin-de-siècle* Vienna was exceedingly proud of its cultural history, and the rising middle class clamored to display their long-sought sophistication by emulating the aristocracy and publicly demonstrating their interest in the arts by attending the symphony and the opera in droves. These new audiences viewed enjoying music and art as a marker of sophistication that could publicly declare their newly achieved social status, particularly in Vienna with its long-held position as the cultural capital of Europe.[29] Mere attendance at the concert hall did not, however, ensure comprehension of the works performed. At the same time that more and more people were attending performances, the development of new modernist techniques began producing increasingly complex music.[30] So more and more people were in the audience, but fewer and fewer really appreciated what they experienced. Their presence was more "to be seen" rather than "to see." Theodor Helm reported on the January 14, 1900 concert of the Vienna Philharmonic in which Mahler premiered several of his *Wunderhorn* songs: "Mahler's purpose was to draw attention to himself as a composer. The fashion-conscious public responded with insatiable applause."[31] One can imagine the scenario as that from the fable of "The Emperor's New Clothes," in which the middle class would risk exposing their "vulgar, peasant roots" by admitting that they did not comprehend the music they heard. And so, while the seats remained full and the spectators feigned interest, the true message behind Mahler's music failed to be understood by the majority of his audience. Leon Botstein equates this lack of "musical literacy" among Viennese middle-class audiences with

Mahler's Responses to Critics and Audiences   213

the new-found popularity of lighter genres, such as the operetta, and increased performances of programmatic works.[32] This requirement to pander to an overwhelmingly ignorant audience seeking a "road map for music" explains, in part, Mahler's well-documented ambivalence toward concert programs. Unlike the cuckoo in "Lob des hohen Verstandes," Mahler indicated that he would never compose his music to cater to the whims of his audience. As he wrote to his future wife:

> If, one day, one of my works should finally come to be heard and understood, (I've already been fighting against shallowness and incomprehension and experiencing all the disappointments, nay misery of a pioneer for fifteen years), and particularly in Vienna, where, after all, people have an instinctive conception of my personality, this should no more bother you or make you distrust my work than does the incomprehension and hostility. The important thing is never to let oneself be guided by the opinion of one's contemporaries and, in both one's life and one's work, to continue steadfastly on one's way without letting oneself be either defeated by failure or diverted by applause.[33]

A similarly nondiscerning audience to that in Vienna is forced to make an important musical decision in "Ablösung im Sommer." The animals of the glen have learned that the cuckoo, who always provided their musical entertainment, has died, and they are forced to find a new source of amusement. "Who then should help us pass the time all summer long?" The very next line of text recommends the nightingale as the new performer: "Oh, that should be Mrs. Nightingale! She sits on a green branch... She sings and springs, is always happy!" The animals do not select the nightingale on the merits of her musical prowess, which would clearly be an improvement over the deceased cuckoo, but instead she is chosen based on her proximity and pleasant demeanor.

Arnim and Brentano identified the text as originating in a "Musikbuch," and Bode specifies that Johann Ott wrote the song lyrics in 1544.[34] Mahler's adaptation supplies an additional stanza, furthering the story.

Sharing many musical similarities with "Lob des hohen Verstandes," "Ablösung im Sommer" nonetheless utilizes a different formal structure to

214   HIDDEN TREASURES

Table 8.2: Text comparison for "Ablösung im Sommer"

Ablösung (Boxberger)	Ablösung im Sommer (Mahler)	Change in Summer
Kuckuk hat sich zu Tod gefallen	Kukuk hat sich zu Tode gefallen,	The cuckoo has fallen to its death
An einer hohlen Weiden;	Tode gefallen	Fallen to its death
Wer soll uns diesen Sommer lang	an einer grünen Weiden! Weiden! Weiden!	On a green willow, willow, willow!
Die Zeit und Weil vertreiben	Kukuk ist tot! Kukuk ist tot! hat sich zu Tod' gefallen!	The cuckoo is dead! The cuckoo is dead! Fallen to its death
	Wer soll uns denn den Sommer lang	Who then should help us pass the time
	die Zeit und Weil' vertreiben?	All summer long?
	Kukuk! Kukuk!	Cuckoo! Cuckoo!
	Wer soll uns denn den Sommer lang	Who then should help us pass the time
	die Zeit und Weil' vertreiben?	All summer long?
Ei, das soll thun Frau Nachtigall,	Ei! Das soll thun Frau Nachtigall!	Oh, that should be Mrs. Nightingale!
Die sitzt auf grünem Zweige;	Die sitzt auf grünem Zweige!	She sits on a green branch!
Sie singt und springt, ist allzeit froh,	Die kleine, feine Nachtigall, die liebe, süße Nachtigall!	The small, fine nightingale, The lovely, sweet nightingale!
Wenn andre Vögel schweigen.	Sie singt und springt, ist all'zeit froh,	She sings and springs, is always happy,
	Wenn andre Voegel schweigen!	When other birds are silent!
	Wie warten auf Frau Nachtigall,	We wait for Mrs. Nightingale,
	die wohnt im grünen Hage,	Who lives in a green glen,
	und wenn der Kukuk zu Ende ist,	And when the cuckoo is at its end,
	dann fängt sie an zu schlagen!	Then she will begin to sing!

portray these very different sounding birds. The musical materials heard in the contrasting sections of "Ablösung" represent a changing of the guard in terms of musical dominance in the meadow.

Two quatrains make up the source poem. Mahler expands the first stanza into two separate verses, six and five lines respectively, supplements the second stanza with an additional two lines of repeated text, and adds an original quatrain at the end. The instability of Mahler's rhythm and rhyme corresponds to the unsettling truth of the story. Despite the tragic death of their neighbor and friend, the animals of the meadow seem more concerned about their own entertainment than the loss of the cuckoo. Their reasoning for selecting Mrs. Nightingale as his replacement further demonstrates their failure to hear music as anything more meaningful than a pleasant pastime. They ignore the superior musical gifts of the nightingale and choose her merely for convenience.

Mahler imitates the cuckoo call using variations of a simple theme. When represented in the accompaniment, the cuckoo call is comprised of a descending perfect fourth. In the voice, the interval becomes a descending minor third (the conventional interval associated with the creature) (see Examples 8.4 and 8.5).[35]

Even as the text announces that the cuckoo has died, his call continues to serve as the predominant music heard by the animals in the meadow. The call only ceases to dominate the musical space when the animals begin to wonder who can take his place.[36] While the entire glen waits anxiously for the nightingale song to begin, the call of the fallen performer still rings in the animals' minds, as the cuckoo motive appears five more times in the accompaniment before the nightingale's song can finally establish itself as the glen's sole new soundtrack. While the promise of better music lies just on the horizon, and, in fact, has been among them all along, this audience cares not about the quality of musical performance, but only that they hear something, and any song will do. The lack of discernment on the part of the forest animals resonates with what Mahler perceived as ignorance among the members of his audiences, who sought little more than an evening of light entertainment.

Mahler inserts a chromatic passage to accompany those moments where the cuckoo's replacement is discussed. This passage comes to usher in the reign of the nightingale in measures 17–20 and represents the

Example 8.4: "Ablösung im Sommer," m. 1

Example 8.5: "Ablösung im Sommer," mm. 10–11

changing of musical supremacy in measures 50–53 and again in the postlude (see Example 8.6).

The song of the nightingale does not provide as easily recognizable a musical equivalent as that of the cuckoo, but in "Ablösung im Sommer," as in "Lob des hohen Verstandes," the other song that compares the two birds, the nightingale song is more lyrical and complex than that of her cuckoo counterpart. Mahler notates her song in a variety of ways, just as he did for the cuckoo. Each is characterized by a small upward leap followed by three or more descending stepwise pitches (see Example 8.7).

We witness the final struggle for musical hegemony during the final line of the song and the postlude. The cuckoo motives continue to recur, even as the text states "Wenn der Kukuk zu Ende ist, dann fängt sie

Example 8.6: "Ablösung im Sommer," mm. 17–21

Example 8.7: "Ablösung im Sommer," mm. 39–41

an zu schlagen" (As the cuckoo has finished, the nightingale begins). While the first two measures of the postlude use the cuckoo theme, the third measure replaces it with that of the nightingale. Even in death the struggle continues, but the nightingale song always has the final say (see Example 8.8).

In spite of the final triumph of the nightingale, the concerns of the creatures of the meadow seem far more related to the maintaining of their personal entertainment than the actual musical abilities of either songbird. The lack of musical discernment demonstrated by the animals echoes that of Mahler's audiences, who simply attended concerts to show off their social status but failed to embrace the intrinsic value of the music that they heard. Their "shallowness and incomprehension," as Mahler called it, translated to boredom, which critics in turn could use to further justify their negative reviews.

Example 8.8: "Ablösung im Sommer," mm. 63–67

218   HIDDEN TREASURES

"Des Antonius von Padua Fischpredigt"

Viewing the song as a commentary on both audiences and the music press, Mahler confronts another lack of discernment in "Des Antonius von Padua Fischpredigt." The story told by this song and its text have already appeared in Chapter 4, where its ironic telling of the story of a Catholic saint was revealed. However, the song can also be explored as another opportunity for Mahler to speak out against negative critics and audiences.

Upon composing "Antonius," Mahler discussed the song with Bauer-Lechner, saying, "Not one of [the fish] is one iota the wiser for it, even though the Saint has *performed for them*! But only a few people will understand my satire on mankind."[37] With this comment, Mahler provides the opportunity to view the song as more than a story of a lonely priest. Both critics and audiences, as portrayed by the fish, could hear Mahler's, i.e. the saint's, music, but whether they were just not really listening or could not comprehend what was happening, they could not appreciate what the composer had to say. They left the concert hall just as they had entered it, uninformed and filled with negativity.

Many of the most viciously negative reviews Mahler endured came from anti-Semitic critics. These figures, often writing for openly anti-Semitic papers such as the *Deutsche Zeitung, Deutsches Volksblatt, Östdeutsche Rundschau*, and *Kikeriki*, typically refused to give a performance the opportunity to move them, arriving on the scene with preconceived notions that they would not allow themselves to be changed by the sermon, that is, Mahler's music. They only wished to be seen by the gathering crowd and be entertained by whatever negative response may unfold, just like St. Anthony's fish.

Mahler uses a particularly clever musical device to poke fun at inattentive and biased audiences. Much of the song features a swirling motive that on the surface resembles the sound of a flowing river, as seen in measures 16–24 (see Example 8.9.). While one might easily dismiss this motive as setting the scene of Anthony's miraculous sermon, it could also be interpreted as the reeling confusion an uninformed listener might feel when being confronted with something beyond their understanding, as they are intellectually swept away by the current of Mahler's music and

Example 8.9: "Des Antonius von Padua Fischpredigt," mm. 16–24

drown in ideas beyond their capacity. Mahler described this motive as the "thoroughly tipsy-sounding language" of the fish and imagined the aquatic audience "sticking their stiff immovable necks out from the water, and gazing up at St. Anthony with their stupid faces."[38] Neither fish nor humans who made the effort to experience a performance but refused to be moved by it were safe from Mahler's mockery, whether their failure to connect to the message was the result of ignorance or stubbornness.

Mahler's final jab at uninformed listeners begins at measure 132. The text claims, "Fisch' große, Fisch' kleine! Vornehm' und Gemeine! Erheben die Köpfe wie verständ'ge Geschöpfe! Auf Gottes Begehren die Predigt anhören!" (Large fish, little fish! Distinguished and common! Raised their heads like understanding creatures! At God's command to hear the sermon!). This noble proclamation is immediately followed by an extremely chromatic clarinet melody marked "mit humor" (with humor) (see Example 8.10). This passage bears many of the same qualities as the *klezmer*-sounding passage identified in Chapter 4, but its confinement to a single instrument strikes the listener as if only one voice is in on the joke. Once this instrumental interlude ends, the text goes on to describe how the fish returned to their sinful ways as soon as the sermon was over, and only then does the song reveal that despite the appearance of comprehension, the fish left the sermon as foolish as they were before. Similarly, the

Example 8.10: "Des Antonius von Padua Fischpredigt," mm. 148–54, clarinet melody

crowds who flocked to theaters to hear Mahler's music but failed to appreciate and understand what it had to say would leave in the same state as Anthony's fish.

Mahler's music tended to have a polarizing effect on his listeners: most remained either unwaveringly enthusiastic or violently opposed to his works. The composer, for the most part, did not take the opinions of his negative critics and audiences to heart, seeing their response as either ignorance and miscomprehension or even religious bigotry. His light-hearted attitude to negative criticism appears in "Lob des hohen Verstandes," "Ablösung im Sommer," and "Des Antonius von Padua Fischpredigt," among the most amusing examples of Mahler's *Humoresken*. These songs represent the composer's subtly veiled response to his critics and audiences, providing him with a way to defend his music and point out others' misconceptions about his work. Mahler is often quoted as saying "My time will come."[39] Given these responses to those who seemed to believe that his time had not yet arrived, it seems that Mahler was willing to wait.

CHAPTER NINE

Conclusion

Mahler's treatment of the poems he selected from *Des Knaben Wunderhorn* reflected a desire to create something far more meaningful than a collection of quasi-*völkisch* art songs. At every stage of perfecting these songs, from the smallest textual alteration to the grandest musical gesture, Mahler engaged in a subtle and complex act of storytelling. The textual and musical narratives of those stories themselves offered more than simple aesthetic enjoyment; they provided reflections on the cultural, social, and political worlds in which Mahler lived and worked. Yet these situations and the problems they reveal extend beyond Mahler's own place and time. The fact that the origins of these poems were far earlier than Mahler's own age, in a collection of poems with medieval roots, is the first indication of the long history of the themes that he chose to develop. Rumination on war, romantic fidelity, religion, gender roles, psychology, poverty, and the appreciation of art neither began in the latter half of the nineteenth century nor ended at the start of the twentieth. These songs have a certain sense of transcending time and place that lies at the heart of what initially attracted Mahler to their texts.

For each song included, this book has examined the building blocks: the literature Mahler utilized to create his *Wunderhorn* lieder and his methods of musical storytelling. The original poems are products of the folk tradition that have undergone what Vladimir Propp calls the "morphological chain," the gradual changes that occur to an artifact when

222   HIDDEN TREASURES

it is transmitted orally.[1] Mahler entered into this chain, viewing the poems in *Des Knaben Wunderhorn* as material that he could freely adapt to his own purposes without distorting their perpetually evolving essence, or as he himself put it, as "Blocks of stone, which anyone might make his own."[2] Examination of contemporaneous editions of *Des Knaben Wunderhorn* establishes a new hypothesis regarding which versions of the Arnim and Brentano anthology Mahler used as textual sources for each of his songs, which in turn enables us to identify Mahler's often extensive revisions to the poetry and the effect of those changes on the stories being told, which often held significant consequences for the commentary on the world Mahler embedded within the songs.

Detailed examination of the compositional and narrative devices Mahler uses in the songs illustrates his richly varied approach to musical storytelling. In the emulation of the style of a poetic narrator, Mahler often employed his music as a nonverbal authoritative voice, using musical sound to distort the temporal progression of a story, allowing the events to "fast forward" during an instrumental interlude or to allow a theme to serve as a recall device of events from the past. Words, sounds, and their subtle interactions each lend a distinct layer of hermeneutic meaning. Many of these examples have grappled with Mahler's inherent musical and textual tension between the traditional and the modern and his narrative use of song form. The various techniques, both textual and musical, that Mahler employed to bring these stories to life served to make these songs reflections of his cultural, social, and political environments.

Scholars frequently view *fin-de-siècle* Vienna, with its development in music, art, literature, and science, as the birthplace of cultural modernism. Though we have since granted Mahler a central role in these developments, his work has not always been so well regarded. His music's reception speaks to many complex issues at play during this period. Mahler used some of his *Wunderhorn* songs as platforms to express his frustration with his detractors, for instance by using the foolish donkey called upon to judge a woodland singing contest in "Lob des hohen Verstandes" to represent his less informed, anti-modernist critics; by equating the undiscerning woodland creatures in "Ablösung im Sommer" with Viennese audiences more concerned with "seeing and being seen" at the concert hall than in actually listening to quality

CONCLUSION   223

music; and by comparing the inattentive fish in "Des Antonius von Padua Fischpredigt" to critics and audiences who failed to even attempt to understand his proto-modernist style. These songs represent Mahler's side of an ongoing dialogue with his critics and audience, enabling him to respond to negative criticism by musical means.

The meanings in folk poetry and fairy tales such as those found in *Des Knaben Wunderhorn* have long been the focus of psychoanalytic approaches which examine fairy tales as, among other things, tools for teaching culturally important values to the young.[3] Particularly fruitful Freudian insights emerge from analysis of songs such as "Wo die schönen Trompeten blasen" and "Der Schildwache Nachtlied," which we can interpret and understand on a deeper level by applying Freud's work on dreams and the unconscious, while "Selbstgefühl" and "Lied des Verfolgten im Turm" serve as instances of Freud's defense mechanisms in action.

This poetry also offered observations that Mahler could apply to various other situations in his life. He explored aspects of Christianity prior to his 1896 baptism in three songs which he utilized as symphonic movements: "Urlicht," "Das himmlische Leben," and "Es sungen drei Engel." "Starke Einbildungskraft" and "Verlor'ne Müh'!" can be interpreted as tools for the cultural indoctrination of young girls and women in his life, keeping with the tradition of folk songs used as didactic tools. "Um schlimme Kinder artig zu machen," "Ich ging mit Lust," "Trost im Unglück," "Aus! Aus!," and "Scheiden und Meiden" shed light on how Mahler viewed his relationships with women, particularly in the area of romantic fidelity. Some songs served the purpose of giving release to his feelings about being "the other man" and in an adulterous affair, others expressed his frustrations concerning the unrequited love of Natalie Bauer-Lechner, and still others demonstrated the intensity of his own feelings when in love.

Some of the *Wunderhorn* lieder also reflect Mahler's youthful interest in politics, particularly utopian socialism and anti-militarism. "Das irdische Leben" serves most obviously as a commentary on a society that allows the poor to suffer needlessly, but also suggests a further significance, which is evidenced by his comment to Bauer-Lechner that the song disguises more a metaphysical than an economic interpretation.[4] We see similar references to the poor in "Rheinlegendchen" and "Wer hat dies Liedlein erdacht?" Mahler privileges spiritual nourishment above physical

224   HIDDEN TREASURES

necessity, betraying practicality for enlightenment, which, one might argue, indicates that he never truly understood the plight of the poor in the first place.

Mahler expressed his political views, particularly with regard to anti-militarism, in several of the *Wunderhorn* lieder. Analyses of "Revelge," "Der Tamboursg'sell," "Zu Straßburg auf der Schanz," and "Nicht Wieder-sehen!" call into question familiar theories about Mahler's fascination with military music and encourage a rethinking of the connections between his pacifist views and the philosophical readings he encountered as a student at the University of Vienna.

While I have attempted to categorize each song within a specific category for the purpose of analysis and to simplify organization, many of these songs could easily be applied to several of the groupings I have identified. Allowing each song to be examined through different lenses would allow for new interpretations and observations to emerge. As an example, "Wo die schönen Trompeten blasen," with its story of a late-night visit to a maiden from her soldier who is off at war, could easily be identified as a story speaking out against the horrors of war (espe-cially if one accepts the interpretation that it is not the soldier himself but his ghost, as I have suggested in Chapter 6). The same song could be viewed from the perspective of Mahler on love and romance. The distinct musical soundscapes afforded the characters of the maiden and the soldier could contribute to a discussion of gender roles. One could even argue that, as the Torah forbids attempting to communicate with the dead, the ghostly visitor might be part of Mahler's spiritual journey to move beyond his Jewish upbringing. Through each of these lenses, different characteristics of the single song might be brought to light, and this same exercise could prove equally fruitful with many of the *Wunder-horn* lieder. In short, the songs are endlessly complex and connect to one another in countless ways.

One topic that has been referenced less than one might expect up to this point is Mahler's *Wunderhorn* symphonies. His Second, Third, and Fourth Symphonies were composed between 1888 and 1900, concurrently with the songs. The reasoning for this lacuna is simple; the songs deserve to be viewed in their own right, not merely as what Raymond Knapp calls

CONCLUSION 225

"a decidedly odd compositional crutch" or a stepping stone to works that Knapp believes "simply matter more than songs, in terms of not only his career and legacy, but also of their dramatic possibilities, cultural status, expressive power, and capacity to make a difference."[5] As several of the songs are either explicitly or conceptually borrowed in the symphonies, it can nonetheless serve our understanding of both the songs and the works that use them to see if the commentaries embedded in Mahler's combinations of music and text provided in the previous chapters are able to withstand their "symphonic metamorphoses."

The use of a song in a symphony is not simply a matter of musical borrowing, especially for a composer as focused on musical meaning as Mahler. Once an established composition is transplanted into a different setting, it takes on a new network of meanings: those implied by the original work, those inferred from the new context, and those that come from any changes made to the original composition. In some ways, the adoption of an earlier work into a new context can serve to reinforce its initial meanings. In other ways, new contextual cues can serve to negate those original word and music relations, leaving the song within the symphony with a completely revised purpose and function.[6] We see examples of these approaches in Mahler's use of "Des Antonius von Padua Fischpredigt" and "Ablösung im Sommer" as the scherzo movements of his Second and Third Symphonies.

The Scherzo of Mahler's Second Symphony relies heavily on the melodic and accompaniment material in "Des Antonius von Padua Fischpredigt." However, as the third movement of a symphony often referred to as the "Resurrection Symphony" due to its reference to Friedrich Gottlieb Klopstock's chorale "Die Auferstehung" (though the subtitle was not specifically given by Mahler), one might more readily identify with the religious aspects of Mahler's song, rather than those based on musical criticism as discussed in Chapter 8. Three different descriptions of the Scherzo written by Mahler have survived; two were written in letters shortly after the symphony was completed, and the third was written years later for a concert program that ultimately was not released to the public. Each of these three descriptions demonstrates Mahler's shifting conceptions of the meaning of this movement, but they hold one theme in common: that of alienation:

226   HIDDEN TREASURES

When you wake out of this sad dream, and must re-enter life, confused as it is, it happens easily that this always-stirring, never-resting, never-comprehensible pushing that is life becomes *horrible* to you, like the motion of dancing figures in a brightly lit ballroom, into which you are peering from outside, in this dark night from such a *distance* that you can *not* hear the *music* they dance to! The life seems *meaningless* to you, like a horrible chimera, that you wrench yourself out of with a horrible cry of disgust.[7]

The second and third movements are episodes from the life of the fallen hero.... What I have expressed in the scherzo can only be described visually. When one watches a dance from a distance, without hearing the music, the revolving motions of the partners seem absurd and pointless. Likewise, to someone who has lost himself and his happiness, the world seems crazy and confused, as if deformed by a concave mirror. The scherzo ends with the fearful scream of a soul that has experienced this torture.[8]

A spirit of disbelief and negation has seized him. He is bewildered by the bustle of appearances and he loses his perception of childhood and the profound strength that love alone can give. He despairs both of himself and of God. The world and life begin to seem unreal. Utter disgust for every form of existence and evolution seizes him in an iron grasp, torments him until he utters a cry of despair.[9]

In all of these descriptions, the protagonist finds himself disgusted by circumstances he cannot understand. The distant dancers' moving and spinning to an unheard accompaniment renders their motions "absurd and pointless." Similar themes of a spurned lover watching his beloved dance with another and grappling with the same sense of alienation appear in other works, and Mahler subtly addresses those commonalities. The final bars of Mahler's song and the related passage in the symphonic movement feature a brief quotation from the conclusion of Schumann's ninth song from *Dichterliebe*, "Das ist ein Flöten und Geigen," in which

CONCLUSION   227

the protagonist watches as the woman he loves celebrates her wedding to another man with dancing. The 3/8 meter of Mahler's song and movement also echoes that of the second movement of Berlioz's *Symphonie fantastique*, wherein the protagonist encounters the object of his obsession at a ball, longingly watching her dance from a distance. The same "absurd and pointless" interpretation of an event might be attributed to a listener who hears new music being praised as innovative, which, alas, he cannot comprehend. Not unlike the children's fable "The Emperor's New Clothes," rather than admit ignorance about music on the cusp of modernity, many critics and audience members simply wrote it off. Rather than despairing about a "world [that] seems crazy and confused," these critics could simply seek to destroy the person who made them feel that way in the first place. Given this explanation, Mahler's movement might even be seen to be sympathizing with his critics, while at the same time pointing out their ignorance. Knapp uses the core idea of alienation as an interpretive tool for Mahler's Scherzo, and one of his observations ties the interpretation of "Des Antonius von Padua Fischpredigt" in Chapters 4 and 8 to the Scherzo quite nicely:

> This was Mahler's perspective, as a Jew contemplating conversion, extended through melodramatically romantic sensibilities to project the experiences of someone forced to wander the world without a home of his own, disgusted by the emptiness he sees around him.... The scherzo suggests even more vitally a perspective that is indelibly Jewish, which in a resisting outsider fights against the tide of absorption into the dominant flow of a hostile culture.[10]

Just as Mahler's critics experienced alienation when hearing his music, the composer himself lived with that sense of disconnection every day. And so, Mahler's symphonic movement both reinforces the message of his song and inverts it, demonstrating that, as oxymoronic as it may seem, alienation is a universal tendency.

Mahler's next instance of song-borrowing for a symphony also served to create a scherzo, this time for the third movement of Symphony no. 3. For this movement, Mahler returned to a song he had composed several

228   HIDDEN TREASURES

years earlier, "Ablösung im Sommer." Rather than using it to generate music for the entire movement, as he had done with "Antonius" in his Second Symphony, Mahler only uses themes from "Ablösung" for the opening and closing sections of his scherzo form, including a newly composed trio section featuring the well-known posthorn solo. Just like in the song, the forest animals in the symphonic movement are confronted by something new; in the song, the dead cuckoo is hesitantly replaced by the nightingale, bringing a different, more aesthetically pleasing (though seemingly unappreciated) sound. The arrival of the posthorn in the Scherzo also represents a change, though this new element is potentially more threatening. John J. Sheinbaum suggests that the posthorn represents an "intrusion of modernity" into the forest.[11] Timothy Freeze views the disruption as something far more complex: "The posthorn episodes thus hang in an interpretational balance poised between mutually exclusive alternatives: rural and urban, past and present, metaphysical and material, the epitome of beauty and vulgarity."[12] To the animals of the forest, however, the true nature of the sound is in fact irrelevant; it is an ominous presence that will disrupt their peaceful existence forever. Unlike in the song, where the animals appreciate the availability of the nightingale (if not necessarily her gifts), the intrusion of the posthorn is met with fear and trepidation. But the new arrival also represents change, and slowly, the animals of the Scherzo will be forced to learn to adapt to life with their new companion, as their soundscape will never be the same. Whereas Mahler's song spoke of a lack of discernment among his audiences, his Scherzo trumpets in (quite literally) the arrival of musical modernity, posing it as an unstoppable force to which audiences will have to adapt.

Donald Mitchell provides perhaps the most succinct description of the merging of the *Wunderhorn* aesthetic with Mahler's first four symphonies. He identifies quotations and allusions to the songs in the works and sums up his findings by observing that:

> It seems that Mahler regarded the four symphonies as a "perfectly self-contained tetralogy." If they are such—and perhaps "perfectly self-contained" is something of an exaggeration—it is surely because they all in various ways employ song, and more

CONCLUSION   229

particularly *Wunderhorn* songs, or songs in the *Wunderhorn* manner (i.e. the *Gesellen* cycle), as a principal compositional technique.[13]

The sheer variety of tone colors, thematic areas, use of popular and *völkisch* tunes contrasted with elegant and lush orchestral flourishes, and formal constructions found in the symphonies owes its origins to those found in the poetry of Arnim and Brentano's *Des Knaben Wunderhorn* and Mahler's interpretations of those texts.

Indubitably, Mahler's use of *Wunderhorn* songs in his symphonies greatly manipulates the meanings one finds in the musical materials themselves. Nonetheless, it is striking that the commentaries embedded in the songs, described in earlier chapters, continue to resonate in their new symphonic contexts. It is for this reason that the songs themselves hold the key to understanding Mahler's critiques of the world around him. It was there that these judgments first appeared, and his reuse of some of the musical characteristics of the songs does not diminish or alter their ability to challenge his surroundings but instead intensifies their reach and scope.

After he composed his final *Wunderhorn* setting, "Der Tamboursg'sell," in 1901, Mahler's choices in song texts took a dramatic shift. He took the texts of his next ten songs, including the five songs from the cycle *Kindertotenlieder*, composed between 1901 and 1904, from Friedrich Rückert. In 1908 and 1909, he set translations of Chinese poetry as the cycle *Das Lied von der Erde*. Mahler did not allow himself the same level of freedom with the texts in these later songs as he did with the *Wunderhorn* texts, seeming to view these poems as products of an artistic rather than a folk tradition, and as such, no longer open to adaptation. The later songs also lack much of the innocence and naïvety of the *Wunderhorn* texts. It is unclear what might have brought about this change in Mahler's musical style as reflected in his songs, but it may not be entirely coincidental that in 1901, the same year he ceased his *Wunderhorn* composition, Mahler suffered a nearly fatal hemorrhage and met his future wife Alma. One could certainly imagine these life-changing events causing him to develop beyond the need for the child-like and didactic nature of the *Wunderhorn* poetry. His newer songs

230   HIDDEN TREASURES

could then reflect that he had learned the lessons embedded in his earlier work and was ready to focus on his newly found maturity, a sense of his own mortality, and with it his eagerness for marriage and family.

After the composer's death, however, these songs, as with much of Mahler's work, fell dramatically out of favor. Many factors contributed to this decline, including political, religious, and cultural ones, as Peter Franklin explains:

> By the 1920s, tensions that had marked the reception of his music during Mahler's lifetime were ever more explicitly politicized and polarized in a Europe soon to witness the rise of fascism. On the one hand he was a composer whose ethnic origins supposedly prevented him from achieving the Germanic "greatness" to which his symphonies aspired; on the other his achievement was construed, in perhaps no less partisan a fashion, as consisting in his modern, ironizing approach to that very "greatness" of aspiration.[14]

The very characteristics that Mahler instilled in his *Wunderhorn* settings to provide them with a universal and timeless quality were seen by many in the early decades of the twentieth century as an excuse to dismiss the works. Once extracted from their *fin-de-siècle* Viennese context, the folk-like qualities abundant in Mahler's *Wunderhorn* ballads sometimes appeared to be mere kitsch. German audiences, naturally, did not have the opportunity to hear much of Mahler's work during the years of the Third Reich, as his music was blamed by the Nazis and decried by musicologists such as Rudolf Gerber and Hans Joachim Moser for "initiating a period of decline" in German music.[15] As a result, Mahler reception declined dramatically during the 1930s and '40s. The primary exception to this occurred at the Concertgebouw Orchestra in Amsterdam, where Willem Mengelberg continued to champion Mahler's works with performances of his songs and symphonies throughout the 1920s, '30s, and '40s.[16]

Limitations in early recording technology also greatly impacted Mahler's reception at the beginning of the twentieth century. Mitchell writes of listening to the Ninth Symphony and *Das Lied von der Erde* on 78 rpm discs recorded in the late 1930s by Bruno Walter. As this recording of

CONCLUSION   231

the symphony lasts over seventy minutes, and one side of a ten-inch 78 rpm record lasts only about three minutes, this must have been a frustrating exercise.[17] Edward R. Reilly also notes that scholarly attention to Mahler in these early decades of the twentieth century was scanty, noting that only three dissertations on the composer were completed before World War II, and two of them were written under the direction of Mahler's friend, the musicologist Guido Adler, at the University of Vienna.[18]

After the war, however, interest in Mahler's music gradually resumed. The 1948 invention of the 33⅓ rpm long-playing record, combined with the 1957 advent of stereophonic recording, allowed listeners to experience Mahler in a whole new, much more lifelike way. Also influential in the Mahler revival of the 1960s were Leonard Bernstein's recordings and performances and Theodor Adorno's goal to "revise the judgment on Gustav Mahler passed not only by the Hitler regime but by the history of music in the fifty years since the composer's death."[19] This gradual return to public awareness can be observed in the dramatic increase in recordings and concert performances of the songs and the related symphonies during the 1960s to '80s. Though in recent decades those numbers have begun to level out, they remain high, demonstrating the lasting popularity of the songs.

We find in Mahler's *Wunderhorn* songs an unprecedented set of instances in which a composer draws musical inspiration from a text but affords himself such a level of freedom with both text and music that, in some cases ("Ich ging mit Lust," "Um schlimme Kinder artig zu machen," "Scheiden und Meiden," and "Der Schildwache Nachtlied" come immediately to mind), subtle textual changes and musical nuances completely change potential meanings for the resulting story. In other cases, such as "Wer hat dies Liedlein erdacht?" and "Wo die schönen Trompeten blasen," the composer cobbled his lyric out of multiple poems, using someone else's building blocks to create a story all his own. Mahler's free adaptation of the *Wunderhorn* poetry provides a uniquely revealing source for understanding the nature and effect of his artistic interventions. They provide the only example of Mahler approaching well-known poetry as if it were completely mutable, easily adaptable for his own purposes, simply just another link in the chain of its oral tradition. I know of no other example

232 Hidden Treasures

of a composer viewing someone else's poetry with such an extreme level of freedom.

Adding the simplest gestures can take on the most profound meanings when viewed as aspects of storytelling. The simple addition of an onomatopoetic cuckoo call in "Um schlimme Kinder" seems on the surface to be little more than a charming instance of *völkisch* kitsch, but also contains a hidden message to a forbidden lover. Mahler transforms "Der Schildwache Nachtlied" through sweeping musical gestures from a simple dialogue between two lovers during wartime to an elaborate dream, rich in potential for Freudian analysis, or, just as easily, into a commentary on the tragedies of war. Textual changes and musical cues alter the confession of an unfaithful lover in "Ich ging mit Lust" to a somewhat ambiguous admonishment for young women just entering the age of romantic involvement. The song of a nightingale reveals to the young woman in "Wo die schönen Trompeten blasen" that she has not been reunited with her beloved soldier, but rather that his ghost has come to warn her of her own impending doom.

Seemingly minor changes have enormous hermeneutic consequences in these songs, which Mahler used to create critical observations of his environment. These critiques are not always apparent to the casual observer; they are the true "hidden treasures" of these songs.

Notes

Chapter One: Gustav Mahler's Lieder from *Des Knaben Wunderhorn*: Questions of Conception, History, and Genre

1   Natalie Bauer-Lechner, *Recollections of Gustav Mahler*, trans. Dika Newlin, ed. Peter Franklin (Cambridge: Cambridge University Press, 1980), 32.

2   E. Mary Dargie, *Music and Poetry in the Songs of Gustav Mahler* (Bern: Peter Lang, 1981), 114.

3   Donald Mitchell, *Gustav Mahler: The Wunderhorn Years* (Woodbridge: Boydell Press, 2005), 113–17, 127–29, 139–44.

4   Letter dated March 2, 1905. Knud Martner, ed. *Selected Letters of Gustav Mahler* (New York: Ferrar, Straus and Giroux, 1979): 284.

5   Jack Zipes, "The Potential of Liberating Fairy Tales for Children," *New Literary History* 13 (1982): 315.

6   Achim von Arnim, "Von Volksliedern," in *Des Knaben Wunderhorn: Alte deutsche Lieder gesammelt von Achim von Arnim und Clemens Brentano*, ed. Heinz Rölleke (Frankfurt am Main: Insel Verlag, 2003), 431.

7   Arnim, "Von Volksliedern," 402.

8   Henry-Louis de La Grange, *Mahler*, vol. 1 (Garden City, NY: Doubleday, 1973), 759; Heinz Rölleke, "Nachwort," in *Des Knaben Wunderhorn: Alte deutsche Lieder gesammelt von Achim von Arnim und Clemens Brentano*, ed. Heinz Rölleke (Frankfurt am Main: Insel Verlag, 2003), 1195–96.

9   Heinz Rölleke is the leading modern-day authority on *Des Knaben Wunderhorn*. His critical edition of the anthology was published in 1987 by Reclam in Stuttgart. An abbreviated edition of his work, published by Insel Verlag, appeared in 2003. In addition, he has published numerous

234   NOTES TO PAGES 10–12

articles and essays about the anthology and Mahler's work with it, including "'Kriegslieder': Achim von Arnims Imitation eines Fliegenden Blattes im Jahre 1806," *Jahrbuch für Volksliedforschung* 17 (1971): 73–80; "Gustav Mahlers 'Wunderhorn' Lieder: Textgrundlagen und Textauswahl," *Jahrbuch des Freien Deutschen Hochstifts* (1981): 370–78; "'Des Knaben Wunderhorn' und seine Stellung zu Volks- und Kirchenlied," *Jahrbuch für Liturgik und Hymnologie* 28 (1984): 27–38; "'Felsblöcke, aus denen jeder das Seine formen darf': Gustav Mahlers Rezeption der Kasseler Literatur: 'Des Knaben Wunderhorn' und Grimms 'Märchen,'" in *Gustav Mahler: Jahre der Entscheidung in Kassel 1883–1885*, eds. Louis Kolitz et al. (Kassel: Weber & Wiedemayer, 1990), 96–103. Karl-Maria Guth published his edition with Hoffenberg in Berlin.

10   Tom Cheesman, *The Shocking Ballad Picture Show: German Popular Literature and Cultural History* (Oxford: Berg, 1994). Cheesman examines the traditions of the "picture singers" who brought news and gossip from town to town, the stories told through their songs, paintings, *fliegende Blätter*, and the impact of this folk tradition on poets such as Goethe.

11   Rölleke, "Nachwort," 1193.

12   Rölleke, "Nachwort," 1193.

13   The image of the white crow signifies a seemingly impossible instance that refutes one's previous assumptions; that is, one only needs to see one white crow to disprove that all crows are black. Arnim is telling his readers that the existence of any remnant of great folk poetry from the illiterate peasant communities is evidence enough to prove that the tradition exists. Arnim, "Von Volksliedern," 420.

14   La Grange, *Mahler*, 1:759.

15   Other members of the Circle included its namesake, the journalist and politician Engelbert Pernerstorfer, poet and journalist Siegfried Lipiner, professor Max von Gruber, composer Hugo Wolf, historian and politician Heinrich Friedjung, historian and poet Richard von Kralik, and politician Victor Adler. The Circle is discussed extensively in William J. McGrath, *Dionysian Art and Populist Politics in Austria* (New Haven, CT: Yale University Press, 1974).

16   La Grange, *Mahler*, 1:759.

17   Quoted in August Heinrich Hoffmann von Fallersleben, "Zur Geschichte des Wunderhorns," *Weimarisches Jahrbuch für Deutsche Sprache, Literatur und Kunst* 2 (1855): 263–65.

18   Karl Bode, *Die Bearbeitung der Vorlagen Des Knaben Wunderhorn*, Palaestra: Untersuchungen und Texte aus der deutschen und englischen Philologie, eds. Alois Brandl, Gustav Roethe, and Erich Schmidt, 76 (1909).

NOTES TO PAGES 12–15   235

19 Ferdinand Reiser, *"Des Knaben Wunderhorn" und seine Quellen: Ein Beitrag zur Geschichte des deutschen Volksliedes und der Romantik* (1908; reprint, Hildesheim: Georg Olms Verlag, 1983).

20 Fallersleben, "Zur Geschichte des Wunderhorns," quoted and translated by Jon W. Finson, "The Reception of Gustav Mahler's *Wunderhorn Lieder*," *Journal of Musicology* 5 (1987): 94. Emphasis mine.

21 La Grange, *Mahler*, 1:171; Guido Adler, "Gustav Mahler," *Biographisches Jahrbuch und deutscher Nekrolog* 16 (1911): 30. The Webers were Captain Karl von Weber, grandson of composer Carl Maria von Weber, and his wife Marion. They had enlisted Mahler to reconstruct the older composer's incomplete opera *Die drei Pintos*.

22 Mitchell, *The Wunderhorn Years*, 118.

23 Herta Blaukopf, "Mahler an der Universität: Versuch, eine biographische Lücke zu schließen," in *Neue Mahleriana: Essays in Honour of Henry-Louis de La Grange on his Seventieth Birthday*, ed. Günther Weiss (New York: Peter Lang, 1997), 1–16; Herta Blaukopf, "The Young Mahler, 1875–1880: Essay in Situational Analysis after Karl R. Popper," in *Mahler Studies*, ed. Stephen E. Hefling (Cambridge: Cambridge University Press, 1997), 1–24.

24 Alma Mahler, *Gustav Mahler: Memories and Letters*, ed. Donald Mitchell, trans. Basil Creighton (Seattle: University of Washington Press, 1975), 93.

25 La Grange, *Mahler*, 1:285.

26 Stuart Feder, "Gustav Mahler: A Composer's Childhood: The Auditory Environment," in *Neue Mahleriana: Essays in Honour of Henry-Louis de La Grange on his Seventieth Birthday*, ed. Günther Weiss (New York: Peter Lang, 1997), 30.

27 Fritz Egon Pamer, "Gustav Mahlers Lieder," *Studien zur Musikwissenschaft: Beihefte der Denkmäler der Tonkunst in Österreich* 16 (1929): 116–38; Ernst Klusen, "Die Liedertexte Gustav Mahlers," *Sudetendeutsche Zeitschrift für Volkskunde* 6 (1933): 178–84; Anne Wadmann, "Gustav Mahler en *Des Knaben Wunderhorn*," *Levende Talen* 53 (1966): 681–99; Peter Hamm, "'Von Euch ich Urlaub nimm'...' Zu den von Gustav Mahler vertonten Texten," *Akzente* 24 (1977): 159–67; Kurt von Fischer, "Gustav Mahlers Umgang mit Wunderhorntexten," *Melos/NZ* 2 (1978): 103–7; Rölleke, "Textgrundlagen und Textauswahl," 370–78.

28 Peter Revers, *Mahlers Lieder: Ein musikalischer Werkführer* (Munich: Verlag C. H. Beck, 2000), 77. In an 1892 letter to his sister Justine, Mahler states that he owns "no fewer than 3 copies" of *Des Knaben Wunderhorn*. Jeremy Barham, "Review of *Des Knaben Wunderhorn*, ed. Renate Hilmar-Voit," *Music and Letters* 83 (2002): 331; Stephen McClatchie, ed., *The Mahler Family Letters* (Oxford: Oxford University Press, 2006), 153.

29 Rölleke, "Textgrundlagen und Textauswahl," 370–78.

236   NOTES TO PAGES 15–18

30   Renate Hilmar-Voit, *Im Wunderhorn-Ton: Gustav Mahlers sprachliches Kompositionsmaterial bis 1900* (Tutzing: Hans Schneider, 1988), 20.

31   I also examined an edition edited by Gustav Wendt, published in 1876 in Berlin, but given its age in 1887, when Mahler began composing to the texts, it wasn't a likely candidate.

32   Heinrich Christoph Koch, "Ballade," in *Musikalisches Lexikon* (1802; reprint, Kassel: Bärenreiter, 2001), 211.

33   Friedrich Bremer, "Ballade," in *Handlexikon der Musik: Eine Encyklopädie der ganzen Tonkunst* (Leipzig: Philipp Reclam, 1882), 37.

34   Hugo Riemann, "Ballade," in *Riemanns Musik-Lexikon*, 3rd ed. (Leipzig: Max Hesse, 1887), 69.

35   Hans Joachim Moser, "Ballade," in *Musikalisches Wörterbuch* (Leipzig: B. G. Teubner, 1923), 9.

36   Koch, "Gesang," in *Musikalisches Lexikon*, 662.

37   Bremer, "Gesang," in *Handlexikon der Musik*, 229.

38   Riemann, "Gesang," in *Riemanns Musik-Lexikon*, 326.

39   "Gesang," in *Brockhaus Kleines Konversations-Lexikon*, 5th ed. (Leipzig: F. A. Brockhaus, 1911), 1:671.

40   Koch, "Lied," in *Musikalisches Lexikon*, 901.

41   Bremer, "Lied," in *Handlexikon der Musik*, 399.

42   Riemann, "Lied," in *Riemanns Musik-Lexikon*, 562.

43   "Humoreske," *Brockhaus*, 836.

44   Heinrich Christoph Koch, "Humoristisch," in *Kurzgefaßtes Handwörterbuch der Musik für praktische Tonkünstler und für Dilettanten* (1807; reprint Hildesheim: Georg Olms, 1981), 137.

45   Günter Schnitzler, "Gustav Mahler und die Romantik in *Des Knaben Wunderhorn*," *Musik-Konzepte* 136 (April 2007): 41.

46   Jean Paul Richter, "Course VII. On Humorous Poetry," in *Horn of Oberon: Jean Paul Richter's School of Aesthetics*, trans. Margaret R. Hale (Detroit: Wayne State University Press, 1973), 88.

47   La Grange, *Mahler*, 1:250.

48   Bauer-Lechner, *Recollections*, 130. In 1843, Carl Loewe composed a set of vocal quartets entitled *Fünf Humoresken*, op. 84, though it was an extremely obscure work.

49   Mahler's unorthodox approaches to the idea of genre have been discussed in Hermann Danuser, *Gustav Mahler und seine Zeit* (Laaber: Laaber-Verlag, 1991), 152–84, and in Vera Micznik, "Mahler and 'The Power of Genre,'" *Journal of Musicology* 12 (1994): 129, who wrote, "While Mahler's materials defy absolute generic commitments, their behavior is dependent on the recognition of their generic models. What takes place here is simultaneous affirmation and negation of genre." Unless the listener recognizes how the piece is *supposed* to function, they will not recognize the significance of that function when it breaks down.

NOTES TO PAGES 18–21   237

50   Of course, simultaneous publication of piano and orchestrated songs may have simply been a commercial consideration, as the singing of art songs was still a common form of household entertainment during Mahler's time.

51   Hermann Danuser details the specific issues brought up in this debate in "Der Orchestergesang des Fin de siècle: Eine historische und ästhetische Skizze," *Die Musikforschung* 30 (1977): 425–52. Elizabeth Schmierer expands on the idea to parse out the differences between *Lied* and *Gesang* in both piano arrangements and those written for orchestra, in *Die Orchesterlieder Gustav Mahlers*, Kieler Schriften zur Musikwissenschaft 38 (Kassel: Bärenreiter, 1991), 2–16.

52   Gillian Rodger writes, "The terms 'Ballade' and 'Romanze' have been fluid even in Bürger's day and Goethe's use of 'Ballade' and 'Lied' is equally inconsistent and therefore to a large extent meaningless." "Goethe's 'Ur-Ei'" in Theory and Practice," *The Modern Language Review* 59 (1964): 227.

53   Bauer-Lechner, *Recollections*, 58–59.

Chapter Two: "A final remnant of a sense of duty": Mahler's Anti-Militarist Commentary

1   Alberto Rizzuti, *Sognatori, utopisti e diertori nei Lieder 'militari' di Gustav Mahler* (Torino: Passigli Editori, 1990); Stefan Hanheide, "Das Schicksal des Soldaten in Gustav Mahlers Liedern nach *Des Knaben Wunderhorn*," *Osnabrücker Jahrbuch Frieden und Wissenschaft* 1 (1994): 105–18; Donald Mitchell, "The Last Two 'Wunderhorn' Songs: 'Revelge' and 'Der Tamboursg'sell,'" in *The Mahler Companion*, ed. Donald Mitchell and Andrew Nicholson (Oxford: Oxford University Press, 1999), 232–35; Peter Franklin, "A Soldier's Sweetheart's Mother's Tale? Mahler's Gendered Musical Discourse," in *Mahler and His World*, ed. Karen Painter (Princeton, NJ: Princeton University Press, 2002), 111–25; Isabelle Werck, "Images de l'armée et de la guerre dans la musique de Gustav Mahler," *Revue Musicale de Suisse Romande* 56 (2003): 32–40; Kordula Kraus, "Der Soldat und das Mädchen: Zu ihrer Darstellung in Gustav Mahlers *Wunderhorn*-Liedern," *Musica Austriaca* 23 (2004): 81–97; Albrecht von Massow, "Romantik als Gesellschaftskritik: Mahlers Soldatenlieder," in *Von Volkston und Romantik: Des Knaben Wunderhorn in der Musik*, ed. Antje Tumat and Internationalen Musikfestival Heidelberger Frühling (Heidelberg: Universitätsverlag Winter, 2008), 141–56.

2   Donald Mitchell, *Gustav Mahler: The Early Years* (Woodbridge: Boydell Press, 2003), 1. The military barracks in Iglau sat on the site of a former Dominican monastery, which is now home to the Hotel Gustav Mahler in Iglau. My thanks go to Tereza Petranova of the Hotel Gustav Mahler for her information on the site's history.

238   NOTES TO PAGES 22–24

3   Paul Stefan, *Gustav Mahler: Eine Studie über Persönlichkeit und Werk* (Munich: R. Piper, 1920), 12. Quoted and translated in Mitchell, *The Early Years*, 19.
4   Natalie Bauer-Lechner, *Recollections of Gustav Mahler*, trans. Dika Newlin, ed. Peter Franklin (Cambridge: Cambridge University Press, 1980), 46.
5   Donald Mitchell follows the recollections of Paul Stefan, whose 1910 biography of Mahler identifies the bands heard by Mahler as a child coming from the barracks of Litoměřice, nearly 200 km northwest of Mahler's childhood home; Mitchell, *The Early Years*, 19–20. In his 2010 dissertation, Jason Stephen Heilman notes that the Austrian army had only used the encampment at Iglau intermittently between 1784 and 1883; "O du mein Österreich: Patriotic Music and Multinational Identity in the Austro-Hungarian Empire" (PhD diss., Duke University, 2010), 4. Also see Eugen Brixel, Gunther Martin, and Gottfried Pils, *Das ist Österreichs Militärmusik* (Graz: Edition Kaleioskop, 1982), 316.
6   Theodor Fischer, "Aus Gustav Mahlers Jugendzeit," *Deutsche Heimat* 7 (1931): 264–68.
7   Michael Kennedy, *Mahler*, ed. Stanley Sadie (Oxford: Oxford University Press, 2000), 7.
8   Henry-Louis de La Grange and Sybille Werner, *Gustav Mahler*, vol. 1, *The Arduous Road to Vienna (1860–1897)* (Turnhout: Brepols, 2020), 29.
9   Hanheide, "Das Schicksal des Soldaten," 109.
10 Nicholas Sambanis, Stergios Skaperdas, and William C. Wohlforth, "Nation-Building Through War," *The American Political Science Review* 109 (2015): 279–96.
11 Stefan Zweig, *The World of Yesterday: An Autobiography* (New York: The Viking Press, 1943), 26, 226.
12 Peter Franklin, *The Life of Mahler* (Cambridge: Cambridge University Press, 1997), 13.
13 Herta Blaukopf, "Mahler unter Soldaten," *Nachrichten zur Mahler-Forschung* 49 (2003): 5.
14 Jacques Kornberg, "Vienna, the 1890s: Jews in the Eyes of Their Defenders. (The Verein zur Abwehr des Antisemitismus)," *Central European History* 28 (1995): 162.
15 Marsha L. Rozenblit, "Assimilation and Affirmation: The Jews of Freud's Vienna," in *The Jewish World of Sigmund Freud*, ed. Arnold D. Richards (Jefferson, NC: McFarland & Co., 2010), 30.
16 Carl E. Schorske, *Thinking with History: Explorations in the Passage to Modernism* (Princeton, NJ: Princeton University Press, 1998), 178.
17 Jens Malte Fischer, *Gustav Mahler*, trans. Stewart Spencer (New Haven, CT: Yale University Press, 2013), 83–84.
18 William J. McGrath, *Dionysian Art and Populist Politics in Austria* (New Haven, CT: Yale University Press, 1974), 246.

NOTES TO PAGES 24–40   239

19   McGrath, *Dionysian Art*, 246.

20   Robert S. Wistrich, *The Jews of Vienna in the Age of Franz Joseph* (Oxford: Oxford University Press, 1989), 160.

21   Allen Janik and Stephen Toulmin, *Wittgenstein's Vienna* (New York: Touchstone Books, 1973), 50.

22   Jon W. Finson, "The Reception of Gustav Mahler's *Wunderhorn* Lieder," *Journal of Musicology* 5 (1987): 101.

23   Richard Wagner, *My Life*, trans. Andrew Gray (Middlesex: Echo Library, 1992), 327.

24   Richard Wagner, "On State and Religion," in *Art and Politics*, trans. William Ashton Ellis (Lincoln: University of Nebraska Press, 1995), 17.

25   Walter A. Kaufmann, *Nietzsche: Philosopher, Psychologist, Antichrist* (Princeton, NJ: Princeton University Press, 1974), 307.

26   Friedrich Nietzsche, *Human, All Too Human*, trans. R. J. Hollingdale (Cambridge: Cambridge University Press, 1996), 163.

27   Quoted in Rebekah S. Perry, *Nietzsche on War* (New York: Algora Publishing, 2009), 82.

28   Quoted in Perry, *Nietzsche on War*, 68.

29   Quoted in Perry, *Nietzsche on War*, 69.

30   Friedrich Nietzsche, *Basic Writings of Nietzsche*, trans. Walter Kaufmann (New York: Random House, 2011), 25.

31   Perry, *Nietzsche on War*, 143, 158.

32   Cesare Vasoli, introduction to *Il Mondo come Volontà e Rappresentazione*, by Arthur Schopenhauer (Bari: Laterza, 1968), xi.

33   Arthur Schopenhauer, *The World as Will and Idea*, trans. R. B. Haldane and John Kemp, 2nd ed. (London: Kegan Paul, Trench, Trübner, & Co., 1891), 2:395.

34   Arthur Schopenhauer, *Parerga and Paralipomena: Short Philosophical Essays*, trans. E. F. J. Payne (Oxford: Clarendon Press, 1974), 2:245–46.

35   Peter Revers, *Mahlers Lieder: Ein musikalischer Werkführer* (Munich: Verlag C. H. Beck, 2000), 77.

36   Donald Mitchell, *Gustav Mahler: The Wunderhorn Years* (Woodbridge: Boydell Press, 2005), 139.

37   "Zu Straßburg auf der Schanz" was orchestrated by Luciano Berio in 1986; Gustav Mahler, *Fünf frühe Lieder für Männerstimme und Orchester*, arr. Luciano Berio (Vienna: Universal Editions, 1986).

38   Karl Bode, *Die Bearbeitung der Vorlagen Des Knaben Wunderhorn*, Palaestra: Untersuchungen und Texte aus der deutschen und englischen Philologie, eds. Alois Brandl, Gustav Roethe, and Erich Schmidt, 76 (1909), 318–21; Ferdinand Reiser, *"Des Knaben Wunderhorn" und seine Quellen: Ein Beitrag zur Geschichte des deutschen Volksliedes und der Romantik* (1908; reprint, Hildesheim: Georg Olms Verlag, 1983), 207–8.

240   NOTES TO PAGES 43–57

39 Newlin, *Bruckner, Mahler, Schoenberg* (New York: W. W. Norton, 1978), 127.

40 Matthias Slunitschek, "Nostalgia oder das Deserteursschicksal in 'Zu Straßburg auf der Schanz,'" *Lied und populäre Kultur* 57 (2012): 82.

41 Angelique Chrisafis, "France Pressured to Remember WWI Soldiers Executed for 'Cowardice,'" *The Guardian*, October 1, 2013, https://www.theguardian.com/world/2013/oct/01/france-first-world-war-soldiers-cowardice-executed-memorial.

42 Johann Gottfried Ebel, *Schilderung der Gebirgsvölker der Schweitz* (Leipzig: Wolf, 1802), 2:153, cited in Slunitschek, "Nostalgia," 92.

43 Bauer-Lechner, *Recollections*, 173. The sketch to which Bauer-Lechner refers is held in the Robert Owen Lehman Collection at the Pierpont Morgan Library. The two-page document shows clear evidence of the rushed activity that she describes, and with the exception of a few minor rhythms, a modulation, and some lengthy instrumental interludes, closely resembles the finished product.

44 Bauer-Lechner, *Recollections*, 50.

45 Mitchell, *The Wunderhorn Years*, 139.

46 Bode, *Bearbeitung der Vorlagen*, 275; Reiser, *Seine Quellen*, 219.

47 Carl E. Schorske, "Mahler and Klimt: Social Experience and Artistic Evolution," *Daedelus* 111, no. 3 (1982): 47.

48 Rufus Hallmark, "The Literary and Musical Rhetoric of Apostrophe in *Winterreise*" (conference paper, Annual Meeting of the American Musicological Society, Quebec City, Quebec, November 2, 2007). My appreciation to Dr. Hallmark for sharing his paper with me.

49 On the cover sheet of Mahler's orchestral manuscript for the piece, Mahler has written: "Der Tamboursg'sell"/**Ballade** aus "des Knaben Wunderhorn"/Gustav Mahler. This manuscript is part of the Robert Owen Lehman Collection on loan to the Pierpont Morgan Library in New York, NY.

50 Christopher Marsh, "'The Pride of Noise': Drums and their Repercussions in Early Modern England," *Early Music* 39 (2011): 205.

51 "Drummers Who Deserted," *Journal of the American Revolution*, May 14, 2018, https://allthingsliberty.com.

52 Hallmark, "Literary and Musical Rhetoric."

Chapter Three: "Vehement and consuming longing, mixed with dread and anxiety": Mahler's Thoughts on Love and Romantic Fidelity

1 Gustav Mahler, *"Mein lieber Trotzkopf, meine süße Mohnblume": Briefe an Anna von Mildenburg*, ed. Franz Willnauer (Vienna: Paul Zsolnay Verlag, 2006); Gustav Mahler, *Gustav Mahler: Letters to His Wife*, ed.

Henry-Louis de La Grange, trans. Anthony Beaumont (Ithaca, NY: Cornell University Press, 1995); Alma Mahler, *Gustav Mahler: Memories and Letters*, ed. Donald Mitchell, trans. Basil Creighton (Seattle: University of Washington Press, 1975).

2   Natalie Bauer-Lechner, *Recollections of Gustav Mahler*, trans. Dika Newlin, ed. Peter Franklin (Cambridge: Cambridge University Press, 1980), 176–77.

3   Knud Martner, ed., *Selected Letters of Gustav Mahler* (New York: Ferrar, Straus and Giroux, 1979), 101.

4   Henry-Louis de La Grange, *Mahler*, vol. 1 (Garden City, NY: Doubleday & Co., 1973), 172.

5   La Grange, *Mahler*, 1:171; Donald Mitchell, *Gustav Mahler: The Wunderhorn Years* (Woodbridge: Boydell Press, 2005), 117–19.

6   Michael Ferber, *A Dictionary of Literary Symbols* (Cambridge: Cambridge University Press, 2007), 48. The German word for "cuckold" is "Hahnrei," a word derived from "Hahn," meaning "cock or rooster"; the rest of the word is thought to have been derived from the word "Reiz," meaning attraction or appeal. *The Online Etymology Dictionary* suggests that the basis of the word may have referred to a "Sexually aggressive hen." And the term "Kuckucksei" (cuckoo's egg) refers to an illegitimate child, as cuckoos typically lay their eggs in the nests of other birds, leaving them to raise their young https://www.etymonline.com/word/cuckold; N. C. W. Spence, "The Human Bestiary," *The Modern Language Review* 96 (2001): 925.

7   Herta Blaukopf, "The Young Mahler, 1875–1880: Essay in Situational Analysis After Karl R. Popper," in *Mahler Studies*, ed. Stephen Hefling (Cambridge: Cambridge University Press, 1997), 17–19.

8   Bauer-Lechner, *Recollections*, 81.

9   Natalie Bauer-Lechner, *Fragmente: Gelerntes und Gelebtes* (Vienna: Rudolf Lechner & Sohn, 1907), 16.

10   Solvik and Hefling, "Natalie Bauer-Lechner on Mahler and Women: A Newly Discovered Document," *Musical Quarterly* 97 (2014): 34.

11   Solvik and Hefling, "Natalie Bauer-Lechner," 36.

12   Steven McClatchie, ed., *The Mahler Family Letters* (Oxford: Oxford University Press, 2006), 217.

13   Solvik and Hefling, "Natalie Bauer-Lechner," 42.

14   McClatchie, *Mahler Family Letters*, 359.

15   Henry-Louis de La Grange, *Gustav Mahler*, vol. 2, *Vienna: Years of Challenge (1897–1904)* (New York: Oxford University Press, 1995), 341.

16   Karl Bode, *Die Bearbeitung der Vorlagen Des Knaben Wunderhorn*, Palaestra: Untersuchungen und Texte aus der deutschen und englischen Philologie, eds. Alois Brandl, Gustav Roethe, and Erich Schmidt, 76 (1909), 307–8; Ferdinand Reiser, *"Des Knaben Wunderhorn" und seine*

242   NOTES TO PAGES 74–87

Quellen: Ein Beitrag zur Geschichte des deutschen Volksliedes und der Romantik (1908; reprint, Hildesheim: Georg Olms Verlag, 1983), 230.

17 Dika Newlin, *Bruckner, Mahler, Schoenberg* (New York: W. W. Norton, 1978), 125.

18 Byron Almén, "The Sacrificed Hero: Creative Mythopoesis in Mahler's Wunderhorn Symphonies," in *Approaches to Meaning in Music*, ed. Byron Almén and Edward Pearson (Bloomington: University of Indiana Press, 2006), 143.

19 Alberto Rizzuti, *Sognatori, utopisti e diertori nei Lieder 'militari' di Gustav Mahler* (Torino: Passigli Editori, 1990); Stefan Hanheide, "Das Schicksal des Soldaten in Gustav Mahlers Liedern nach *Des Knaben Wunderhorn*," *Osnabrücker Jahrbuch Frieden und Wissenschaft* 1 (1994): 105–18; Donald Mitchell, "The Last Two 'Wunderhorn' Songs: 'Revelge' and 'Der Tamboursg'sell,'" in *The Mahler Companion*, ed. Donald Mitchell and Andrew Nicholson (Oxford: Oxford University Press, 1999), 232–35; Peter Franklin, "A Soldier's Sweetheart's Mother's Tale? Mahler's Gendered Musical Discourse," in *Mahler and His World*, ed. Karen Painter (Princeton, NJ: Princeton University Press, 2002), 111–25; Isabelle Werck, "Images de l'armée et de la guerre dans la musique de Gustav Mahler," *Revue Musicale de Suisse Romande* 56 (2003): 32–40; Kordula Kraus, "Der Soldat und das Mädchen: Zu ihrer Darstellung in Gustav Mahlers *Wunderhorn*-Liedern," *Musica Austriaca* 23 (2004): 81–97; Albrecht von Massow, "Romantik als Gesellschaftskritik: Mahlers Soldatenlieder," in *Von Volkston und Romantik: Des Knaben Wunderhorn in der Musik*, ed. Antje Tumat and Internationalen Musikfestival Heidelberger Frühling (Heidelberg: Universitätsverlag Winter, 2008), 141–56.

20 Caldwell Titcomb, "Baroque Court and Military Trumpets and Kettledrums: Technique and Music," *The Galpin Society Journal* 9 (1956): 71.

21 Bode, *Bearbeitung der Vorlagen*, 630–31, Reiser, *Seine Quellen*, 503–5.

22 Several of the earliest *Wunderhorn* songs were treated to orchestral settings by Luciano Berio in 1986 and 1987. "Scheiden und Meiden" was included in the second set. These settings were created at the behest of Henry-Louis de La Grange. Gustav Mahler, *Sechs frühe Lieder für Bariton und Orchester*, arr. Luciano Berio (Vienna: Universal Edition, 1987).

23 Martner, *Selected Letters*, 58.

24 Franz Willnauer, ed., *Gustav Mahler: "In Eile—wie immer!" Neue unbekannte Briefe* (Vienna: Zsolnay, 2016), 59.

25 Henry-Louis de La Grange and Sybille Werner, *Gustav Mahler*, vol. 1, *The Arduous Road to Vienna (1860–1897)* (Turnhout: Brepols, 2020), 144.

26 La Grange and Werner, *The Arduous Road*, 640.

27 Martner, *Selected Letters*, 188.

NOTES TO PAGES 89–93   243

Chapter Four: "Wrestling with God": Mahler and Spirituality

1   Alma Mahler, *Gustav Mahler: Memories and Letters*, 3rd ed., ed. Donald Mitchell, trans. Basil Creighton (Seattle, University of Washington Press, 1975), 101.

2   Alma Mahler, *Memories and Letters*, 20.

3   Eliza Slavet, "Freud's Theory of Jewishness: For Better and For Worse," in *The Jewish World of Sigmund Freud*, ed. Arnold D. Richards (Jefferson, NC: McFarland & Co., 2010), 96.

4   Theodor Adorno, *Mahler: A Musical Physiognomy*, trans. Edmund Jephcott (Chicago: University of Chicago Press, 1992), 149.

5   Caroline A. Kita, *Jewish Difference and the Arts in Vienna: Composing Compassion in Music and Biblical Theater* (Bloomington, IN: Indiana University Press, 2019), 40; William J. McGrath, "Student Radicalism in Vienna," *Journal of Contemporary History* 2 (1967): 198.

6   Richard Wagner, "Religion and Art," in *Prose Works*, vol. 6, trans. William Ashton Ellis (London: Kegen Paul, Trench, Trübner, & Co., 1897), 213.

7   Richard Specht, *Gustav Mahler* (Berlin: Schuster & Loeffler, 1913), 39.

8   A. David Hogarth, "Gustav Mahler," liner notes for Gustav Mahler, Symphony no. 4, Elly Ameling, Concertgebouw Orchestra, cond. Bernard Haitink, 1967, Philips 802 888.

9   Henry-Louis de La Grange and Sybille Werner, *Gustav Mahler*, vol. 1, *The Arduous Road to Vienna (1860–1897)* (Turnhout: Brepols, 2020), 45–46.

10   Martin Eric Vann, "Encounters with Modernity: Jews Music, and Vienna, 1880–1914" (PhD diss., Georgetown University, 2007), 359–60.

11   La Grange and Werner, *The Arduous Road*, 28, 47.

12   Sabine Frerichs, "From Credit to Crisis: Max Weber, Karl Polanyi, and the Other Side of the Coin," *Journal of Law and Society* 40 (2013): 7–26, describes these events through writings of contemporary scholars.

13   Steven K. Baum, *Anti-Semitism Explained* (Lanham, MD: University Press of America, 2012), 17.

14   Marsha L. Rozenblit, "Assimilation and Affirmation: The Jews of Freud's Vienna," in *The Jewish World of Sigmund Freud*, ed. Arnold D. Richards (Jefferson, NC: McFarland & Co., 2010), 23.

15   Alma Maria Mahler, ed., *Gustav Mahler Briefe: 1879–1911* (Hildesheim: Georg Olms Verlag, 1978), 102.

16   Michael Steinberg, "Jewish Identity and Intellectuality in Fin-de-Siècle Vienna: Suggestions for a Historical Discourse," *New German Critique* 43 (1988): 24.

17   K. M. Knittel, "'Ein hypermoderner Dirigent': Mahler and Anti-Semitism in Fin-De-Siècle Vienna," *19th-Century Music* 18 (1995): 267.

18   Sandra McColl, *Music Criticism in Vienna 1896–1897: Critically Moving Forms* (Oxford: Clarendon Press, 1996), 21–22.

244 NOTES TO PAGES 93–96

19 McColl, *Music Criticism*, 22–30.

20 Henry-Louis de La Grange, *Mahler*, vol. 1 (Garden City, NY: Doubleday, 1973), 549.

21 Quoted and translated in La Grange, *Mahler*, 1:553–54.

22 Richard Wagner, "Judaism in Music," in *The Theatre: Richard Wagner's Prose Works* vol. 3, trans. William Ashton Ellis (London: Kegen Paul, Trench, Trübner & Co., 1893), 84.

23 La Grange, *Mahler*, 1:507.

24 La Grange, *Mahler*, 1:655. The comment regarding the Blue Danube refers to the famous waltz "On the Beautiful Blue Danube" by Johann Strauss, Jr., indicating both Strauss' Jewish descent and the work's popularity among the middle class.

25 William Ritter, *Études d'art étranger* (Paris: Mercure de France, 1911), 271. Quoted and translated by La Grange, *Mahler*, 1:651–52.

26 Guido Adler, *Richard Wagner: Vorlesungen gehalten an der Universität zu Wien* (Leipzig: Breitkopf and Härtel, 1904), 189. Quoted and translated in Kevin C. Karnes, *Music, Criticism, and the Challenge of History: Shaping Modern Musical Thought in Late Nineteenth-Century Vienna*, AMS Studies in Music (Oxford: Oxford University Press, 2008), 187.

27 Stephen McClatchie, ed., *The Mahler Family Letters* (Oxford: Oxford University Press, 2006), 257.

28 Knud Martner, ed., *Selected Letters of Gustav Mahler* (New York: Ferrar, Straus and Giroux, 1979), 207.

29 Ludwig Karpath, *Begegnung mit dem Genius*, 2nd ed. (Vienna: Fiba Verlag, 1934), 102. "Pollini's Hamburg inferno" refers to the position Mahler left before beginning his duties in Vienna.

30 Karpath, *Begegnung*, 102.

31 Undated letter to Oskar Fried from 1906, quoted in Vann, "Encounters with Modernity," 404.

32 Though one of the emperor's closest advisors, Prince Rudolf of Liechtenstein, said of hiring Mahler to a position at the Hofoper, "We have not yet reached the point in Vienna that anti-Semitism is a decisive factor here," other officials of the Opera, most notably Cosima Wagner, held firm that no imperial position could be held by a Jew. La Grange and Werner, *The Arduous Road*, 714.

33 Leon Botstein, "Gustav Mahler's Vienna," in *The Mahler Companion*, ed. Donald Mitchell and Andrew Nicholson (Oxford: Oxford University Press, 1999), 18.

34 Sander L. Gilman, *Jewish Self-Hatred: Anti-Semitism and the Hidden Language of the Jews* (Baltimore: The Johns Hopkins University Press, 1986), 225.

35 Robert S. Wistrich, *The Jews of Vienna in the Age of Franz Joseph* (Oxford: Oxford University Press, 1989), 51.

NOTES TO PAGES 96–109   245

36 McClatchie, *Mahler Family Letters*, 158, emphasis mine.

37 Alma Mahler, *Memories and Letters*, 224.

38 La Grange and Werner, *The Arduous Road*, 717.

39 La Grange and Werner, *The Arduous Road*, 718.

40 Ferdinand Pfohl, "Mahler und Nikisch," *Hundertjahrfeier des Hamburger Stadttheaters 1827–1927* (Leipzig: Max Beck Verlag, 1927), 82.

41 Indeed, another version of the folk-song text, published by Ludwig Tobler, begins with the line "Herr Gott, Röseli rott" (Lord God, red rose); Karl Bode, *Die Bearbeitung der Vorlagen Des Knaben Wunderhorn*, Palaestra: Untersuchungen und Texte aus der deutschen und englischen Philologie, eds. Alois Brandl, Gustav Roethe, and Erich Schmidt, 76 (1909), 158. Another well-known song drawing connections between the birth of Christ and the rose is "Es ist ein Ros entsprungen" (Lo, How a Rose e'er Blooming).

42 The chronology of the song's creation is complicated, largely by the fact that the original sketch for voice and piano has not survived, and the orchestrated version for the independent song (completed in summer 1893) differs from the instrumentation of that used in the symphony (which was not created until December 1894 at the earliest). Donald Mitchell, *Gustav Mahler: The Wunderhorn Years* (Woodbridge: The Boydell Press, 2005), 136.

43 Natalie Bauer-Lechner, *Recollections of Gustav Mahler*, trans. Dika Newlin, ed. Peter Franklin (Cambridge: Cambridge University Press, 1980), 44.

44 For that, the listener must wait until the final movement, a chorus singing text beginning with Friedrich Klopstock's poem "Auferstehn" and continuing with text written by Mahler himself.

45 Alma Mahler, *Memories and Letters*, 213. Emphasis mine.

46 La Grange, *Mahler*, 1:654.

47 Bode, *Bearbeitung der Vorlagen*, 185.

48 Bauer-Lechner, *Recollections*, 40–41; Mitchell, *The Wunderhorn Years*, 129.

49 Caroline A. Kita, "Jacob Struggling with the Angel: Siegfried Lipiner, Gustav Mahler, and the Search for Aesthetic-Religious Redemption in Fin-de-Siècle Vienna" (PhD diss., Duke University, 2011), 191–98; Raymond Knapp, "Suffering Children: Perspectives on Innocence and Vulnerability in Mahler's Fourth Symphony," *19th-Century Music* 22 (Spring 1999): 239.

50 Carl Niekerk, *Reading Mahler: German Culture and Jewish Identity in Fin-de-Siècle Vienna* (Rochester, NY: Camden House, 2010), 115.

51 Bauer-Lechner, *Recollections*, 178.

52 Natalie Bauer-Lechner, *Mahleriana*, unpublished manuscript in the collection of the Médiathèque Musicale Mahler in Paris. Quoted in La Grange and Werner, *The Arduous Road*, 480.

246   NOTES TO PAGES 109–20

53   N. Dal-Gal, "St. Anthony of Padua," *The Catholic Encyclopedia*, vol. 1 (New York: Robert Appleton Co., 1907), accessed June 8, 2012, http://www.newadvent.org/cathen/01556a.htm.

54   Abraham worked on *Judas der Erzschelm* for ten years between 1686 and 1695. The work combines a variety of moral reflections with an extensive tracing of the life of Judas.

55   Nikolaus Scheid, "Abraham a Sancta Clara," *Catholic Encyclopedia*, ed. Charles G. Herbermann et al. (New York: The Encyclopedia Press, 1907), accessed June 5, 2012, http://en.wikisource.org/wiki/Catholic_Encyclopedia_(1913)/Abraham_a_Sancta_Clara.

56   Wistrich, *The Jews of Vienna*, 8.

57   Bauer-Lechner, *Recollections*, 33.

58   Oxford Music Online, s.v. "Jewish Music: Non-Liturgical Music: Instrumental Music: Klezmer," by Walter Zev Feldman, accessed January 20, 2010, http://www.oxfordmusiconline.com/subscriber/article/grove/music/41322.

59   Mitchell, *The Wunderhorn Years*, 183.

60   Magnar Breivik, "A Sermon for Fishes in a Secular Age: On the Scherzo Movement of Mahler's Second Symphony," in *Voicing the Ineffable: Musical Representations of Religious Experience*, ed. Siglind Bruhn (Hillsdale, NY: Pendragon Press, 2002), 47–70.

61   Breivik, "A Sermon for Fishes," 58.

62   Breivik, "A Sermon for Fishes," 60.

63   Breivik, "A Sermon for Fishes," 62.

64   David Schiff, "Jewish and Musical Tradition in the Music of Mahler and Schoenberg," *Journal of the Arnold Schoenberg Institute* 9 (1986): 217.

65   Bauer-Lechner, *Recollections*, 30.

66   Bauer-Lechner, *Recollections*, 154.

Chapter Five: "The risky obstacles in society which are quite dangerous for women": Commentary on Gender Roles in the *Wunderhorn* Songs

1   Written in a letter by Natalie Bauer-Lechner in 1917, and translated by Morten Solvik and Stephen E. Hefling, "Natalie Bauer-Lechner on Mahler and Women: A Newly Discovered Document," *Musical Quarterly* 97 (2014): 28.

2   My thanks to German scholars Shelley Hay and Jennifer Bienert for their insight regarding the usage associated with the verb *nehmen*.

3   Paul Reitter, "Carl Schorske and the Dialectics of Viennese Modernism," *Qui Parle* 11 (1997): 161.

4   The manuscript for "Starke Einbildungskraft" is in the key of B-flat major, but the first edition was published in C major and A major. My examples are based on the C major setting.

NOTES TO PAGES 123–34   247

5   Stuart Feder, "Gustav Mahler: The Music of Fratricide," in *Psychoanalytic Explorations in Music*, ed. Stuart Feder, Richard L. Karmel, and George H. Pollock (Madison, CT: International Universities Press, 1990), 341–90; George Pollock, "Mourning Through Music: Gustav Mahler," in *Psychoanalytic Explorations in Music*, 321–39; Pierre Babin, "Gustav Mahler: Un Enfant malade," in *Colloque International Gustav Mahler: 25.26.27 Janvier, 1985* (Paris: Association Gustav Mahler, 1986), 57–61; Dika Newlin, "'The Mahler's Brother Syndrome': Necropsychiatry and the Artist," *Musical Quarterly* 66 (1980): 296–304; Mathias Hansen, "Das irdische Leben: Zum Weltbild des jungen Mahler," *Beiträge zur Musikwissenschaft* 16 (1974): 25–30; William Mooney, "Gustav Mahler: A Note on Life and Death in Music," *Psychoanalytic Quarterly* 37 (1968): 88–101.

6   In a letter written to Max Staegemann, Mahler's employer in Leipzig. Stephen McClatchie, ed., *The Mahler Family Letters* (Oxford: Oxford University Press, 2006), 4.

7   McClatchie, *Mahler Family Letters*, 4.

8   McClatchie, *Mahler Family Letters*, 121.

9   McClatchie, *Mahler Family Letters*, 73.

10   McClatchie, *Mahler Family Letters*, 72.

11   Henry-Louis de La Grange and Sybille Werner, *Gustav Mahler*, vol. 1, *The Arduous Road to Vienna (1860–1897)* (Turnhout: Brepols, 2020), 407.

12   J. B. Foerster, "Gustav Mahler in Hamburg," *Prager Presse*, April 7, 1922.

13   Quoted in La Grange and Werner, *The Arduous Road*, 405.

14   McClatchie, *Mahler Family Letters*, 121.

15   McClatchie, *Mahler Family Letters*, 204.

16   From a letter to her friend Ernestine Löhr, dated February 18, 1897; McClatchie, *Mahler Family Letters*, 6.

17   Letter from April 1891; McClatchie, *Mahler Family Letters*, 122.

18   Letter from February 1893; McClatchie, *Mahler Family Letters*, 216.

19   Letter from Justine to Gustav, dated April 1892; McClatchie, *Mahler Family Letters*, 164–65.

20   Alma Mahler, *Gustav Mahler: Memories and Letters*, trans. Donald Mitchell (Seattle: University of Washington Press, 1975), 13.

21   Byron Almén writes of the use of folk elements in music, "An idealized Volk... both participates in society and is close to nature. This is, of course, a common nineteenth-century reaction to the dehumanization of urban society: the call to return to a social structure centered on the naïve yet spiritually attuned rural peasant"; "The Sacrificed Hero: Creative Mythopoesis in Mahler's Wunderhorn Symphonies," in *Approaches to Meaning in Music*, ed. Byron Almén and Edward Pearson (Bloomington: University of Indiana Press, 2006), 144.

22   Stefan Zweig, *The World of Yesterday: An Autobiography* (New York: The Viking Press, 1943), 77–79.

248   NOTES TO PAGES 135–37

23   Bruno Bettelheim, *The Uses of Enchantment: The Meaning and Importance of Fairy Tales* (New York: Vintage Books, 1977), 231. The story recorded by the Brothers Grimm tells of a princess who falls into a deep sleep after pricking her finger on a spindle, and she is left in her seemingly lifeless state alone in a castle. Some time later, a man is hunting and his prey flies into the castle, where the man discovers the sleeping princess. Infatuated but unable to wake her, he makes love to her and leaves. The sleeping princess gives birth to twins who instinctively suckle until the man's wife discovers the children and decides that they must die.

24   Bettelheim, *The Uses of Enchantment*, 173: "Red is the color of violent emotions, very much including sexual ones. The red velvet cap given by Grandmother... thus can be viewed as a symbol of premature transfer of sexual attractiveness... She is too little... for managing what this cap symbolizes, and what her wearing it invites."

Chapter Six: "Highly complicated activity of the mind": Songs with a Freudian Slant

1   Notable examples include Theodor Reik, *Variations psychanalytiques sur un thème de Gustav Mahler* (Paris: DeNoël, 1953); William J. McGrath, "Mahler and Freud: The Dream of the Stately House," in *Beiträge '79–81: Gustav Mahler Kolloquium 1979*, ed. Rudolf Klein (Basel: Bärenreiter, 1981), 40–51; and Peter Ostwald, "Gustav Mahler from the Viewpoint of Psychoanalysis," in *Des Gustav-Mahler-Fest Hamburg 1989: Bericht über den Internationalen Gustav-Mahler-Kongreß*, ed. Matthias Theodor Vogt (Basel: Bärenreiter, 1991), 89–96. It should be noted that as their meeting was not a formal session, Freud left no notes, and Mahler himself spoke little about the meeting beyond this rather self-serving passage preserved in a letter he wrote to his wife Alma, which she published in her 1949 collection entitled *Gustav Mahler: Erinnerungen und Briefen*: "Freud is quite right—you were always for me the light and the central point! The inner light, I mean, which rose over all; and the blissful consciousness of this—now unshadowed and unconfined—raises all my feelings to the infinite." In Alma Mahler, *Gustav Mahler: Memories and Letters*, trans. Basil Creighton, ed. Donald Mitchell (Seattle: University of Washington Press, 1975), 335. Indeed, the bulk of our knowledge of the events of that afternoon stem from Freud's somewhat faulty recollections shared with others in the years following Mahler's death.

2   McGrath, "Mahler and Freud," 40. Freud wrote of this in a letter to his friend and biographer Ernest Jones.

3   Henry-Louis de La Grange, *Gustav Mahler*, vol. 3, *Vienna: Triumph and Disillusion (1904–1907)* (Oxford: Oxford University Press, 1999), 348. We know that Bruno Walter discussed his treatment with Mahler, as it

NOTES TO PAGES 138–39   249

was through Mahler's assistance that the conductor was able to receive funding to travel to Sicily, as was recommended by Freud as the cure for Walter's chronic arm pain. Walter describes his treatment: "I was attacked by an arm ailment. Medical science called it a professional cramp, but it looked deucedly like incipient paralysis. I went from one prominent doctor to another... and finally decided to call on Professor Sigmund Freud. The consultation took a course I had not foreseen. Instead of questioning me about sexual aberrations in infancy, as my layman's ignorance had led me to expect, Freud examined my arm briefly. I told him my story, feeling certain that he would be professionally interested in a possible connection between my actual physical affliction and a wrong I had suffered more than a year before. Instead, he asked me if I had ever been to Sicily. When I replied that I had not, he said that it was very beautiful, and more Greek than Greece itself. In short, I was to leave that very evening, forget all about my arm and the Opera, and do nothing for a few weeks but use my eyes. I did as I was told." Bruno Walter, *Theme and Variations: An Autobiography*, trans. James A. Galston (New York: Alfred A. Knopf, 1959), 164–65.

4   A. A. van dem Braembussche, *Thinking Art: An Introduction to the Philosophy of Art*, trans. Michael Krassilovsky (Brussels: Springer Science, 2009), 17.

5   Eduard Hanslick, *On the Musically Beautiful: A Contribution Towards the Revision of the Aesthetics of Music*, trans. Geoffrey Payzant (Indianapolis: Hackett, 1986), 9.

6   Written in an 1896 letter to Max Marschalk, quoted in Herta Blaukopf, ed., *Gustav Mahler Briefe*, 2nd ed. (Vienna: Zsolnay, 1996), 171.

7   Susanne K. Langer, *Philosophy in a New Key*, 3rd ed. (Cambridge, MA: Harvard University Press, 1976), 236.

8   This practice, termed "necropsychiatry" by Dika Newlin, is defined by her as "The raping of the minds and spirits of great men and women of the past in the name of 'science.'" Dika Newlin, "'The Mahler's Brother Syndrome': Necropsychiatry and the Artist," *Musical Quarterly* 66 (1980): 297.

9   Bruno Bettelheim and Marie-Luise von Franz study the use of folk songs and fairy tales as tools for passing on life lessons to the young through the lens of psychoanalysis: Bruno Bettelheim, *The Uses of Enchantment: The Meaning and Importance of Fairy Tales* (New York: Vintage Books, 1977); Marie-Luise von Franz, *An Introduction to the Psychology of Fairy Tales* (Irving, TX: Spring, 1978).

10   Karl Bode, *Die Bearbeitung der Vorlagen Des Knaben Wunderhorn*, Palaestra: Untersuchungen und Texte aus der deutschen und englischen Philologie, eds. Alois Brandl, Gustav Roethe, and Erich Schmidt, 76 (1909), 291–92.

250   NOTES TO PAGES 141–60

11   Josef Breuer, "Hysterical Conversion," in Sigmund Freud and Josef Breuer, *Studies in Hysteria*, trans. Nicole Luchhurst (New York: Penguin, 2004), 215.

12   Bode, *Bearbeitung der Vorlagen*, 625–26; Ferdinand Reiser, *"Des Knaben Wunderhorn" und seine Quellen: Ein Beitrag zur Geschichte des deutschen Volksliedes und der Romantik* (1908; reprint, Hildesheim: Georg Olms Verlag, 1983), 530–31.

13   The only earlier song that does not tell of parting lovers is "Zu Straßburg auf der Schanz," which is discussed in Chapter 2.

14   Assuming, of course, that both figures are actually present. Elizabeth Schmierer argues that the woman in this dialogue is merely a figment of the prisoner's imagination; *Die Orchesterlieder Gustav Mahlers*, Kieler Schriften zur Musikwissenschaft 38 (Kassel: Bärenreiter, 1991), 136.

15   Anna Freud, *The Ego and the Mechanisms of Defense* (New York: International Universities Press, 1967), 89.

16   Carolyn Abbate, *Unsung Voices: Opera and Musical Narrative in the Nineteenth Century* (Princeton, NJ: Princeton University Press, 1991), 124–25; Berger, "Diegesis and Mimesis," 407–33.

17   Molly Breckling, "Narrative Strategies in Gustav Mahler's Balladic *Wunderhorn* Lieder" (PhD diss., University of North Carolina—Chapel Hill, 2010), 237–41, 256–71.

18   Julian Johnson explores the idea of musical voices negating one another, whether through structure upheaval, fracturing, language, or through the sound of the voice itself, in "The Breaking of the Voice," *Nineteenth-Century Music Review* 8 (2011): 179–95. In this instance, the voice that destroys the lovers' idyllic reunion is scarcely present but still possesses the power to deliver devastating news.

19   "Frau Nachtigall," "Cedroris Klage," "Schall der Nacht," "Grosse Wasche," "Käuzlein," "Frühlingsblumen," "Maria auf der Reise," "Der lustige Geselle," "Variation," "Hochzeit Lied auf Kaiser Leopoldus und Claudia Felix," "Antwort Mariä auf den Gruss der Engel," "Wettstreits der Kuckuck mit der Nachtigall" (which Mahler used for the text in "Lob des hohen Verstandes"), "Der Schäfers Tageszelten," "Frühlingserwartung," "Wechselgesang," "Ständchen," "Wächter hüt zum Trutz," "Wiederhall," "Warnung," "Waldvöglein" (which Mahler used for the text in "Ich ging mit Lust"), "Liebeswünsche," "Sommerleid," "Die hohe Unterhandlerin," "Ablösung" (which Mahler used for the text in "Ablösung im Sommer"), "Mailied," "Jahrezeiten," "Der verwandelte Einsiedler," "Sonnenblicke," "Eine heilige Familie," "Erziehung durch Natur," "Das Federspiel," "Die zwei Hirten in der Christnacht," and "Mondliedchen."

20   For example, "Als wie ein himmlische Nachtigall, Ich das Magnifikat tu singen," (Like a heavenly nightingale, I sang the Magnificat) from "Maria auf der Reise" (I 375). Arnim and Brentano, *Des Knaben Wunderhorn:*

NOTES TO PAGES 161–66   251

Alte deutsche Lieder gesammelt von Achim von Arnim und Clemens Brentano, ed. Heinz Rölleke (Frankfurt am Main: Insel Verlag, 2003), 353.

21   Oswald A. Erich and Richard Beitl, *Wörterbuch der deutschen Volkskunde* (Stuttgart: Alfred Kröner Verlag, 1955), 547–48. See also Maria Leach, ed., *Funk and Wagnalls Standard Dictionary of Folklore, Mythology and Legend* (New York: Funk & Wagnalls, 1972), 792–93, and Anthony S. Mercatante, *Zoo of the Gods: Animals in Myth, Legend and Fable* (New York: Harper & Row, 1974), 163. The nightingale's connection to death is seen in the Greek myth of Philomela as well as in Hans Christian Andersen's fairy tale "The Nightingale." A medieval story explains the quality of the nightingale's song in that she keeps awake at night by pressing her breast against a thorn. Her mournful tone describes her pain. Lawrence Kramer refers to the extensive references to nightingales in the Romantic art-song tradition in *Franz Schubert: Sexuality, Subjectivity, Song* (Cambridge: Cambridge University Press, 1998), 121, 144–45.

22   John Keats, "Ode to a Nightingale," in *The Poetical Works and Other Writings of John Keats*, ed. H. Buxton Forman (New York: Charles Scribner's Sons, 1939), 145–51.

23   Constantin Floros, *Gustav Mahler*, vol. 2, *Mahler und die Symphonik des 19. Jahrhunderts in neuer Deutung* (Wiesbaden: Breitkopf & Härtel, 1985), 207.

24   Sigmund Freud, *The Interpretation of Dreams*, trans. James Strachey (London: George Allen & Unwin, 1971), 421.

25   Freud, *Interpretation*, 111.

26   Freud, *Interpretation*, 424.

27   Freud, *Interpretation*, 421.

28   David Buchan, "Talerole Analysis and Child's Supernatural Ballads," in *The Ballad and Oral Tradition*, ed. Joseph Harris (Cambridge, MA: Harvard University Press, 1991), 65–67.

29   Siegfried Lipiner and Albert and Nina Spiegler, friends of Mahler.

30   Natalie Bauer-Lechner, *Mahleriana* (partly unpublished journals), January 14, 1900, Collection of the Bibliothèque Gustav Mahler, Paris. I am grateful to the Bibliothèque Gustav Mahler, in particular to Alena Parthonnaud, for making this material available to me.

31   I further discuss the incongruities of Mahler's interpretation of "Trompeten" with musical and literary evidence in my article "Tears from a Nightingale: Analytical Duality in Gustav Mahler's 'Wo die schönen Trompeten blasen,'" *Music Research Forum* 19 (2004): 49–70.

32   Freud, *Interpretation*, 122.

33   Freud, *Interpretation*, 126.

252   NOTES TO PAGES 171–77

Chapter Seven: "The brutal bourgeoisie": Mahler and Socioeconomic Equality

1   "I am thrice homeless: as a Bohemian among Austrians; as an Austrian among Germans; and as a Jew: everywhere." Recorded by Alma Mahler, *Gustav Mahler: Memories and Letters*, ed. Donald Mitchell, trans. Basil Creighton (Seattle: University of Washington Press, 1975) , 109.

2   William J. McGrath, *Dionysian Art and Populist Politics in Vienna* (New Haven, CT: Yale University Press, 1974). McGrath traces the entire history of the Pernerstorfer Circle and its subsequent political and philosophical movements.

3   William J. McGrath, "Student Radicalism in Vienna," *Journal of Contemporary History* 2 (1967): 183. Quoting from Richard von Kralik, "Geschichte und Gestalten—Victor Adler und Pernerstorfer," Collected Papers, Vienna State Library, Ms. I. N. 106.071, f. 2.

4   McGrath, *Dionysian Art*, 20. Quoting from Gruber, "Kleine Mitteilungen," *Münchener medizinische Wochenschrift* 70 (August 3, 1923): 1038.

5   McGrath, *Dionysian Art*, 34.

6   McGrath, *Dionysian Art*, 82.

7   Herta Blaukopf, "The Young Mahler, 1875–1880: Essay in Situational Analysis After Karl R. Popper," in *Mahler Studies*, ed. Stephen Hefling (Cambridge: Cambridge University Press, 1997), 18–19.

8   Johannes Volkelt, "Mein philosophischer Entwicklungsgang," *Die deutsche Philosophie der Gegenwart in Selbstdarstellung*, ed. Raymund Schmidt (Leipzig: Felix Meiner, 1921), 205.

9   Caroline Kita, *Jewish Difference and the Arts in Vienna: Composing Compassion in Music and Biblical Theater* (Bloomington, IN: Indiana University Press, 2019), 13.

10   Natalie Bauer-Lechner, *Recollections of Gustav Mahler*, trans. Dika Newlin, ed. Peter Franklin (Cambridge: Cambridge University Press, 1980), 232–33.

11   Bauer-Lechner, *Recollections*, 51.

12   Alma Mahler, *Memories and Letters*, 82.

13   La Grange, *Mahler*, 1:311, 442–43, 514, 520.

14   Bauer-Lechner, *Recollections*, 36–37.

15   Stephen McClatchie, ed., *The Mahler Family Letters* (Oxford: Oxford University Press, 2006), 183. Emphasis mine.

16   Franz Hermann Franken, "Gustav Mahler," in *Die Krankheiten großer Komponisten*, vol. 3 (Wilhelmshaven: Florian Noetzel Verlag, 1991), 157.

17   Henry-Louis de La Grange, *Mahler*, vol. 1 (Garden City, NY: Doubleday, 1973), 10–11.

18   Stefan Zweig, *The World of Yesterday: An Autobiography* (New York: The Viking Press, 1943), 11: "It is generally accepted that getting rich is the

NOTES TO PAGES 177–89   253

only and typical goal of the Jew. Nothing could be further from the truth. Riches are to him merely a stepping stone, a means to the true end, and in no sense the real goal. The real determination of the Jew is to rise to a higher cultural plane in the intellectual world."

19 Blaukopf, "The Young Mahler," 5.

20 McClatchie, *Mahler Family Letters*, 164.

21 McClatchie, *Mahler Family Letters*, 163.

22 Sander L. Gilman, *Jewish Self-Hatred: Anti-Semitism and the Hidden Language of the Jews* (Baltimore: The Johns Hopkins University Press, 1986).

23 Bauer-Lechner, *Recollections*, 32.

24 Karl Bode, *Die Bearbeitung der Vorlagen Des Knaben Wunderhorn*, Palaestra: Untersuchungen und Texte aus der deutschen und englischen Philologie, eds. Alois Brandl, Gustav Roethe, and Erich Schmidt, 76 (1909), 276–77; Ferdinand Reiser, *"Des Knaben Wunderhorn" und seine Quellen: Ein Beitrag zur Geschichte des deutschen Volksliedes und der Romantik* (1908; reprint, Hildesheim: Georg Olms Verlag, 1983), 470.

25 Bauer-Lechner, *Recollections*, 147.

26 William E. Lake, "Hermeneutic Music Structures in 'Das irdische Leben' by Gustav Mahler," *In Theory Only* 12, no. 7 (November 1994): 4.

27 Bauer-Lechner, *Recollections*, 32.

28 Theodor Adorno, *Mahler: A Musical Physiognomy*, trans. Edmund Jephcott (Chicago: University of Chicago Press, 1992), 29.

29 These markings appear in the critical edition of the piano/vocal arrangements of "Das irdische Leben." The critical edition and manuscript of the orchestral setting (held in the Mary Flagler Cary Collection at the Pierpont Morgan Library) omit the articulation markings. The manuscript of the piano/vocal arrangement was most recently in the possession of musicologist Dika Newlin and since her passing in 2006 has remained unavailable. I express my thanks to Dr. Sabine Feisst for her information regarding the location of the manuscript.

30 Bode, *Bearbeitung der Vorlagen*, 595–96; Reiser, *Seine Quellen*, 543–44.

31 Elizabeth Schmierer identifies the dance as having a "typical *Ländler* rhythm" (der typische Ländlerrhythmus) and a "waltz effect" (Walzerfolge). The triple meter and accent on the first beat heard in "Rheinlegendchen" conforms to both dances, but the lack of arpeggiations and first-beat accents (such as those identified in "Verlor'ne Müh'!") frequently heard in the *Ländler* aligns this more closely with the waltz. Schmierer, *Die Orchesterlieder Gustav Mahlers*, Kieler Schriften zur Musikwissenschaft 38 (Kassel: Bärenreiter, 1991), 107.

32 La Grange has observed the similarity between this melody and that of the minuet of Schubert's Piano Sonata in G, D. 894; "Music About Music in Mahler: Reminiscences, Allusions or Quotations?" in *Mahler Studies*,

254 NOTES TO PAGES 190–202

ed. Stephen Hefling (Cambridge: Cambridge University Press, 1997), 152.

33 Zoltan Roman writes extensively about the formal structures found in Mahler's songs: "Structure as a Factor in the Genesis of Gustav Mahler's Songs," in *Gustav Mahler*, ed. Hermann Danuser (Darmstadt: Wissenschaftliche Buchgesellschaft Darmstadt, 1992), 82–95.

34 Kita, *Jewish Difference and the Arts in Vienna*, 13.

Chapter Eight: "The misery of a pioneer": Mahler's Responses to Critics and Audiences

1 Natalie Bauer-Lechner, *Recollections of Gustav Mahler*, trans. Dika Newlin, ed. Peter Franklin (Cambridge: Cambridge University Press, 1980), 130.

2 Stefan Zweig, *The World of Yesterday: An Autobiography* (New York: The Viking Press, 1943), 44.

3 Zweig, *The World of Yesterday*, 100.

4 Quoted in Henry-Louis de La Grange, *Mahler*, vol. 1 (Garden City, NY: Doubleday & Co., 1973), 617. Emphasis mine.

5 Gustav Mahler, *Gustav Mahler: Letters to His Wife*, ed. Henry-Louis de La Grange, trans. Anthony Beaumont (Ithaca, NY: Cornell University Press, 1995), 261; Gustav Mahler, *Gustav Mahler—Richard Strauss: Correspondence 1888–1911*, ed. Herta Blaukopf, trans. Edmund Jephcott (Chicago: University of Chicago Press, 1984), 40; La Grange, *Mahler*, 1:661.

6 Bauer-Lechner, *Recollections*, 54.

7 Eduard Hanslick, "Fünftes Philharmonisches Konzert," *Neue Freie Presse* 12714 (January 16, 1900): 8. Translation mine.

8 Hermann Danuser, "Der Orchestergesang des Fin de siècle: Eine historische und ästhetische Skizze," *Die Musikforschung* 30 (1977): 425–31. Mahler, in fact, used many genre labels on manuscripts and publications of the *Wunderhorn* lieder, regardless of their accompaniment, referring to them at different times as *Lieder, Humoresken, Balladen*, and *Gesängen*, as discussed in Chapter 1.

9 Bauer-Lechner, *Recollections*, 130.

10 Bauer-Lechner, *Recollections*, 34.

11 Eduard Hanslick, *On the Musically Beautiful: A Contribution Towards the Revision of the Aesthetics of Music*, trans. Geoffrey Payzant (Indianapolis: Hackett, 1986), 65.

12 Hanslick, "Fünftes Philharmonisches Konzert," 8.

13 Eduard Hanslick, *Aus meinem Leben* (Berlin: Allgemeiner Verein für Deutsche Literatur, 1894), 308. Quoted in and translated by Kevin C. Karnes, *Music, Criticism, and the Challenge of History: Shaping Modern*

NOTES TO PAGES 203–11   255

Musical Thought in Late Nineteenth-Century Vienna, AMS Studies in Music (Oxford: Oxford University Press, 2008), 72–73.

14 Quoted and translated by La Grange, *Mahler*, 1:263.

15 La Grange, *Mahler*, 1:264.

16 Stephen McClatchie, ed., *The Mahler Family Letters* (Oxford: Oxford University Press, 2006), 191.

17 Max Burckhard, "Feuilleton: Der Begriff des Modernen in der Kunst," *Neue Freie Presse* 13019 (November 20, 1900): 1–3.

18 Bauer-Lechner, *Recollections*, 96.

19 Hanslick, *On the Musically Beautiful*, 72.

20 Dan Cohn-Sherbock, *Anti-Semitism: A History* (Stroud: Sutton, 2002), 244.

21 Cohn-Sherbock, *Anti-Semitism*, 246.

22 Karl Bode, *Die Bearbeitung der Vorlagen Des Knaben Wunderhorn*, Palaestra: Untersuchungen und Texte aus der deutschen und englischen Philologie, eds. Alois Brandl, Gustav Roethe, and Erich Schmidt, 76 (1909), 47, 264; Ferdinand Reiser, *"Des Knaben Wunderhorn" und seine Quellen: Ein Beitrag zur Geschichte des deutschen Volksliedes und der Romantik* (1908; reprint, Hildesheim: Georg Olms Verlag, 1983), 419.

23 Bauer-Lechner, *Recollections*, 58.

24 This sketch is held with the Moldenhauer Archives collection at the Bayerische Staatsbibliothek in Munich. Günther Wiess, Sigrid von Moisy, and Hartmut Schaefer, *Gustav Mahler: Briefe und Musikautographen aus den Moldenhauer-Archiven in der Bayerischen Staatsbibliothek* (Munich: Kulturstiftung der Länder Freistaat Bayern and Bayern Landesstiftung Bundesministerium des Innern, 2003), 108–9.

25 Precisely transcribing the song of a nightingale has remained a difficult exercise, as nightingales sing different songs depending on their mood, the time of year, and often from one bird to the next. See Orlando A. Mansfield, "The Cuckoo and the Nightingale in Music," *The Musical Quarterly* 7 (1921): 271, and Daniel W. Leger, Katherine E. Brooks, and Judith E. O'Brien, "Versatility from a Single Song: The Case of the Nightingale Wren," *The Auk* 117 (2000): 1039–41.

26 Bauer-Lechner, *Recollections*, 118. Emphasis mine.

27 Felix von Bonin, "Esel," *Kleines Handlexikon der Märchensymbolik* (Stuttgart: Kreuz Verlag, 2001), 39.

28 Jean Chevalier and Alain Gheerbrant, *The Penguin Dictionary of Symbols* (London: Penguin Books, 1996), 268. The relationship between the cuckoo and jealousy relates to the bird's habit of laying eggs in the nests of other species so that the other birds will care for the young. This also connects the word "cuckoo" to "cuckold," a man whose wife is unfaithful, as, if the cheating spouse were to become pregnant from an affair, the cuckolded husband would be left to care for the offspring of another man.

256   NOTES TO PAGES 212–26

29   Carl E. Schorske. *Thinking with History: Explorations in the Passage to Modernism* (Princeton, NJ: Princeton University Press, 1998), 127.
30   Carl E. Schorske, "Mahler and Klimt: Social Experience and Artistic Evolution," *Daedulus* 111, no. 3 (1982): 46.
31   Theodor Helm, "Theater, Kunst, und Literatur," *Deutsche Zeitung* (January 15, 1900): 3.
32   Leon Botstein, "Listening Through Reading: Musical Literacy and the Concert Audience," *19th-Century Music* 16 (1992): 143.
33   La Grange, *Mahler*, 1:663.
34   Bode, *Bearbeitung der Vorlagen*, 166.
35   Mansfield, "The Cuckoo and the Nightingale in Music," 263. Mansfield points out that the natural cuckoo call changes throughout the season, ranging from an augmented fourth to a minor third.
36   Julian Johnson discusses Mahler's musical treatments of the voices of the dead in "The Breaking of the Voice," *Nineteenth-Century Music Review* 8 (2011): 194.
37   Quoted by Bauer-Lechner, *Recollections*, 33. Emphasis mine.
38   Bauer-Lechner, *Recollections*, 32.
39   Georg Borchardt et al., *Gustav Mahler: "Meine Zeit wird kommen": Aspekte der Mahler-Rezeption* (Hamburg: Dölling und Galitz Verlag, 1996).

Chapter Nine: Conclusion

1   Vladimir Propp, *Morphology of the Folktale*, 2nd ed., trans. Laurence Scott, ed. Louis A. Wagner, American Folklore Society Bibliographical and Special Series 9 (Austin: University of Texas Press, 1968).
2   Alma Mahler, *Gustav Mahler: Erinnerungen und Briefe*, ed. Donald Mitchell (Frankfurt am Main: Ullstein, 1949), 120.
3   Bruno Bettelheim, *The Uses of Enchantment: The Meaning and Importance of Fairy Tales* (New York: Vintage Books, 1977); Marie-Louise von Franz, *An Introduction to the Psychology of Fairy Tales* (Irving, TX: Spring Publications, 1978).
4   Quoted by Natalie Bauer-Lechner, *Recollections of Gustav Mahler*, trans. Dika Newlin, ed. Peter Franklin (Cambridge: Cambridge University Press, 1980), 32.
5   Raymond Knapp, *Symphonic Metamorphoses: Subjectivity and Alienation in Mahler's Re-Cycled Songs* (Middletown, CT: Wesleyan University Press, 2003), 1, 207.
6   Knapp, *Symphonic Metamorphoses*, 6.
7   Alma Maria Mahler, ed., *Gustav Mahler Briefe: 1879–1911* (Vienna: Paul Zsolnay Verlag, 1925), 189.
8   Henry-Louis de La Grange, *Mahler*, vol. 1 (Garden City, NY: Doubleday, 1973), 171; Guido Adler, "Gustav Mahler," *Biographisches Jahrbuch und deutscher Nekrolog* 16 (1911): 784–85.

NOTES TO PAGES 226–31   257

9   La Grange, *Mahler*, 1:785.

10 Knapp, *Symphonic Metamorphoses*, 118–19.

11 John J. Sheinbaum, "Adorno's Mahler and the Timbral Outsider," *Journal of the Royal Music Association* 131 (2006): 62.

12 Timothy Freeze, "Popular Music and the Colloquial Tone in the Posthorn Solos of Mahler's Third Symphony," in *Rethinking Mahler*, ed. Jeremy Barham (Oxford: Oxford University Press, 2017). Many thanks to Dr. Freeze for sharing his work with me in advance of publication.

13 Donald Mitchell, *Gustav Mahler: The Wunderhorn Years* (Woodbridge: Boydell Press, 2005), 311.

14 Peter Franklin, "Socio-Political Landscapes: Reception and Biography," in *The Cambridge Companion to Mahler*, ed. Jeremy Barham (Cambridge: Cambridge University Press, 2007), 8.

15 Pamela Potter, "Musicology Under Hitler: New Sources in Context," *Journal of the American Musicological Society* 49 (1996): 88.

16 Oxford Music Online, s.v. "Mengelberg, Willem," by José A. Bowen et al., accessed March 31, 2010, http://www.oxfordmusiconline.com./subscriber/article/grove/music/18402.

17 Mark Katz, *Capturing Sound: How Technology has Changed Music* (Berkeley: University of California Press, 2004), 3.

18 Edward R. Reilly, "Mahler and Guido Adler," *Musical Quarterly* 58 (1972): 468.

19 Theodor Adorno, *Mahler: A Musical Physiognomy*, trans. Edmund Jephcott (Chicago: University of Chicago Press, 1992), 3. See also Leon Botstein, "Whose Gustav Mahler? Reception, Interpretation, and History," in *Mahler and His World*, ed. Karen Painter (Princeton, NJ: Princeton University Press, 2002), 2.

Index

Abraham a Sancta Clara 109
Adler, Guido 13, 22, 95, 199, 231
Adler, Victor 172, 173, 234
Adorno, Theodor 90, 182, 231
Alberti bass 67, 68
Amsterdam 230
Anthony of Padua, St. 109, 112, 113, 114, 218, 219, 220
anti-Semitism 24, 25, 27, 89, 90, 92–95, 96, 112, 113, 205, 218, 244
   by music critics 93–95, 218
Arnim, Bettina von 75
Arnim, Ludwig Achim von 1, 3, 5, 7, 8, 10–13, 14, 21, 23, 40, 44, 71, 75, 139, 145, 180, 186, 200, 213, 222, 229, 234
art as religion 24, 25, 27, 29, 91, 227
Austrian Imperial 5th Infantry Regiment 22
Austrian Imperial 13th Battalion of Light Infantry 22
Austro-Prussian War 23

Balladen 16, 18, 237, 240
bar form 41, 49, 54
Bauer-Lechner, Natalie 5, 14, 17, 21, 44, 46, 58, 68–70, 98, 109, 112, 115, 124,

161, 162, 174, 175, 178, 180, 182, 186, 194, 198, 199, 202, 204, 209, 223
   diaries 5, 44, 46, 68–69, 162
   romantic feelings toward Mahler 68–70, 223
Bayerische Staatsbibliothek, Munich 255
Berio, Luciano 242
Berlin 10, 113, 174, 203
Berlin Philharmonic 113, 203
Berliner Staatsbibliothek 3, 10
Berlioz, Hector 42, 48, 200, 227
Bernstein, Leonard 231
Bettelheim, Bruno 249
birdsong 55, 66, 67, 68, 122, 160, 189, 211, 215, 216, 217, 255
Blaukopf, Herta 13, 23
Blech, Leo 93
Bode, Karl 12, 100, 186, 213
Botstein, Leon 95, 212
Boxberger, Robert, editor of 1883 edition of *Des Knaben Wunderhorn* 15, 36
Brahms, Johannes 133, 161
Bremer, Friedrich, editor of 1878 edition of *Des Knaben Wunderhorn* 15, 36
Brenta River 113

259

260 INDEX

Brentano, Clemens 1, 3, 5, 7, 8, 10–13,
  14, 20, 23, 40, 44, 75, 139, 145, 180,
  200, 213, 222, 229
Breuer, Josef 141
Bruckner, Anton 74
Budapest Royal Hungarian Opera 123,
  124
Bülow, Hans von 203
Burckhard, Max 204

Catholicism 25, 89, 91–93, 97, 112, 114,
  218
cholera epidemic of 1892 69, 97, 176
Christian Social Party 25
Christianity 28, 29, 89–92, 96–97, 98,
  100, 103, 109, 114–15
Clement V, Pope 92
Committee for the Protection of
  German Emigrants 97
Concertgebouw, Amsterdam 230
cuckoos 61–64, 205, 207–12, 213,
  215–17

Dehmel, Ida 13
*Des Knaben Wunderhorn: Alte deutsche
  Lieder* 1, 5, 9, 10–15, 21, 23, 25, 36,
  59, 75, 117, 180, 222, 233
Deutsche Zeitung 93, 218
Deutsches Volksblatt 93, 218
"Deutschland, Deutschland über alles"
  172
didactic nature of folk stories 3, 6, 8–9,
  68, 117–18, 119–20, 123, 127, 134,
  138–39, 184, 223, 229–30, 249
Die Zeit 198
donkeys 207, 208–11, 222

Ebel, Johann Gottfried 43
"The Emperor's New Clothes" 212, 226

Feder, Stuart 14
feuilletons 198–203, 204
Fischer, Jens Malte 24
Fischer, Theodor 22
Fleischl-Marxow, Ernst von 161

fliegende Blätter (broadsides) 10, 40, 71,
  139, 144
Franco-Prussian War 26
Frank, Betty 58, 87
Franklin, Peter 21, 230
Freeze, Timothy 2, 228
Freud, Anna 141, 145
Freud, Sigmund 90, 134, 137–39, 141,
  161, 166–67, 223, 232, 248, 249
  conversion disorder 139
  defense mechanisms 141, 145
  Die Traumdeutung 139
  dream theory 161, 166–67
  Psychopathologie des Alltagslebens 139
  Studien über Hysterie 139
Friedjung, Heinrich 172

gender roles 117–18, 120, 123, 126–27,
  130–31, 133–35
genre 16–19, 51, 104, 200–2, 236, 254
Gesellschaft der Musikfreunde 2, 125
Gewandhaus Leipzig 59
Gilman, Sander L. 96
Goethe, Johann Wolfgang von 10, 11, 12,
  19, 91, 162, 181, 184, 200–1, 234, 237
Grimm, Jacob and Wilhelm 7, 248
Gropius, Walter 68
Gruber, Max von 172, 234
Guth, Karl-Maria 10, 234

Hamburg 69, 87, 89, 93, 95, 97–98, 176,
  203
Hamburg Stadttheater 97–98
Hanheide, Stefan 21
Hanslick, Eduard 138, 198, 200–3, 205
Hefling, Stephen E. 69
Helm, Theodor 93–94, 212
Herder, Johann Gottfried 11, 208
Hilmar-Voit, Renate 15
Hitler, Adolf 27, 124, 230–31
Hofer, Johannes 43
Hogarth, A. David 91
Horn, Camillo 93
Hotel Gustav Mahler 2, 237
Humoresken 16, 17, 18, 47, 104, 236

Iglau 21–22, 23, 30, 74, 86, 91, 124, 125, 176, 237, 238

Jewish self-hatred 95–96, 177–78
Joachim, Amalie 203
Judaism
   biological constant 25, 27, 89–90, 95
   cause of career issues 93, 95, 197, 227
   religious practice 24, 89–90, 103, 224
   stereotypes 27, 92–95, 176–77, 197, 205, 227, 244

Karpath, Ludwig 5, 95
Kassel State Theater 58, 87
Keats, John 161
Kikeriki 93, 218
Kinderlieder, volume of *Des Knaben Wunderhorn* 10
Kleffel, Arno 203
Klezmer 112–13, 219
Klopstock, Friedrich Gottlieb 225, 245
Knapp, Raymond 224–25, 227
Kralik, Richard von 172, 234
Kraus, Kordula 21
Krisper, Anton 86
Kunstballaden 11
Kurz, Selma 200

La Grange, Henry-Louis de 12, 13, 22, 59
Ländler 130, 133, 153, 157, 159, 195, 253
Langer, Susanne 138
Leiden, Netherlands 137
Leipzig 58–59
Leipzig Opera House 58
Leseverein der deutschen Studenten Wiens 172–73
Lieder 16–17, 18, 19, 85, 93, 104, 153, 200–2
Lipiner, Siegfried 162, 172, 174, 194, 234, 251
Loewe, Carl 17, 201, 236
Löhr, Friedrich 58, 93, 124
Löhr, Uda 124
Ludwig II, King of Bavaria 26
Lueger, Karl 25, 92–93

Mahler, Alma Schindler 69, 70, 89, 96, 126, 127, 161, 175, 229, 248, 252
Mahler, Alois 123–24, 125
Mahler, Bernhard 14, 92, 123
Mahler, Ernst 123
Mahler, Gustav
   "Ablösung im Sommer" 6, 197, 212–17, 220, 222, 225, 228, 250
   anti-Semitism 95–97, 178
   "Aus! Aus!" 6, 57, 75–81, 223
   baptism 89–90, 93, 95–97, 103, 114, 115, 126, 223
   "Das himmlische Leben" 6, 91, 103–9, 113, 114, 115, 223
   "Das irdische Leben" 6, 104, 174, 178–86, 223
   Das klagende Lied 14
   Das Lied von der Erde 229, 230
   "Der Schildwache Nachtlied" 6, 139, 162–69, 203, 223, 231, 232
   "Der Tamboursg'sell" 6, 15, 30, 36, 37, 44–51, 224, 229, 240
   "Des Antonius von Padua Fischpredigt" 6, 91, 109–14, 115, 197, 218–20, 223, 225, 227
   economic status 176–78
   "Es sungen drei Engel" 6, 91, 100–3, 113, 114, 115, 223
   as guardian of his younger siblings 117, 123–27
   "Ich ging mit Lust" 6, 57, 64–68, 223, 231, 232, 250
   Judaism 24–25, 89, 90, 91, 92, 93–97, 103, 178, 197, 224, 227, 251
   Kindertotenlieder 46
   "Lied des Verfolgten im Turm" 6, 139, 145–52, 223
   Lieder eines fahrenden Gesellen 14, 58, 175, 200
   "Lob des hohen Verstandes" 6, 62, 197, 205–12, 213, 216, 220, 222, 250
   musical characterization 9, 68, 71, 79, 80, 127, 145, 148, 150, 160, 163, 185, 190, 216, 221, 222, 224

262 INDEX

"Nicht Wiedersehen" 6, 30, 51–56
orchestration 18, 37, 71, 85, 93–94,
    100, 104, 107, 108, 109, 189, 194,
    200–1, 229, 237, 240, 245, 253
poetic editing 12, 14, 15, 41, 44, 46,
    47, 51, 64, 71, 82, 98, 104, 139,
    144, 148, 153, 162, 163, 181, 191,
    194, 208, 212, 213, 221, 222, 229,
    231, 232
"Revelge" 6, 15, 30–37, 44, 47, 224
"Rheinlegendchen" 6, 174, 186–91,
    223, 253
romantic life 15, 57–59, 68–70,
    86–87, 127, 223, 229, 248
"Scheiden und Meiden" 6, 57, 82–86,
    223, 231, 242
"Selbstgefühl" 6, 139–44, 223
song–symphony relationships 1, 19,
    21, 37, 44, 91, 94, 98, 100, 103–4,
    109, 113–15, 210, 223, 224–29,
    231, 245
"Starke Einbildungskraft" 6, 118–23,
    127, 133, 134 223, 246
Symphony no. 1 ("Titan") 59, 175,
    176, 204
Symphony no. 2 ("Resurrection")
    6, 91, 99, 100, 113–14, 200, 210,
    225–27, 245
Symphony no. 3 6, 87, 100, 104, 225,
    227–28
Symphony no. 4 6, 94–95, 104
Symphony no. 9 230–31
"Trost im Unglück" 6, 57, 70, 71–75,
    223
"Um schlimme Kinder artig zu
    machen" 6, 57, 59–64, 68, 223,
    231, 232
"Urlicht" 6, 91, 98–100, 102, 113, 114,
    115, 223
"Verlor'ne Müh'!" 6, 70, 127–34, 203,
    223, 253
views on audiences 6, 9, 19, 114,
    118, 138, 144, 197, 198, 199, 203,
    212–17, 218, 219–20, 222, 227,
    228

views on criticism 10, 114, 197,
    198–203, 205–11, 212, 217, 218,
    220, 222–23, 227
views on economic equality 10, 171,
    172–76, 178, 186, 191, 194, 195,
    196, 221, 223
views on militarism 9, 21–24, 25,
    29–30, 56, 223–24, 237
views on spirituality 9, 29, 89, 90–91,
    92, 97, 100, 112, 114–15, 178, 186,
    221, 223, 224, 225
"Wer hat dies Liedlein erdacht?" 6,
    174, 191–96, 223, 231
"Wo die schönen Trompeten blasen"
    6, 37, 139, 152–62, 223, 224, 231,
    232
"Zu Straßburg auf der Schanz" 6, 30,
    37–44, 47, 49, 224, 239, 250
Mahler, Marie Hermann 92, 123
Mahler, Otto 123–24, 125, 126
Mahler Quittner, Leopoldine 123
Mahler Rosé, Emma 97, 123–24, 125–26,
    127, 134
Mahler Rosé, Justine 17, 69–70, 95, 96,
    97, 123–24, 125, 126–27, 134, 176,
    177, 235
    closeness with Gustav 126–27
    financial irresponsibility 124, 176–77
    frail health 124
Mannheim 191
Marschalk, Max 95
Marx, Karl 28, 174
Massow, Albrecht von 21
Matzek, Dominik 22
May Day 175
Médiathèque Musicale Mahler 2
Meynberg, Theodor 97
Mildenburg, Anna von 15, 87
military
    children in 47–48
    desertion from 40, 44, 48
Mitchell, Donald 13, 21, 37, 44, 228, 230,
    238
modernism 9, 197, 198–205, 212, 222,
    223, 227, 228, 230

modified strophic form 133, 152, 163, 184

Monteverdi, Claudio 74

moto perpetuo 181–82, 184, 185

Muntz, Maximillian 93, 94

Napoleonic Wars 8, 11, 25

narrative voice 1, 8, 9, 68, 71, 78, 79, 80, 99, 114, 127, 145, 148, 150, 160, 163, 181, 184, 185, 190, 216, 221, 222, 224

Neue Berliner Musikzeitung 203

Neue freie Presse 198, 204

New York Public Library 2

Newlin, Dika 74, 249

Nietzsche, Friedrich 25, 27–29, 30, 59, 89, 90, 172

 Also sprach Zarathustra 28

 Gay Science, The 27

 Human, All Too Human 27

nightingales 160–61, 205, 207–8, 210, 211, 212, 213, 215, 216, 217, 228, 232, 250, 251, 255

Nikisch, Arthur 58

"O du Deutschland, ich muss marschieren" 172

oral tradition 12, 222, 231

orchestral songs 18, 37, 71, 85, 93–94, 100, 104, 107, 108, 109, 189, 194, 200–1, 229, 237, 240, 245, 253

Östdeutche Rundschau 93, 218

Ostjuden 96

Pan-Germanism 7, 11–12, 24–25, 172, 196

Panic of 1893 25, 92

Pattberg, Frau Auguste 186

Pernerstorfer, Engelbert 172, 234

Pernerstorfer Circle 12, 24–25, 29, 172–74, 196, 234, 252

Perry, Rebekah S. 28

Pierpont Morgan Library 2, 240

Plato 138

Poisl, Josephine 86–87

Pollini, Bernhard 95, 97–98, 244

Prague State Opera House 58, 87

Propp, Vladimir 221

psychoanalysis 137–39, 170, 223

Puchstein, Hans 93

radical socialism 172–74, 176, 194, 195, 196, 223

Reilly, Edward R. 231

Reiser, Ferdinand 12, 186

Richter, Jean Paul 17, 104

Richter, Johanna 58, 87

Riehl, Hans 69, 70

Riemann, Hugo 16

Ritter, William 94–95

Rölleke, Heinz 10, 15, 233–34

romantic infidelity 57, 58–59, 64, 67, 68

rondo form 78, 80, 153

Rosé, Alfred 124

Rosé, Arnold 126, 127

Rosé, Eduard 126

Rotterdam 191

Rückert, Friedrich 46, 229

Sankt Jakobkirche 92

Schiff, David 114

Schopenhauer, Arthur 28, 29, 30, 56, 89, 90, 172

 Parerga and Paralipomena 29

 World as Will and Representation, The 28

Schorske, Carl E. 24, 46

Schubert, Franz 82, 184, 253

 "Erlkönig" 82, 84, 184

Schumann, Robert 17, 226

Secessionist art 93, 197, 202

Seidl, Arthur 100

Shakespeare, William 74

Sheinbaum, John J. 228

Slunitschek, Matthias 43

Smyth, Ethel 59

Solvik, Morten 69

song forms 16, 34, 35, 41–42, 49, 54–56, 67–68, 78, 94, 107–9, 133, 145, 152, 153, 160, 180, 181, 184, 190, 194, 200, 213–14, 222, 254

264 INDEX

Specht, Richard 90
Spiegler, Nina 162, 251
Stefan, Paul 21, 238
Stimmen der Völker 11
Strauss, Johann 94, 244
Strauss, Richard 202
strophic form 16, 35, 41, 120, 145, 180, 181
Swider, Vicar Zygmunt 97

ternary form 190, 194 –95
through-composed form 16

Unger, Rabbi Jakob Joachim 91–92
University of Vienna 12, 13, 24, 29, 56, 62, 171, 172–73, 178, 196, 224, 231
University of Western Ontario 2
utopian socialism 172–74, 176, 194, 195, 196, 223

Vann, Martin 92
Vienna 2, 24–25, 88–89, 92–93, 95–96, 119, 124, 134, 137, 138, 161, 176, 198–99, 200, 202–3, 212–13, 222, 230, 244
   audiences 198, 202–3, 212–13, 222
   Conservatory 125, 172, 177

Hofoper 87, 93, 95, 97, 197
Philharmonic 204, 212
Volkelt, Johannes 173–74

Wagner, Cosima 244
Wagner, Richard 25, 30, 56, 90, 94, 172
   anti-Semitism 27, 94
   views on militarism 26–27
Walter, Bruno 230
Weber, Adolf von 59, 64, 117
Weber, Captain Karl von 13, 58, 59, 62, 117, 118, 235
Weber, Carl Maria von 58, 235
   Die drei Pintos 58, 59, 113, 235
Weber, Katharina von 59, 64, 117, 118, 123
Weber, Marion von 13, 58–59, 62, 64, 68, 117, 118, 235
Weber, Marion von (daughter) 59, 64, 117, 118, 123
Weininger, Otto 120
Werner, Sybille 22
Wiener Allgemeine Zeitung 198
Wolf, Hugo 172, 202, 234
Wörthersee 70

Zipes, Jack 8
Zweig, Stefan 23, 134, 176, 198, 252–53